Microsoft
ACCESS 7
FOR WINDOWS 95

Gary B. Shelly
Thomas J. Cashman
Philip J. Pratt

SHELLY
CASHMAN
SERIES®

boyd & fraser

A DIVISION OF COURSE TECHNOLOGY
ONE MAIN STREET
CAMBRIDGE MA 02142

an International Thomson Publishing company I(T)P®

CAMBRIDGE • ALBANY • BONN • CINCINNATI • LONDON • MADRID • MELBOURNE

MEXICO CITY • NEW YORK • PARIS • SAN FRANCISCO • TOKYO • TORONTO • WASHINGTON

© 1996 boyd & fraser publishing company
A Division of Course Technology
One Main Street
Cambridge, Massachusetts 02142

I(T)P® International Thomson Publishing
boyd & fraser publishing company is an ITP company.
The ITP trademark is used under license.

Printed in the United States of America

For more information, contact boyd & fraser publishing company:

boyd & fraser publishing company
A Division of Course Technology
One Main Street
Cambridge, Massachusetts 02142, USA

International Thomson Editores
Campos Eliseos 385, Piso 7
Colonia Polanco
11560 Mexico D.F. Mexico

International Thomson Publishing Europe
Berkshire House
168-173 High Holborn
London, WC1V 7AA, United Kingdom

International Thomson Publishing GmbH
Konigswinterer Strasse 418
53227 Bonn, Germany

Thomas Nelson Australia
102 Dodds Street
South Melbourne
Victoria 3205 Australia

International Thomson Publishing Asia
Block 211, Henderson Road #08-03
Henderson Industrial Park
Singapore 0315

Nelson Canada
1120 Birchmont Road
Scarborough, Ontario
Canada M1K 5G4

International Thomson Publishing Japan
Hirakawa-cho Kyowa Building, 3F
2-2-1 Hirakawa-cho, Chiyoda-ku
Tokyo 102, Japan

ISBN 0-7895-1154-1

SHELLY CASHMAN SERIES® and **Custom Edition**® are trademarks of International Thomson Publishing, Inc. Names of all other products mentioned herein are used for identification purposes only and may be trademarks and/or registered trademarks of their respective owners. International Thomson Publishing, Inc. and boyd & fraser publishing company disclaim any affiliation, association, or connection with, or sponsorship or endorsement by such owners.

PHOTO CREDITS: *Project 1, page A 1.4* ESPNET TO GO, Motorola Inc.; *page A 1.5* Satellite Dish, Jim Zuckerman/Westlight; *Project 2, page A 2.2* PeaPod, PeaPod LP; *Project 3, page A 3.2* Motorola Mobile Workstation 9100-386, Motorola Inc.; *page A 3.3*, Employee Using a Mobile Workstation, Northern Illinois Gas Company

1 2 3 4 5 6 7 8 9 10   BC   0 9 8 7 6

Microsoft
ACCESS 7
FOR WINDOWS 95

CONTENTS

Microsoft Access 7   A 1.1

▶ PROJECT ONE
CREATING A DATABASE USING DESIGN AND DATASHEET VIEWS

Objectives	A 1.3
Introduction	A 1.6
Project One – Mason Clinic	A 1.8
What Is Microsoft Access?	A 1.8
Overview of Project Steps	A 1.9
Mouse Usage	A 1.9
Starting Access and Creating a New Database	A 1.10
The Access Desktop and the Database Window	A 1.12
Creating a Table	A 1.13
Defining the Fields	A 1.16
Correcting Errors in the Structure	A 1.18
Saving a Table	A 1.19
Adding Records to a Table	A 1.20
Closing a Table and a Database and Exiting Access	A 1.23
Opening a Database	A 1.24
Adding Additional Records	A 1.26
Correcting Errors in the Data	A 1.28
Previewing and Printing the Contents of a Table	A 1.28
Creating Additional Tables	A 1.32
Adding Records to the Therapist Table	A 1.34
Using a Form to View Data	A 1.35
Closing and Saving the Form	A 1.36
Opening the Saved Form	A 1.37
Using the Form	A 1.38
Switching Between Form View and Datasheet View	A 1.39
Creating a Report	A 1.40
Selecting the Fields for the Report	A 1.42
Completing the Report	A 1.43
Printing the Report	A 1.45
Closing the Database	A 1.46

Access Online Help	A 1.46
Using the Contents Sheet to Obtain Help	A 1.46
Using the Index Sheet to Obtain Help	A 1.49
Using the Find Sheet to Obtain Help	A 1.50
Using the Answer Wizard to Obtain Help	A 1.52
Designing a Database	A 1.54
Project Summary	A 1.56
What You Should Know	A 1.56
Test Your Knowledge	A 1.57
Use Help	A 1.60
Apply Your Knowledge	A 1.61
In the Lab	A 1.64
Cases and Places	A 1.73

▶ PROJECT TWO
QUERYING A DATABASE USING THE SELECT QUERY WINDOW

Objectives	A 2.1
Introduction	A 2.4
Project Two – Mason Clinic	A 2.4
Overview of Project Steps	A 2.6
Opening the Database	A 2.7
Creating a New Query	A 2.7
Using the Select Query Window	A 2.10
Displaying Selected Fields in a Query	A 2.10
Running a Query	A 2.12
Printing the Results of a Query	A 2.13
Returning to the Select Query Window	A 2.14
Closing a Query	A 2.15
Including All Fields in a Query	A 2.16
Clearing the Design Grid	A 2.17
Entering Criteria	A 2.18
Using Text Data in Criteria	A 2.18
Using Wildcards	A 2.19
Criteria for a Field Not in the Result	A 2.20
Using Numeric Data in Criteria	A 2.22
Using Comparison Operators	A 2.23
Using Compound Criteria	A 2.24

Sorting Data in a Query   A 2.27
Sorting on Multiple Keys   A 2.28
Omitting Duplicates   A 2.30
Joining Tables   A 2.32
Restricting Records in a Join   A 2.35
Using Computed Fields in a Query   A 2.36
Calculating Statistics   A 2.38
Using Criteria in Calculating Statistics   A 2.41
Grouping   A 2.42
Saving a Query   A 2.43
Closing the Database   A 2.45
Project Summary   A 2.45
What You Should Know   A 2.45
Test Your Knowledge   A 2.46
Use Help   A 2.50
Apply Your Knowledge   A 2.52
In the Lab   A 2.53
Cases and Places   A 2.57

▶ PROJECT THREE

MAINTAINING A DATABASE USING THE DESIGN AND UPDATE FEATURES OF ACCESS

Objectives   A 3.1
Introduction   A 3.4
Project Three – Mason Clinic   A 3.4
Overview of Project Steps   A 3.5
Opening the Database   A 3.6
Adding, Changing, and Deleting   A 3.6
    Adding Records   A 3.6
    Searching for a Record   A 3.8
    Changing the Contents of a Record   A 3.10
    Switching Between Views   A 3.10
    Deleting Records   A 3.12
Changing the Structure   A 3.13
    Changing the Size of a Field   A 3.13
    Adding a New Field   A 3.15
    Updating the Restructured Database   A 3.17
    Resizing Columns   A 3.18
    Using an Update Query   A 3.20
    Using a Delete Query to Delete a Group of
        Records   A 3.22
Creating Validation Rules   A 3.24
    Specifying a Required Field   A 3.25
    Specifying a Range   A 3.26
    Specifying a Default Value   A 3.27
    Specifying a Collection of Legal Values   A 3.27
    Using a Format   A 3.28
    Saving Rules, Values, and Formats   A 3.29
    Updating a Table that Contains Validation Rules A 3.30
    Making Individual Changes to a Field   A 3.33

Specifying Referential Integrity   A 3.35
Ordering Records   A 3.39
    Ordering Rows on Multiple Fields   A 3.40
Creating and Using Indexes   A 3.42
    What Is an Index?   A 3.42
    How Does Access Use an Index?   A 3.44
    When Should You Create an Index?   A 3.44
    Creating Single-Field Indexes   A 3.45
    Creating Multiple-Field Indexes   A 3.46
Closing the Database   A 3.49
Project Summary   A 3.49
What You Should Know   A 3.49
Test Your Knowledge   A 3.50
Use Help   A 3.54
Apply Your Knowledge   A 3.56
In the Lab   A 3.57
Cases and Places   A 3.62

▶ INTEGRATION FEATURE

INTEGRATING EXCEL WORKSHEET DATA INTO AN ACCESS DATABASE

Introduction   AI 1.1
    Opening an Excel Workbook   AI 1.3
Converting an Excel Worksheet to an
    Access Database   AI 1.4
Using the Access Table   AI 1.7
Summary   AI 1.7
What You Should Know   AI 1.7
In the Lab   AI 1.8

Preface

Shelly Cashman Series® Microsoft Windows 95 Books

The Shelly Cashman Series Microsoft Windows 95 books reinforce the fact that you made the right choice when you use a Shelly Cashman Series book. The Shelly Cashman Series Microsoft Windows 3.1 books were used by more schools and more students than any other series in textbook publishing. Yet the Shelly Cashman Series team wanted to produce even better books for Windows 95, so the books were thoroughly redesigned to present material in an even easier to understand format and with more project-ending activities. Features such as Other Ways and More Abouts were added to give in-depth knowledge to the student. The opening of each project provides a fascinating perspective of the subject covered in the project. Completely redesigned student assignments include the unique Cases and Places. This book provides the finest educational experience for a student learning about computer software.

Objectives of This Textbook

Microsoft Access 7 for Windows 95 Double Diamond Edition is intended for a course that covers a brief introduction to Microsoft Access 7. No experience with a computer is assumed and no mathematics beyond the high school freshman level is required. The objectives of this book are:

- ▶ To teach the fundamentals of Microsoft Access 7 for Windows 95
- ▶ To provide a knowledge base of Microsoft Access 7 on which students can build
- ▶ To expose students to examples of the computer as a useful tool
- ▶ To help students who are working on their own

When students complete the course using this textbook, they will have a basic knowledge and understanding of Access 7.

The Shelly Cashman Approach

Features of the Shelly Cashman Series Windows 95 books include:

- ▶ **Project Orientation:** Each project in the book uses the unique Shelly Cashman Series screen-by-screen, step-by-step approach.
- ▶ **Screen-by-Screen, Step-by-Step Instructions:** Each of the tasks required to complete a project is identified throughout the development of the project and is shown screen by screen, step by step.
- ▶ **Multiple Ways to Use the Book:** This book can be used in a variety of ways, including: (a) Lecture and textbook approach; (b) Tutorial approach; (c) Many teachers lecture on the material and then require their students to perform each step in the project, reinforcing the material lectured. The students then complete one or more of the In the Lab exercises at the end of the project; and (d) Reference: Each task in a project is clearly identified. Therefore, the material serves as a complete reference.

◆ More *About* Creating a Table

If you have not already determined the fields that comprise your table, you can use **Table Wizards**, which are tools that guide you through the table creation by suggesting some commonly used tables and fields. If you already know the fields you need, however, it usually is easier to just create the table yourself.

v

> **Other Ways Boxes for Reference:** Access 7 provides a wide variety of ways to carry out a given task. The Other Ways boxes displayed at the end of most of the step-by-step sequences specify the other ways to do the task completed in the steps.

Organization of This Textbook

Microsoft Access 7 for Windows 95 Double Diamond Edition provides detailed instruction on how to use Access 7 for Windows 95. The material is divided into three projects and one integration feature as follows:

Project 1 – Creating a Database Using Design and Datasheet Views   In Project 1, students are introduced to Access terminology, the Access window, and the basic characteristics of databases. Topics include starting and exiting Access; creating a database; creating a table; defining fields; opening a table; adding records to a table; closing a table; opening and closing a database; and previewing and printing the contents of a table. Other topics in this project include using a form to view data; creating a report using the Report Wizard; and using online Help. Students also learn how to design a database to eliminate redundancy.

Project 2 – Querying a Database Using the Select Query Window   In Project 2, students learn how to ask questions concerning the data in their databases by using queries. Topics include creating and running queries; printing the results of queries; displaying only selected fields; using character data in criteria; using wildcards; using numeric data in criteria; using various comparison operators; and creating compound criteria. Other topics include sorting; joining tables; and restricting records in a join. Students learn to use computed fields, statistics, grouping, and also how to save a query.

Project 3 – Maintaining a Database Using the Design and Update Features of Access
In Project 3, students learn how to maintain a database. Topics include using Datasheet view and Form view to add new records, to change existing records and to delete records; and searching for a record. Students also learn how to change the structure of a table; how to add additional fields and to change characteristics of existing fields; how to create a variety of validation rules; and how to specify referential integrity. Students perform mass changes and deletions using queries. They also create single-field and multiple-field indexes.

Integration Feature – Integrating Excel Worksheet Data into an Access Database   In this section, students learn how to use the Import Spreadsheet Wizard to integrate an Excel worksheet into an Access database. Topics include opening an Excel workbook; converting an Excel worksheet to an Access database; and using the Access table.

End-of-Project Student Activities

A notable strength of the Shelly Cashman Series Windows 95 books is the extensive student activities at the end of each project. Well-structured student activities can make the difference between students merely participating in a class and students retaining the information they learn. The activities in the Shelly Cashman Series Windows 95 books include:

> **What You Should Know**   A listing of the tasks completed within a project together with the pages where the step-by-step, screen-by-screen explanations appear. This section provides a perfect study review for the student.

▶ **Test Your Knowledge** Four pencil-and-paper activities designed to determine the student's understanding of the material in the project. Included are true/false questions, multiple-choice questions, and two short-answer activities.

▶ **Use Help** Any user of Windows 95 must know how to use Help. Therefore, this book contains two Help exercises per project. These exercises alone distinguish the Shelly Cashman Series from any other set of Windows 95 instructional materials.

▶ **Apply Your Knowledge** This exercise requires the student to open and manipulate a file from the Student Floppy Disk that accompanies the book.

▶ **In the Lab** Three in-depth assignments per project that require the student to apply the knowledge gained in the project to solve problems on a computer.

▶ **Cases and Places** Seven unique case studies allow students to apply their knowledge to real-world situations.

Instructor's Support Package

A comprehensive Instructor's Support Package accompanies this textbook in the form of an electronic Instructor's Manual and teaching and testing aids on CD-ROM. The Instructor's Manual and most of the aids also are available to registered instructors on the Shelly Cashman Online home page (http://www.bf.com/scseries.html). The CD-ROM (ISBN 0-7895-1152-5) is available through your Course Technology representative or by calling 1-800-648-7450. The contents of the Instructor's Manual and additional support materials on the CD-ROM are listed below.

▶ **Instructor's Manual** The Instructor's Manual includes the following for each project: project objectives; project overview; detailed lesson plans with page number references; teacher notes and activities; answers to the end-of-project exercises; test bank of 110 questions for every project (50 true/false, 25 multiple-choice, and 35 fill-in-the blanks); and transparency references.

▶ **CD-ROM** The CD-ROM includes the following:

● **Figures on CD-ROM** Illustrations for every screen in the textbook are available. Use this ancillary to create a slide show from the illustrations for lecture or to print transparencies for use in lecture with an overhead.

● **ElecMan** ElecMan stands for *Elec*tronic *Man*ual. ElecMan is a Microsoft Word version of the Instructor's Manual, including all lecture notes and the test bank. The files allow you to modify the lecture notes or generate quizzes and exams from the test bank using your word processor.

● **Course Test Manager** Designed by Course Technology, this cutting edge Windows-based testing software helps instructors design and administer tests and pre-tests. The full-featured online program permits students to take tests at the computer where their grades are computed immediately following completion of the exam. Automatic statistics collection, student guides customized to the student's performance, and printed tests are only a few of the features.

● **Lecture Success System** Lecture Success System files are for use with the application software, a personal computer, and projection device to explain and illustrate the step-by-step, screen-by-screen development of a project in the textbook without entering large amounts of data.

● **Lab Tests** Tests that parallel the In the Lab assignments are supplied for the purpose of testing students in the laboratory on the material covered in the project.

- **Instructor's Lab Solutions**   Solutions and required files for all of the In the Lab assignments at the end of each project are available.

- **Student Files**   All the files that are required by the student to complete the Apply Your Knowledge exercises or advanced projects are included.

Shelly Cashman Online

Shelly Cashman Online is a World Wide Web service available to instructors and students of computer education. Visit Shelly Cashman Online at http://www.bf.com/scseries.html. Shelly Cashman Online is divided into four areas:

- **Series Information**   Information on the Shelly Cashman Series products.

- **The Community**   Opportunities to discuss your course and your ideas with instructors in your field and with the Shelly Cashman Series team.

- **Teaching Resources**   This area includes password-protected data from Instructor's Floppy Disks that can be downloaded, course outlines, teaching tips, and ancillaries such as ElecMan and Lab Tests.

- **Student Center**   Dedicated to students learning about computers with Shelly Cashman Series textbooks and software. This area includes cool links, data from Student Floppy Disks that can be downloaded, and much more.

Acknowledgments

The Shelly Cashman Series would not be the leading computer education series without the contributions of outstanding publishing professionals. First, and foremost, among them is Becky Herrington, director of production and designer. She is the heart and soul of the Shelly Cashman Series, and it is only through her leadership, dedication, and tireless efforts that superior products are made possible. Becky created and produced the award-winning Windows 95 series of books.

Under Becky's direction, the following individuals made significant contributions to these books: Peter Schiller, production manager; Ginny Harvey, series administrator and manuscript editor; Ken Russo, senior illustrator and cover artist; Mike Bodnar, Stephanie Nance, Greg Herrington, and Dave Bonnewitz, Quark artists and illustrators; Patti Garbarino, editorial assistant; Jeanne Black, Quark expert; Cristina Haley, indexer; Debora Christy, Cherilyn King, Nancy Lamm, Lyn Markowicz, and Marilyn Martin, proofreaders; Nancy Lamm, Susan Sebok, Tim Walker, and Peggy Wyman and Jerry Orton, contributing writers; Sarah Evertson of Image Quest, photo researcher; Henry Blackham, cover photographer; and Kent Lauer, cover glass work. Special mention must go to Suzanne Biron, Becky Herrington, and Michael Gregson for the outstanding book design. Particular thanks to Jim Quasney, series editor, whose talents and energy are unmatched in publishing. Without Jim's efforts and dedication, none of this happens.

Gary B. Shelly
Thomas J. Cashman
Philip J. Pratt

Visit Shelly Cashman Online at
http://www.bf.com/scseries.html

▶ **PROJECT ONE**

CREATING A DATABASE USING DESIGN AND DATASHEET VIEWS

Objectives   A 1.3
Introduction   A 1.6
Project One – Mason Clinic   A 1.8
What Is Microsoft Access?   A 1.8
Overview of Project Steps   A 1.9
Mouse Usage   A 1.9
Starting Access and Creating a New Database   A 1.10
The Access Desktop and the Database Window   A 1.12
Creating a Table   A 1.13
Saving a Table   A 1.19
Adding Records to a Table   A 1.20
Closing a Table and a Database and Exiting Access   A 1.23
Opening a Database   A 1.24
Adding Additional Records   A 1.26
Previewing and Printing the Contents of a Table   A 1.28
Creating Additional Tables   A 1.32
Adding Records to the Therapist Table   A 1.34
Using a Form to View Data   A 1.35
Creating a Report   A 1.40
Closing the Database   A 1.46
Access Online Help   A 1.46
Designing a Database   A 1.54
Project Summary   A 1.56
What You Should Know   A 1.56
Test Your Knowledge   A 1.57
Use Help   A 1.60
Apply Your Knowledge   A 1.61
In the Lab   A 1.64
Cases and Places   A 1.73

▶ **PROJECT TWO**

QUERYING A DATABASE USING THE SELECT QUERY WINDOW

Objectives   A 2.1
Introduction   A 2.4
Project Two – Mason Clinic   A 2.4
Overview of Project Steps   A 2.6
Opening the Database   A 2.7
Creating a New Query   A 2.7
Running a Query   A 2.12
Printing the Results of a Query   A 2.13
Returning to the Select Query Window   A 2.14
Closing a Query   A 2.15
Clearing the Design Grid   A 2.17
Entering Criteria   A 2.18
Using Text Data in Criteria   A 2.18
Using Wildcards   A 2.19
Criteria for a Field Not in the Result   A 2.20
Using Numeric Data in Criteria   A 2.22
Using Comparison Operators   A 2.23
Using Compound Criteria   A 2.24
Sorting Data in a Query   A 2.27
Sorting on Multiple Keys   A 2.28
Omitting Duplicates   A 2.30
Joining Tables   A 2.32
Restricting Records in a Join   A 2.35
Using Computed Fields in a Query   A 2.36
Calculating Statistics   A 2.38
Using Criteria in Calculating Statistics   A 2.41
Grouping   A 2.42
Saving a Query   A 2.43
Closing the Database   A 2.45
Project Summary   A 2.45
What You Should Know   A 2.45
Test Your Knowledge   A 2.46
Use Help   A 2.50
Apply Your Knowledge   A 2.52
In the Lab   A 2.53
Cases and Places   A 2.57

▶ **PROJECT THREE**

MAINTAINING A DATABASE USING THE DESIGN AND UPDATE FEATURES OF ACCESS

Objectives   A 3.1
Introduction   A 3.4
Project Three – Mason Clinic   A 3.4
Overview of Project Steps   A 3.5
Opening the Database   A 3.6
Adding, Changing, and Deleting   A 3.6
Changing the Structure   A 3.13
Creating Validation Rules   A 3.24
Specifying Referential Integrity   A 3.35
Ordering Records   A 3.39
Creating and Using Indexes   A 3.42
Closing the Database   A 3.49
Project Summary   A 3.49
What You Should Know   A 3.49
Test Your Knowledge   A 3.50
Use Help   A 3.54
Apply Your Knowledge   A 3.56
In the Lab   A 3.57
Cases and Places   A 3.62

▶ **INTEGRATION FEATURE**

INTEGRATING EXCEL WORKSHEET DATA INTO AN ACCESS DATABASE

Introduction   AI 1.1
Converting an Excel Worksheet to an Access Database   AI 1.4
Using the Access Table   AI 1.7
Summary   AI 1.7
What You Should Know   AI 1.7
In the Lab   AI 1.8

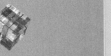

Microsoft Access 7

Windows 95

Creating a Database Using Design and Datasheet Views

Objectives

You will have mastered the material in this project when you can:

◗ Describe databases and database management systems

◗ Start Access

◗ Describe the features of the Access screen

◗ Create a database

◗ Create a table

◗ Define the fields in a table

◗ Open a table

◗ Add records to an empty table

◗ Close a table

◗ Close a database

◗ Open a database

◗ Add records to a non-empty table

◗ Print the contents of a table

◗ Use a form to view data

◗ Create a custom report

◗ Use online Help

◗ Understand how to design a database to eliminate redundancy

THE SPORTS FAN'S *ULTIMATE* DATABASE

Sports Scores on Your Pager

BASKETBALL

FOOTBALL

BASEBALL

HOCKEY

GOLF

BOXING

AUTO RACING

You are at your school's conference championship game. As you cheer the team to victory, your thoughts turn to professional sports. What is the score of the Lakers' game? How is Michael Jordan's injured calf muscle? Is it raining at the Western Open?

Until a few years ago, you would have had to leave the game, buy one or more newspapers, and comb the sports pages to satisfy your curiosity. Today, however, you can reach in your pocket, pull out your pager, and find the answers to these questions, along with the latest sports news, scores, game information, and trivia. It is part of ESPNET TO GO, a new wireless service on Motorola's EMBARC sports receiver.

All this information is found in a database located in Florida. A database is an organized collection of data that provides access to information in a variety of ways. The database management system used to create, maintain, and report on the sports information is so sophisticated that twenty-nine computers are needed to run it. Data covering professional and collegiate sports, including

Team Names
Visiting Team First

Scoring
Play

```
MIA   14              FGoal
NYG < 10 ^ 4          3Q9:22
ON:   MIAMI 23        4TH & 6
TREADWELL            40 YDS
READ      MODE
ESPNET TO.GO
```

basketball, football, baseball, hockey, golf, boxing, and auto racing, is kept in more than 200 storage areas, or fields. Statistics, game schedules, injury and weather reports, and point spreads are part of the service, which also includes play situations (such as who is batting or who has the ball) for Major League Baseball and National Football League games in progress.

The data for the ESPNET database comes from many feeds, including ESPN, the largest cable network in America. Score updates, late-breaking sports news, other sports information, and commentary are transmitted to a satellite, which then relays the data to the database.

The data is checked continually for errors, sorted, and then integrated into the database. The fields in the database are updated when new information is received. For example, the field containing the halftime score of the USC-UCLA game is updated when either team scores.

Approximately every five minutes, the computer uplinks the revised database information to a satellite. This satellite then delivers the data to a network of land-based transmitters located in more than 230 metropolitan areas across the United States and Canada. These transmitters, in turn, broadcast the data to pager-like receivers or to personal computers. The wireless sports information service also is available internationally.

ESPNET TO GO was introduced in August 1995 after four years of development. The product is targeted for two groups: avid sports fans and professionals in the sports industry, such as coaches, players, and sports writers. It is used more than a million times daily by subscribers. In the future, ESPNET might be customized so users can obtain only the sports information they desire. For example, subscribers who are not interested in golf could choose to delete all information regarding that sport.

Ultimate sports fans who want to follow all the action, anywhere and anytime, find the virtual real-time information in the ESPNET database a welcome supplement to their minimum daily sports diet.

WBN NETWORK

Project

Microsoft
Access 7
Windows 95

Creating a Database Using Design and Datasheet Views

Case Perspective

The management of Mason Clinic, a physical therapy clinic, has determined that the practice has grown to the point that the maintenance of patient and therapist data can no longer be done manually. By placing the data in a database, managed by a database management system like Access, management will be able to ensure that the data is more current and more accurate than in the present manual system. They also will be able to produce a variety of useful reports. In addition, they need to be able to ask questions concerning the data in the database and obtain answers to these questions easily and rapidly.

Introduction

Creating, storing, sorting, and retrieving data are important tasks. In their personal lives, many people keep a variety of records such as names, addresses, and phone numbers of friends and business associates, records of investments, records of expenses for tax purposes, and so on. These records must be arranged for quick access. Businesses also must be able to store and access information quickly and easily. Personnel and inventory records, payroll information, patient records, order data, and accounts receivable information all are crucial and must be readily available.

The term **database** describes a collection of data organized in a manner that allows access, retrieval, and use of that data. A **database management system**, like Access, allows you to use a computer to create a database; add, change, and delete data in the database; sort the data in the database; retrieve data in the database; and create forms and reports using the data in the database.

In Access, a database consists of a collection of tables. Figure 1-1 shows a sample database for Mason Clinic. It consists of two tables. The Patient table contains information about the patients in a multiple-therapist clinic. The Therapist table contains information about the therapists in the clinic.

The rows in the tables are called records. A **record** contains information about a given person, product, or event. A row in the Patient table, for example, contains information about a specific patient.

FIGURE 1-1

fields

patients of therapist Mary Hughes

Patient Table

records

PATIENT NUMBER	LAST NAME	FIRST NAME	ADDRESS	CITY	STATE	ZIP CODE	BALANCE	INSURANCE	THER NUMBER
AL26	Alardyce	Lisa	311 Birchwood	Lamont	MI	49160	$196.62	$180.00	05
AT73	Acton	Thomas	312 Newcastle	Homer	MI	49162	$726.42	$550.00	08
BR31	Bryce	Roger	617 College	Lamont	MI	49160	$96.00	$0.00	08
DI32	Dalton	Irene	41 Lafayette	Madison	IN	42909	$875.00	$600.00	14
GC92	Gutierez	Carlos	476 Fulton	Jackson	OH	49401	$273.00	$150.00	05
GT43	Grant	Thomas	247 Fuller	Lamont	MI	49160	$276.00	$0.00	08
JG22	Jenkins	Glen	201 Plymouth	Madison	IN	42909	$0.00	$0.00	08
LI66	Lawrence	Irving	912 Devonshire	Beulah	MI	45621	$346.50	$175.00	05
PE33	Pezato	Eduardo	346 Vernor	Homer	MI	49162	$467.12	$500.00	14
PE76	Perez	Enzo	216 Four Mile	Perry	MI	47211	$216.00	$0.00	08

Therapist Table

therapist 05 - Mary Hughes

THER NUMBER	LAST NAME	FIRST NAME	ADDRESS	CITY	STATE	ZIP CODE	BILLING	PAID
05	Hughes	Mary	4613 Essex	Burnips	MI	49277	$62,277.00	$46,245.25
08	Foster	Richard	6621 Eastern	Stockton	IN	47962	$71,245.00	$65,121.33
14	Galvez	Juanita	684 Valley	Leland	MI	47205	$34,252.50	$22,645.90

The columns in the tables are called fields. A **field** contains a specific piece of information within a record. In the Patient table, for example, the fourth field, City, contains the city where the patient is located.

The first field in the Patient table is the Patient Number. This is a code assigned by the clinic to each patient. Like many organizations, this clinic calls it a "number" even though it actually contains letters. The patient numbers have a special format. They consist of two uppercase letters followed by a two-digit number.

These numbers are *unique*; that is, no two patients will be assigned the same number. Such a field can be used as a **unique identifier**. This simply means that a given patient number will appear only in a single record in the table. Only one record exists, for example, in which the patient number is BR31. A unique identifier also is called a **primary key**. Thus, the Patient Number field is the primary key for the Patient table.

More *About* **Creating a Database**

In Access, a database is stored in a single file on disk. The file has an extension of MDB. All the tables, queries, forms, reports, and programs that you create for this database are stored in this one file.

The next eight fields in the Patient table include the Last Name, First Name, Address, City, State, Zip Code, Balance, and Insurance. The Balance field contains the patient's current balance; that is, the amount the patient owes to the clinic. The Insurance field contains the portion of the balance that is expected to be covered by the patient's health insurance.

For example, patient AL26 is Lisa Alardyce. She is located at 311 Birchwood in Lamont, Michigan. The Zip Code is 49160. Her current balance (the amount she owes to the clinic) is $196.62. The portion of this amount that should be paid by her insurance company is $180.00.

Each patient is assigned to a single therapist. The last field in the Patient table, Ther Number, gives the number of the patient's therapist.

The first field in the Therapist table, Ther Number, is the number assigned by the clinic to each therapist. These numbers are unique, so Ther Number is the primary key of the Therapist table.

The other fields in the Therapist table are Last Name, First Name, Address, City, State, Zip Code, Billing, and Paid. The Billing field contains the total amount that has been billed by the therapist for the therapist's services so far this year. The Paid field contains the portion of this amount that already has been paid, either by patients or by insurance companies.

For example, therapist 05 is Mary Hughes. She lives at 4613 Essex in Burnips, Michigan. Her Zip Code is 49277. So far this year, she has billed $62,277.00, of which $46,245.25 already has been paid.

The Ther Number appears in both the Patient table and the Therapist table. It is used to relate patients and therapists. For example, in the Patient table, you see that the Ther Number for patient AL26 is 05. To find the name of this therapist, look for the row in the Therapist table that contains 05 in the Ther Number field. Once you have found it, you know the patient is assigned to Mary Hughes. To find all the patients assigned to Mary Hughes, look through the Patient table for all the patients that contain 05 in the Ther Number field. Her patients are AL26 (Lisa Alardyce), GC92 (Carlos Gutierez), and LI66 (Irving Lawrence).

Project One – Mason Clinic

Together with the management of Mason Clinic, you have determined that the data that must be maintained in the database is the data shown in Figure 1-1 on page A 1.7. You first must create the database and the tables it contains. In the process, you must define the fields contained in the two tables, including the type of data each field will contain. You then must add the appropriate records to the tables. You also must print the contents of the tables. Finally, you must create a report containing the patient number, first name, last name, balance, and insurance amount fields for each patient of Mason Clinic. Other reports and requirements for the database at Mason Clinic will be addressed with the Mason Clinic management in the future.

What Is Microsoft Access?

Microsoft Access is a powerful database management system (DBMS) that functions in the Windows environment and allows you to create and process data in a database. To illustrate the use of Access, this book presents a series of projects.

The projects use the database of patients and therapists. In Project 1, the two tables that comprise the database are created and the appropriate records are added to them. The project also uses a form to display the data in the tables. In addition, the project prepares and prints a custom report that represents the data in the database.

Overview of Project Steps

The database preparation steps give you an overview of how the database consisting of the Patient table and the Therapist table shown in Figure 1-1 will be built in this project. The following tasks will be completed in this project.

1. Start Access.
2. Create a database called Mason Clinic.
3. Create the Patient table by defining its fields.
4. Save the Patient table in the database called Mason Clinic.
5. Add data records to the Patient table.
6. Print the contents of the Patient table.
7. Create the Therapist table, save it, and add data records to it.
8. Create a form to display data in the Patient table.
9. Create and print a report that presents the data in the Patient table.

The following pages contain a detailed explanation of each of these steps.

Mouse Usage

In this book, the mouse is the primary way to communicate with Access. You can perform six operations with a mouse: point, click, right-click, double-click, drag, and right-drag.

Point means you move the mouse across a flat surface until the mouse pointer rests on the item of choice on the screen. As you move the mouse, the mouse pointer moves across the screen in the same direction. **Click** means you press and release the left mouse button. The terminology used in this book to direct you to point to a particular item and then click is, Click the particular item. For example, Click the Primary Key button on the toolbar, means point to the Primary Key button on the toolbar and then click.

Right-click means you press and release the right mouse button. As with the left mouse button, you normally will point to an item on the screen prior to right-clicking. Right-clicking produces a **shortcut menu**, which is a menu of the most frequently used commands that relate to the portion of the screen to which you are pointing. You then can select one of these commands by pointing to it and clicking the *left* mouse button.

Double-click means you quickly press and release the left mouse button twice without moving the mouse. In most cases, you must point to an item before double-clicking. **Drag** means you point to an item, hold down the left mouse button, move the item to the desired location on the screen, and then release the left mouse button. **Right-drag** means you point to an item, hold down the right mouse button, move the item to the desired location, and then release the right mouse button.

The use of the mouse is an important skill when working with Microsoft Access for Windows 95.

Starting Access and Creating a New Database

To start Access, Windows 95 must be running. Perform the following steps to start Access and create a new database.

Steps   To Start Access

1 Place a formatted floppy disk in drive A, click the Start button, and point to New Office Document near the top of the Start menu.

The Start menu displays (Figure 1-2).

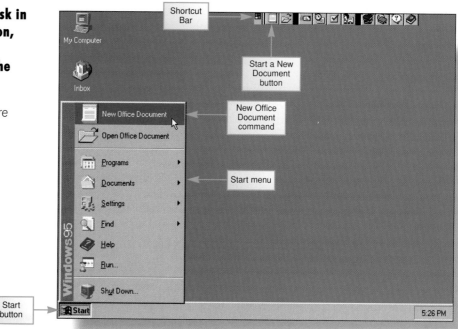

FIGURE 1-2

2 Click New Office Document. If the General tab is not selected, that is, if it does not display in front of the other tabs, click the General tab. Make sure the Blank Database icon is selected, and then point to the OK button.

The New dialog box displays (Figure 1-3). The Blank Database icon is selected.

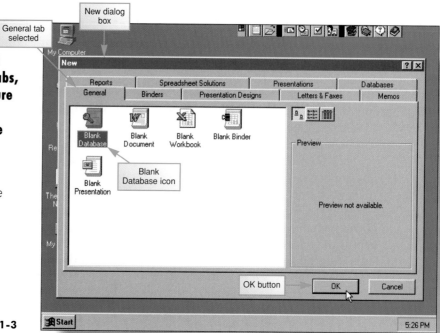

FIGURE 1-3

3 Click the OK button, and then point to the Save in box arrow.

The File New Database dialog box displays (Figure 1-4).

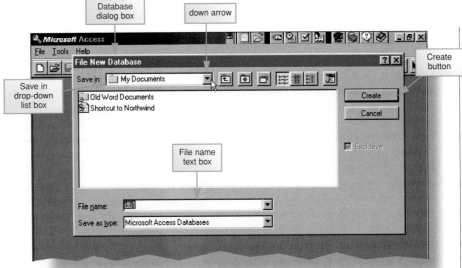

FIGURE 1-4

4 Click the down arrow and then point to 3½ Floppy [A:].

The Save in drop-down list displays (Figure 1-5).

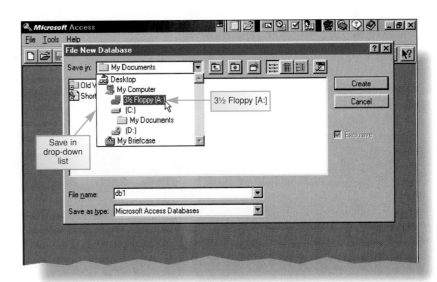

FIGURE 1-5

5 Click 3½ Floppy [A:].

The Save in text box contains 3½ Floppy [A:] (Figure 1-6).

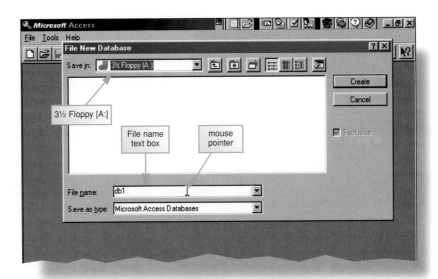

FIGURE 1-6

6 **Click in the File name text box. Repeatedly press the BACKSPACE key to delete db1, and then type Mason Clinic as the filename. Point to the Create button.**

The filename is changed to Mason Clinic (Figure 1-7).

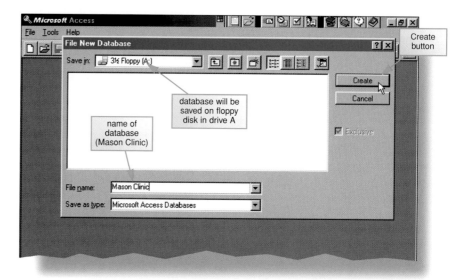

FIGURE 1-7

7 **Click the Create button to create the database.**

The Mason Clinic database is created. The Mason Clinic : Database window displays on the desktop (Figure 1-8).

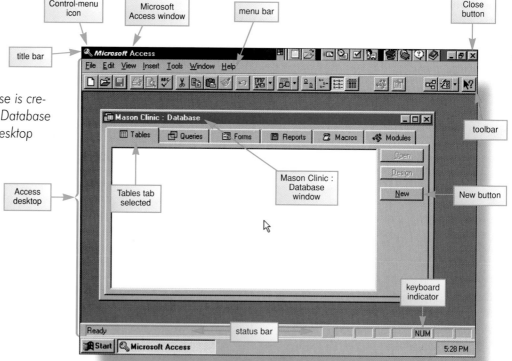

FIGURE 1-8

OtherWays

1. Right-click Start button, click Open, double-click New Office Document
2. On Office Shortcut Bar, click Start a New Document button
3. On Start menu click Programs, click Microsoft Access

The Access Desktop and the Database Window

The first bar on the desktop (Figure 1-8) is the **title bar**. It displays the title of the product, Microsoft Access. The **Control-menu icon** (the key) at the left end of the title bar is used to access the **Control menu**. The button on the right is the **Close button**. Clicking a Close button closes the window.

The second bar is the **menu bar**. It contains a list of menus. You select a menu from the menu bar by clicking the menu name.

The third bar is the **toolbar**. The toolbar contains buttons that allow you to perform certain tasks more quickly than using the menu bar. Each button contains a picture, or icon, depicting its function. The specific buttons on the toolbar will vary, depending on the task on which you are working.

The **taskbar** at the bottom of the screen displays the Start button, any active windows, and the current time.

Immediately above the Windows 95 taskbar is the **status bar** (Figure 1-8). It contains special information that is appropriate for the task on which you are working. Currently, it contains the word, Ready, which means Access is ready to accept commands. Other keyboard indicators may appear such as NUM shown in Figure 1-8.

The **Database window**, referred to in Figure 1-8 as the Mason Clinic : Database window, is a special window that allows you to easily and rapidly access a variety of objects such as tables, queries, forms, and reports. To do so, you will use the various components of the window.

Creating a Table

An Access database consists of a collection of tables. Once you have created the database, you must create each of the tables within it. In this project, for example, you must create both the Patient and Therapist tables shown in Figure 1-1 on page A 1.7.

To create a table, you describe the **structure** of the table to Access by describing the fields within the table. For each field, you indicate the following:

1. **Field name** — Each field in the table must have a unique name. In the Patient table (Figure 1-9 on the next page), for example, the field names are Patient Number, Last Name, First Name, Address, City, State, Zip Code, Balance, Insurance, and Ther Number.
2. **Data type** — Data type indicates to Access the type of data the field will contain. Some fields can contain only numbers. Others, such as Balance and Insurance, can contain numbers and dollar signs. Still others, such as Last Name, First Name, and Address, can contain letters.
3. **Description** — Access allows you to enter a detailed description of the field.

You can also assign field widths to text fields (fields whose data type is Text). This indicates the maximum number of characters that can be stored in the field. If you do not assign a width to such a field, Access assumes the width is 50.

You also must indicate which field or fields make up the **primary key**; that is, the unique identifier, for the table. In the sample database, the Patient Number field is the primary key of the Patient table and the Ther Number field is the primary key of the Therapist table.

The rules for field names are:

1. Names can be up to 64 characters in length.
2. Names can contain letters, digits, spaces, as well as most of the punctuation symbols.
3. Names cannot contain periods, exclamation points (!), or square brackets ([ ]).
4. The same name cannot be used for two different fields in the same table.

Structure of Patient Table

FIELD NAME	DATA TYPE	FIELD SIZE	PRIMARY KEY?	DESCRIPTION
Patient Number	Text	4	Yes	Patient Number (Primary Key)
Last Name	Text	10		Patient Last Name
First Name	Text	8		Patient First Name
Address	Text	15		Street Address
City	Text	15		City
State	Text	2		State (Two-Character Abbreviation)
Zip Code	Text	5		Zip Code (Five-Character Version)
Balance	Currency			Current Balance
Insurance	Currency			Expected Amount from Insurance
Ther Number	Text	2		Number of Patient's Therapist

Data for Patient Table

PATIENT NUMBER	LAST NAME	FIRST NAME	ADDRESS	CITY	STATE	ZIP CODE	BALANCE	INSURANCE	THER NUMBER
AL26	Alardyce	Lisa	311 Birchwood	Lamont	MI	49160	$196.62	$180.00	05
AT73	Acton	Thomas	312 Newcastle	Homer	MI	49162	$726.42	$550.00	08
BR31	Bryce	Roger	617 College	Lamont	MI	49160	$96.00	$0.00	08
DI32	Dalton	Irene	41 Lafayette	Madison	IN	42909	$875.00	$600.00	14
GC92	Gutierez	Carlos	476 Fulton	Jackson	OH	49401	$273.00	$150.00	05
GT43	Grant	Thomas	247 Fuller	Lamont	MI	49160	$276.00	$0.00	08
JG22	Jenkins	Glen	201 Plymouth	Madison	IN	42909	$0.00	$0.00	08
LI66	Lawrence	Irving	912 Devonshire	Beulah	MI	45621	$346.50	$175.00	05
PE33	Pezato	Eduardo	346 Vernor	Homer	MI	49162	$467.12	$500.00	14
PE76	Perez	Enzo	216 Four Mile	Perry	MI	47211	$216.00	$0.00	08

FIGURE 1-9

More *About*
Data Types

The list of data types that are available varies slightly from one database management system to another. In addition, the names can vary. The Access Text data type, for example, is referred to as Character in some systems.

Each field has a data type. This indicates the type of data that can be stored in the field. The data types you will use in this project are:

1. **Text** — The field can contain any characters.
2. **Number** — The field can contain only numbers. The numbers can be either positive or negative. Fields are assigned this type so they can be used in arithmetic operations. Fields that contain numbers but will not be used for arithmetic operations are usually assigned a data type of Text. The Ther Number field, for example, is a text field because the Ther Numbers will not be involved in any arithmetic.
3. **Currency** — The field can contain only dollar amounts. The values will be displayed with dollar signs, commas, decimal points, and with two digits following the decimal point. Like numeric fields, you can use currency fields in arithmetic operations. Access automatically assigns a size to currency fields.

The field names, data types, field widths, primary key information, and descriptions for the Patient table are shown in Figure 1-9. With this information, you are ready to begin creating the table. To create the table, use the following steps.

Steps To Begin Creating the Table

1 **Click the New button in the Mason Clinic : Database window (see Figure 1-8 on page A 1.12). Point to Design View.**

The New Table dialog box displays (Figure 1-10).

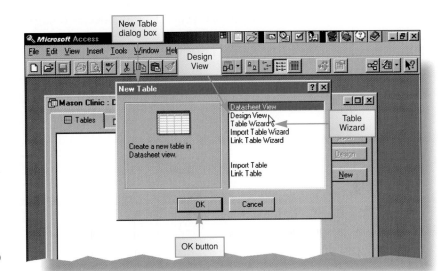

FIGURE 1-10

2 **Click Design View, and then click the OK button.**

The Table1 : Table window displays (Figure 1-11).

3 **Click the Maximize button for the Table1 : Table window.**

A maximized Table1 : Table window displays.

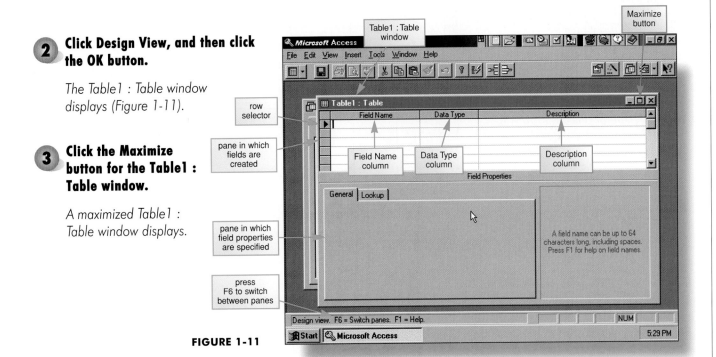

FIGURE 1-11

*Other***Ways**

1. Click New Object button down arrow on toolbar, click New Table
2. On Insert menu click Table
3. Press ALT+N

Defining the Fields

The next step in creating the table is to define the fields by specifying the required details in the Table window. To do so, make entries in the Field Name, Data Type, and Description columns. Enter additional information in the Field Properties box in the lower portion of the Table window. To do so, press F6 to move from the upper **pane** (portion of the screen), the one where you define the fields, to the lower pane, the one where you define field properties. Enter the appropriate field size, and then press F6 to return to the upper pane. As you define the fields, the **row selector** (Figure 1-11 on page A 1.15) indicates the field you are currently describing. It currently is positioned on the first field, indicating Access is ready for you to enter the name of the first field in the Field Name column.

Perform the following steps to define the fields in the table.

Steps To Define the Fields in the Table

1 **Type** Patient Number **(the name of the first field) in the Field Name column and press the TAB key.**

The words, Patient Number, display in the Field Name column and the highlight advances to the Data Type column, indicating you can enter the data type (Figure 1-12). The word, Text, one of the possible data types, currently displays. There also is an arrow you can click to display a list of available data types.

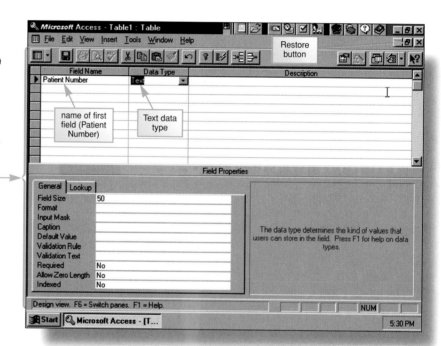

FIGURE 1-12

2 Because Text is the correct data type, press the TAB key to move the highlight to the Description column, type Patient Number (Primary Key) as the description, and then point to the Primary Key button on the toolbar (Figure 1-13).

*A **tooltip** displays, which is a description of the button, partially obscuring the description of the first field.*

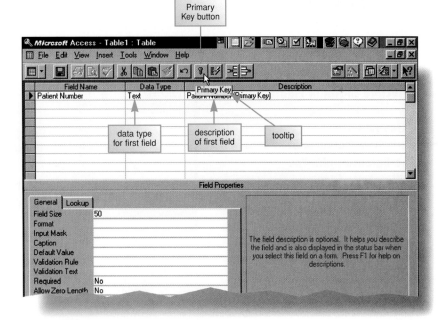

FIGURE 1-13

3 Click the Primary Key button to make Patient Number the primary key and then press F6 to move the highlight to the Field Size text box.

The Patient Number field is the primary key as indicated by the key symbol that appears in front of the field (Figure 1-14). The current entry in the Field Size text box (50) is highlighted.

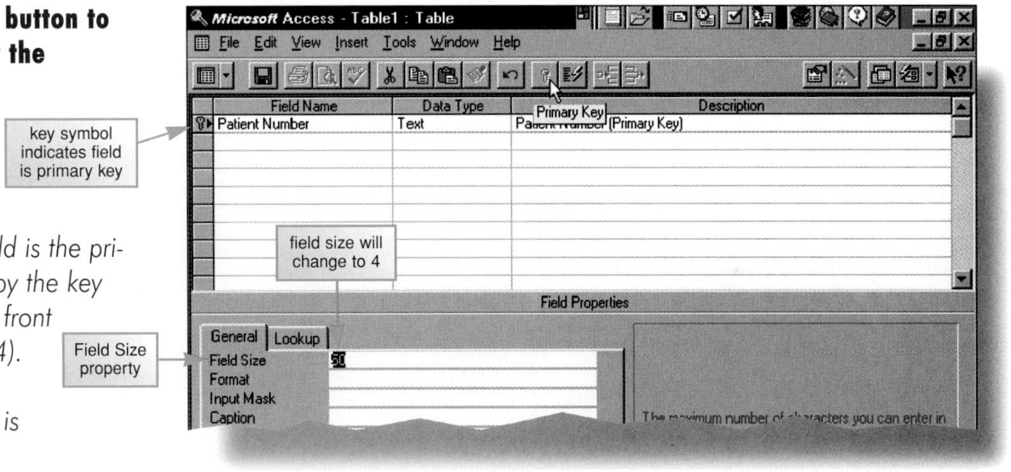

FIGURE 1-14

4 Type 4 as the size of the Patient Number field. Press F6 to return to the Description column for the Patient Number field, and then press the TAB key to move to the Field Name column in the second row.

The row selector moves to the second row just below the field name Patient Number (Figure 1-15).

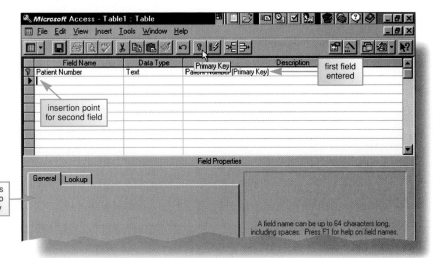

FIGURE 1-15

5 Use the techniques illustrated in Steps 1 through 4 to make the entries from the Patient table structure shown in Figure 1-9 on page A 1.14 up through and including the name of the Balance field. You will not need to click the Primary Key button for any of these fields. Click the Data Type column down arrow and then point to the Currency data type.

The additional fields are entered (Figure 1-16). A list of available data types displays in the Data Type column for the Balance field.

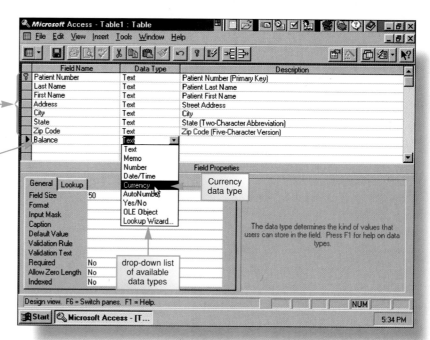

FIGURE 1-16

6 Click the Currency data type, and then press the TAB key. Make the remaining entries from the Patient table structure shown in Figure 1-9.

The fields are all entered (Figure 1-17)

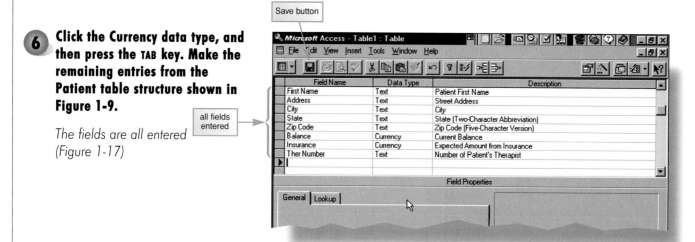

FIGURE 1-17

More *About*
Correcting Errors

It is possible to correct errors in the structure even after you have entered data. Access will make all the necessary adjustments to the structure of the table as well as to the data within it. (It is simplest to make the correction, however, before any data is entered.)

Correcting Errors in the Structure

When creating a table, check the entries carefully to ensure they are correct. If you make a mistake and discover it before you press the TAB key, you can correct the error by repeatedly pressing the BACKSPACE key until the incorrect characters are removed. Then, type the correct characters. If you do not discover a mistake until later, you can click the entry with the mouse, type the correct value, and then press the ENTER key.

If you accidentally add an extra field to the structure, select the field, by clicking the leftmost column on the row that contains the field to be deleted. Once you have selected the field, press the DELETE key. This will remove the field from the structure.

If you forget a field, select the field that will follow the field you wish to add, click Edit on the menu bar, and then click Insert Row. The remaining fields move down one row, making room for the missing field. Make the entries for the new field in the usual manner.

If you made the wrong field a key field, click the correct primary key entry for the field, and then click the Primary Key button on the toolbar.

As an alternative to these steps, you may want to start over. To do so, click the Close button for the Table1 : Table window and then click No. The original desktop displays and you can repeat the process you used earlier.

Saving a Table

The Patient table structure is now complete. The final step is to **save the table** within the database. To do so, you must give the table a name.

Table names are from one to sixty-four characters in length and can contain letters, numbers, and spaces. The two table names in this project are Patient and Therapist.

To save the table, complete the following steps.

 Steps To Save the Table

① **Click the Save button on the toolbar (see Figure 1-17). Type** Patient **as the name of the table in the Save As dialog box, and then point to the OK button.**

The Save As dialog box displays (Figure 1-18). The name of the table is entered in the Table Name text box.

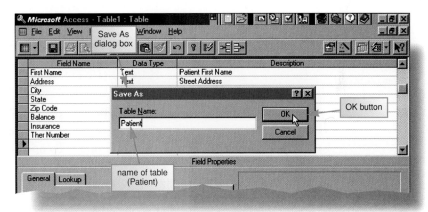

FIGURE 1-18

② **Click the OK button, and then point to the Close button for the Patient : Table window.**

The Table is saved on the floppy disk in drive A. The name of the table is now Patient as indicated in the title bar (Figure 1-19).

FIGURE 1-19

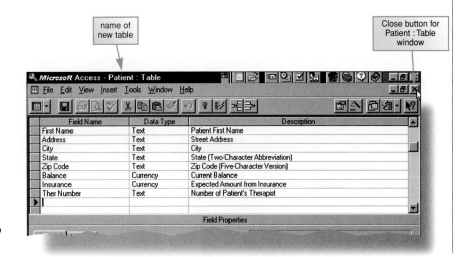

3 **Click the Close button for the Patient : Table window. (Be sure not to click the Close button on the first line, because this would close Microsoft Access.)**

The Patient : Table window no longer displays (Figure 1-20). The Mason Clinic : Database window displays. It is maximized because the previous window, the Patient : Table window, was maximized.

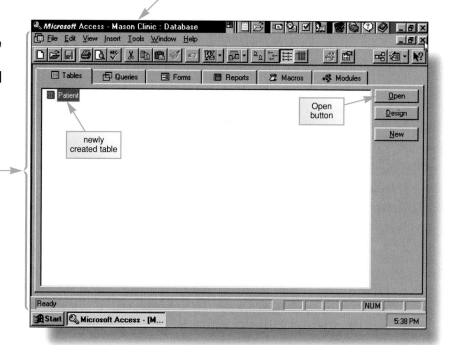

FIGURE 1-20

Other Ways

1. On File menu click Save As
2. Press CTRL+S

If you want to restore the Database window to its original size, click the window's Restore button.

Adding Records to a Table

More *About*
Adding Records

When adding records to a table, each new record is saved as soon as it is entered. This is different from other tools. The rows entered in a worksheet, for example, are not saved until the entire worksheet is saved.

Creating a table by building the structure and saving the table is the first step in a two-step process. The second step is to **add records** to the table. To add records to a table, the table must be open. To **open a table**, select the table in the Database window and then click the Open button. The table displays in Datasheet view. In **Datasheet view**, the table is represented as a collection of rows and columns called a datasheet. It looks very much like the tables shown in Figure 1-1 on page A 1.7.

You often add records in phases. You may, for example, not have enough time to add all the records in one session. To illustrate this process, this project begins by adding the first two records in the Patient table (Figure 1-21). The remaining records are added later.

Patient Table (first 2 records)

PATIENT NUMBER	LAST NAME	FIRST NAME	ADDRESS	CITY	STATE	ZIP CODE	BALANCE	INSURANCE	THER NUMBER
AL26	Alardyce	Lisa	311 Birchwood	Lamont	MI	49160	$196.62	$180.00	05
AT73	Acton	Thomas	312 Newcastle	Homer	MI	49162	$726.42	$550.00	08

FIGURE 1-21

To open the Patient table and then add records, use the following steps.

Steps To Add Records to the Table

1 **Click the Open button in the Mason Clinic : Database window (see Figure 1-20).**

The Patient : Table window displays (Figure 1-22). The window contains the Datasheet view for the Patient table. The current record indicator is positioned on the first record. The status bar at the bottom of the window also indicates that the indicator is positioned on record 1.

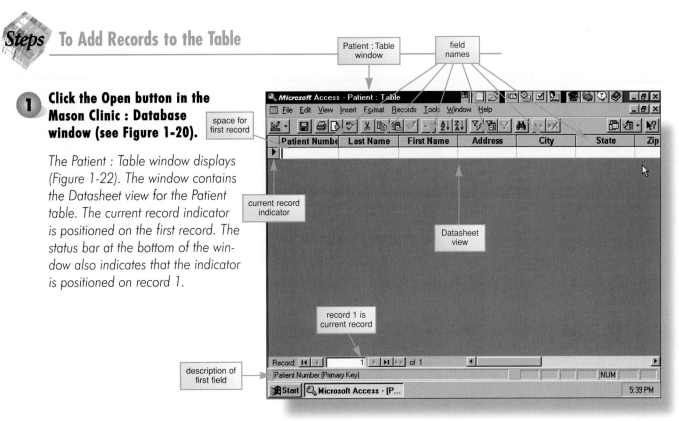

FIGURE 1-22

2 **If your window is not already maximized, click the Maximize button to maximize the window containing the table. Type AL26 as the first Patient Number, as shown in Figure 1-21. Be sure you type the letters in uppercase, because that is the way they are to be entered in the database.**

The Patient Number is entered, but the insertion point is still in the Patient Number field (Figure 1-23).

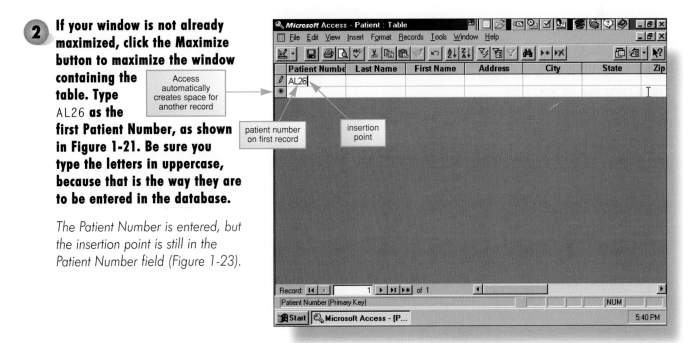

FIGURE 1-23

3 Press the TAB key to complete the entry for the Patient Number field. Type Alardyce as the last name and then press the TAB key. Type Lisa as the first name and then press the TAB key. Type 311 Birchwood as the address and then press the TAB key. Type Lamont as the city and then press the TAB key. Type MI as the State name.

The Last Name, First Name, Address, and City fields are entered. The data for the State displays on the screen (Figure 1-24), but the entry is not complete because you have not yet pressed the TAB key.

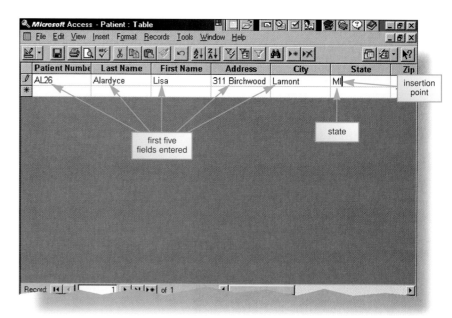

FIGURE 1-24

4 Press the TAB key.

The fields shift to the left (Figure 1-25). The Zip Code field displays.

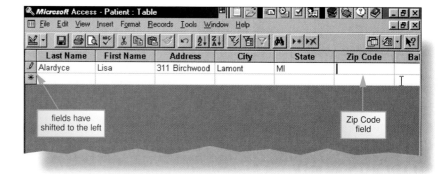

FIGURE 1-25

5 Type 49160 as the Zip Code and then press the TAB key. Type 196.62 as the Balance and then press the TAB key. (You do not need to type dollar signs or commas. In addition, if the digits to the right of the decimal point were both zeros, you would not need to type the decimal point.) Type 180 as the Insurance amount and then press the TAB key. Type 05 as the Ther Number to complete the record.

The fields have shifted to the left (Figure 1-26). The Balance and Insurance values display with dollar signs and decimal points. The value for the Ther Number has been entered, but the insertion point is still positioned on the field.

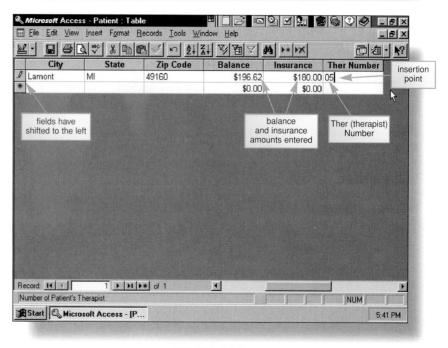

FIGURE 1-26

6 **Press the TAB key.**

The fields shift back to the right, the record is saved, and the insertion point moves to the Patient Number on the second row (Figure 1-27).

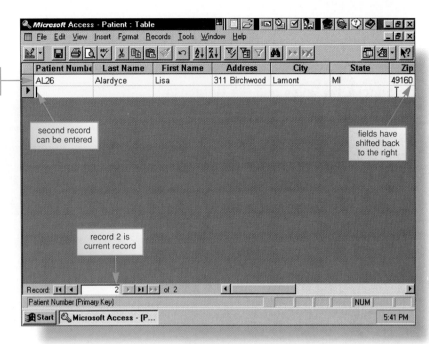

FIGURE 1-27

7 **Use the techniques shown in Steps 2 through 6 to add the data for the second record in Figure 1-21 on page A 1.20.**

The second record is added and the insertion point moves to the Patient Number on the third row (Figure 1-28).

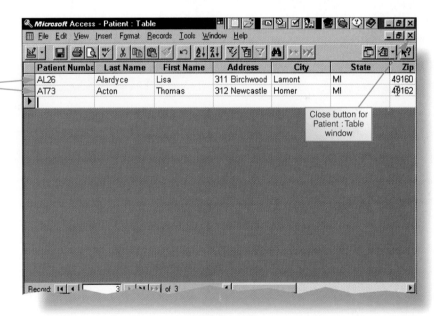

FIGURE 1-28

Closing a Table and a Database and Exiting Access

It is a good idea to close a table as soon as you have finished working with it. It keeps the screen from getting cluttered and also prevents you from making accidental changes to the data in the table. If you will no longer work with the database, you should close the database as well. With the creation of the Patient table complete, you can exit Access at this point.

Perform the following steps to close the table and the database and then exit Access.

Steps To Close the Table and the Database

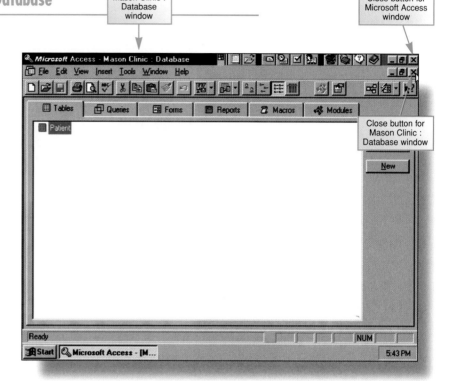

FIGURE 1-29

1 **Click the Close button for the Patient : Table window (see Figure 1-28 on page A 1.23).**

The datasheet for the Patient table no longer displays (Figure 1-29).

2 **Click the Close button for the Mason Clinic : Database window (see Figure 1-29).**

The Mason Clinic : Database window no longer displays.

3 **Click the Close button for the Microsoft Access window.**

The Microsoft Access window no longer displays.

OtherWays

1. Double-click Control-menu icon on title bar for the window
2. On File menu click Close
3. Press CTRL+W or press CTRL+F4

Opening a Database

In order to work with any of the tables, reports, or forms in a database, the database must be open. To open a database from the Windows 95 desktop, click Open Office Document on the Start menu by performing the following steps. (The Other Ways box indicates ways to open a database from within Access.)

 **To Open a Database**

1 **Click the Start button and then point to Open Office Document (Figure 1-30).**

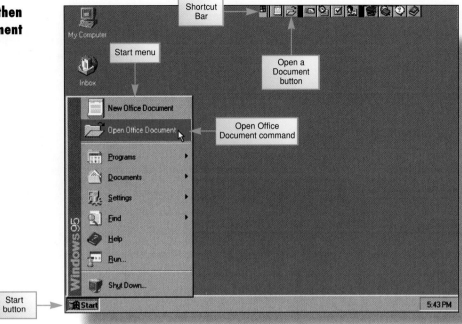

FIGURE 1-30

2 **Click Open Office Document. If necessary, click the Look in box arrow and then click 3½ Floppy [A:] in the Look in drop-down list box. If it is not already selected, click the Mason Clinic database name. Point to the Open button.**

The Open dialog box displays (Figure 1-31). The 3½ Floppy [A:] folder displays in the Look in box and the files on the floppy disk in drive A display. Your list may be different.

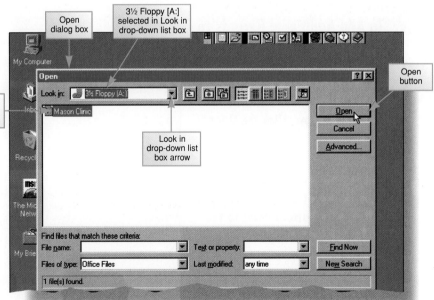

FIGURE 1-31

3 **Click the Open button.**

The database is open and the Mason Clinic : Database window displays.

Other Ways

1. Click Open Database button on toolbar
2. On File menu click Open Database
3. Press CTRL+O

Adding Additional Records

You can add records to a table that already contains data using a process almost identical to that used to add records to an empty table. The only difference is that you place the highlight after the last data record before you enter the additional data. To do so, use the **Navigation buttons** found near the lower left-hand corner of the screen. The purpose of each of the Navigation buttons is described in Table 1-1.

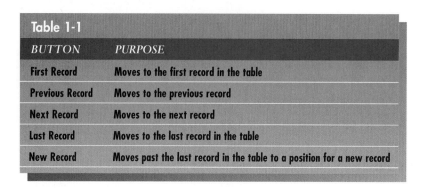

Table 1-1	
BUTTON	*PURPOSE*
First Record	Moves to the first record in the table
Previous Record	Moves to the previous record
Next Record	Moves to the next record
Last Record	Moves to the last record in the table
New Record	Moves past the last record in the table to a position for a new record

Complete the following steps to add the remaining records to the Patient table.

Steps To Add Additional Records to the Table

1 With the Patient table selected in the Mason Clinic : Database window, click the Open button.

2 When the Patient table displays, maximize the window by clicking the Maximize button. Point to the New Record button.

The datasheet displays (Figure 1-32).

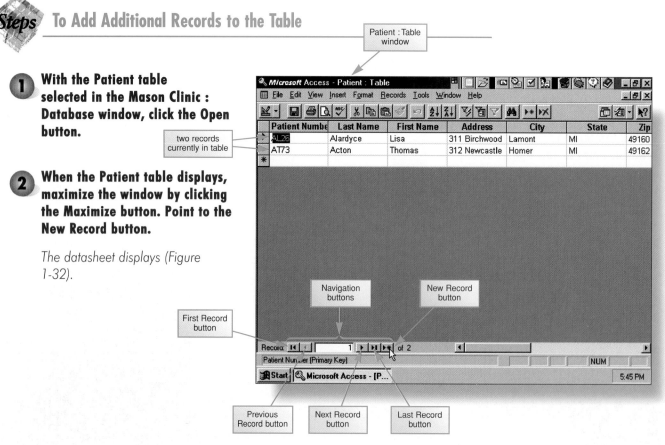

FIGURE 1-32

3 **Click the New Record button.**

Access places the insertion point in position to enter a new record (Figure 1-33).

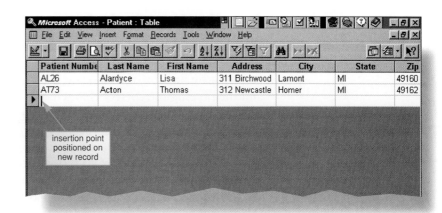

insertion point positioned on new record

FIGURE 1-33

4 **Add the remaining records from Figure 1-34 using the same techniques you used to add the first two records.**

The additional records are added (Figure 1-35).

Patient Table (last 8 records)

PATIENT NUMBER	LAST NAME	FIRST NAME	ADDRESS	CITY	STATE	ZIP CODE	BALANCE	INSURANCE	THER NUMBER
BR31	Bryce	Roger	617 College	Lamont	MI	49160	$96.00	$0.00	08
DI32	Dalton	Irene	41 Lafayette	Madison	IN	42909	$875.00	$600.00	14
GC92	Gutierez	Carlos	476 Fulton	Jackson	OH	49401	$273.00	$150.00	05
GT43	Grant	Thomas	247 Fuller	Lamont	MI	49160	$276.00	$0.00	08
JG22	Jenkins	Glen	201 Plymouth	Madison	IN	42909	$0.00	$0.00	08
LI66	Lawrence	Irving	912 Devonshire	Beulah	MI	45621	$346.50	$175.00	05
PE33	Pezato	Eduardo	346 Vernor	Homer	MI	49162	$467.12	$500.00	14
PE76	Perez	Enzo	216 Four Mile	Perry	MI	47211	$216.00	$0.00	08

FIGURE 1-34

5 **Close the table by clicking its Close button.**

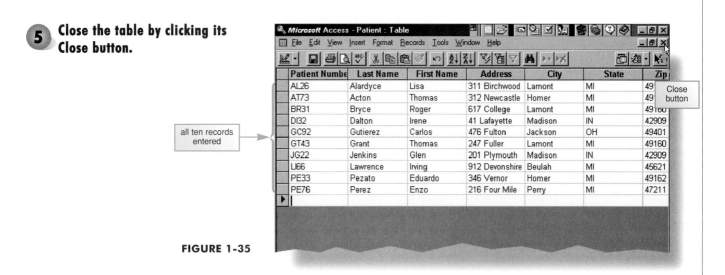

all ten records entered

Close button

FIGURE 1-35

Correcting Errors in the Data

Just as when you created the table, check the entries carefully to ensure they are correct. If you make a mistake and discover it before you press the TAB key, correct it by pressing the BACKSPACE key until the incorrect characters are removed and then typing the correct characters.

If you discover an incorrect entry later, correct the error by clicking the incorrect entry, and then making the appropriate correction. If the record you must correct is not on the screen, use the Navigation buttons (Next Record, Previous Record, and so on) to move to it. If the field you want to correct is not visible on the screen, use the horizontal scroll bar along the bottom of the screen to shift all the fields until the one you want displays. Then make the correction.

If you accidentally add an extra record, select the record by pointing to the box that immediately precedes the record and clicking the left mouse button. Then, press the DELETE key. This will remove the record from the table. If you forget a record, add it using the same procedure as for all the other records. Access will automatically place it in the correct location in the table.

If you cannot determine how to correct the data, you have a problem. Access will neither allow you to move to any other record until you have made the correction, nor will it allow you to close the table. You are, in effect, stuck on the record. If you should ever find yourself in this situation, simply press the ESC key. This will remove the record you are trying to add from the screen. You can then move to any other record, close the table, or take any other action you desire.

<table>
<tr><td>

◆ **More** *About*
Printing the
Contents of a Table

Using the Page sheet in the Page Setup dialog box, you can change the paper size, paper source, or the printer that will be used to print the report. To change either of these, click the appropriate down arrow and select the desired size.

</td></tr>
</table>

Previewing and Printing the Contents of a Table

When working with a database, you often will need to **print** a copy of the table contents. Figure 1-36 shows a printed copy of the contents of the Patient table. (Yours may look slightly different, depending on your printer.) Because the Patient table is substantially wider than the screen, it also will be wider than the normal printed page in portrait orientation. **Portrait orientation** means the printout is across the width of the page. **Landscape orientation** means the printout is across the length of the page. Thus, to print the wide database table, use landscape orientation. If you are printing the contents of a table that fits on the screen, you will not need landscape orientation. A convenient way to change to landscape orientation is to **preview** what the printed copy will look like by using Print Preview. This allows you to determine whether landscape orientation is necessary and, if it is, to easily change the orientation to landscape. In addition, you also can use Print Preview to determine whether any adjustments are necessary to the page margins.

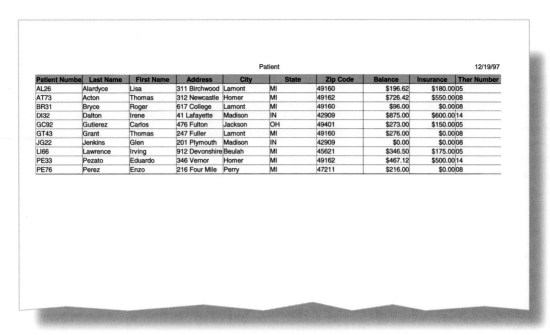

Patient Number	Last Name	First Name	Address	City	State	Zip Code	Balance	Insurance	Ther Number
AL26	Alardyce	Lisa	311 Birchwood	Lamont	MI	49160	$196.62	$180.00	05
AT73	Acton	Thomas	312 Newcastle	Homer	MI	49162	$726.42	$550.00	08
BR31	Bryce	Roger	617 College	Lamont	MI	49160	$96.00	$0.00	08
DI32	Dalton	Irene	41 Lafayette	Madison	IN	42909	$875.00	$600.00	14
GC92	Gutierez	Carlos	476 Fulton	Jackson	OH	49401	$273.00	$150.00	05
GT43	Grant	Thomas	247 Fuller	Lamont	MI	49160	$276.00	$0.00	08
JG22	Jenkins	Glen	201 Plymouth	Madison	IN	42909	$0.00	$0.00	08
LI66	Lawrence	Irving	912 Devonshire	Beulah	MI	45621	$346.50	$175.00	05
PE33	Pezato	Eduardo	346 Vernor	Homer	MI	49162	$467.12	$500.00	14
PE76	Perez	Enzo	216 Four Mile	Perry	MI	47211	$216.00	$0.00	08

Patient   12/19/97

FIGURE 1-36

Perform the following steps to use Print Preview to preview and then print the Patient table.

Steps **To Preview and Print the Contents of the Table**

1 **Make sure the Patient table is selected, and then point to the Print Preview button on the toolbar (Figure 1-37).**

FIGURE 1-37

2 **Click the Print Preview button, click File on the menu bar, and then point to Page Setup.**

The preview of the report displays (Figure 1-38). In the figure, the report displays in portrait orientation, which will not display all fields on a page. The File menu displays.

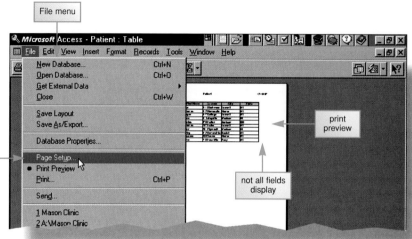

FIGURE 1-38

3 **Click Page Setup, and then point to the Page tab.**

The Page Setup dialog box displays (Figure 1-39).

FIGURE 1-39

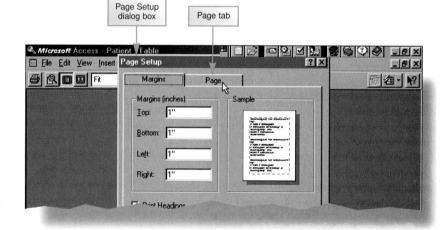

4 **Click the Page tab.**

The Page options display (Figure 1-40). The Portrait option button currently is selected.

FIGURE 1-40

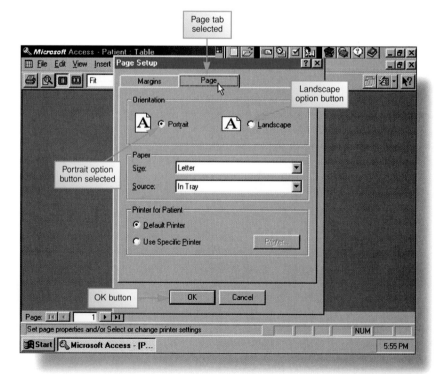

5 **Click Landscape and then click the OK button.**

The orientation is changed to landscape as shown by the report that displays on the screen (Figure 1-41). The characters in the report are so small that it is difficult to determine whether all fields currently display. To zoom in on a portion of the report, click the desired portion of the report.

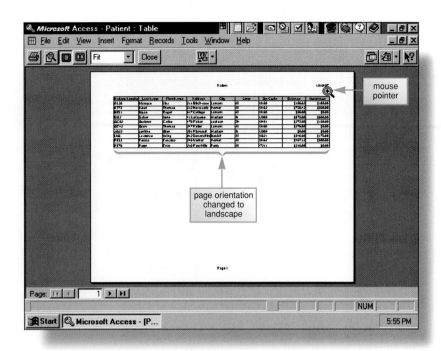

FIGURE 1-41

6 **With the mouse pointer, which displays as a magnifying glass, in the position shown in Figure 1-41, click the left mouse button.**

*The portion surrounding the mouse pointer is magnified (Figure 1-42). The last field that displays is the Insurance field. The Ther Number field does not display. To make it display, decrease the **left** and **right** margins, the amount of space left by Access on the left and right edges of the report. (You may need to experiment with the left and right margins to find appropriate numbers.)*

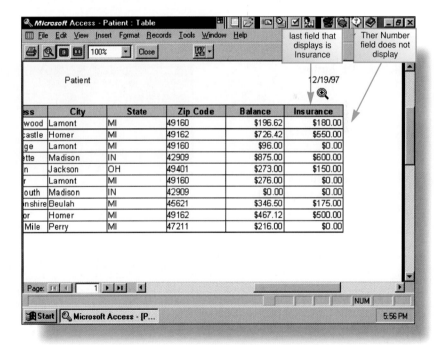

FIGURE 1-42

7 Click File on the menu bar and then click Page Setup. Click the Left text box in the Margins (inches) area, use the BACKSPACE key to delete the current entry, and then type .333 as the new entry. Repeat the process with the Right text box.

The Page Setup dialog box displays (Figure 1-43). The Left and Right margins have been changed to .333".

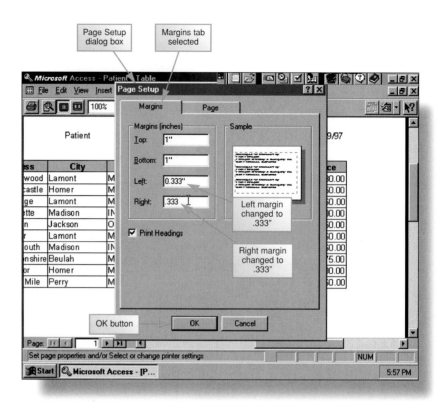

FIGURE 1-43

8 Click the OK button.

All fields now display in the report (Figure 1-44).

9 Click the Print button to print the report. Click the Close button when the report has been printed to close the Preview window.

The Preview window no longer displays.

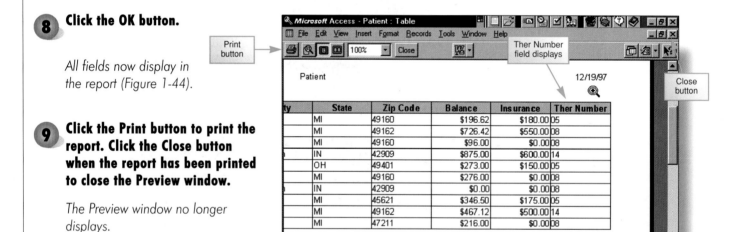

FIGURE 1-44

Other Ways

1. On File menu click Print Preview to preview; on File menu click Print to print
2. Press CTRL+P to print

Creating Additional Tables

A database typically consists of more than one table. The sample database contains two, the Patient table and the Therapist table. You need to repeat the process of creating a table and adding records for each table in the database. In the sample database, you need to create and add records to the Therapist table. The structure and data for the table are given in Figure 1-45. The steps to create the table follow.

Structure of Therapist Table

FIELD NAME	DATA TYPE	FIELD SIZE	PRIMARY KEY?	DESCRIPTION
Ther Number	Text	2	Yes	Therapist Number (Primary Key)
Last Name	Text	10		Last Name of Therapist
First Name	Text	8		First Name of Therapist
Address	Text	15		Street Address
City	Text	15		City
State	Text	2		State (Two-Character Abbreviation)
Zip Code	Text	5		Zip Code (Five-Character Version)
Billing	Currency			Total Billing Amount of Therapist
Paid	Currency			Amount Already Paid by Patient or Insurance Company

Data for Therapist Table

THER NUMBER	LAST NAME	FIRST NAME	ADDRESS	CITY	STATE	ZIP CODE	BILLING	PAID
05	Hughes	Mary	4613 Essex	Burnips	MI	49277	$62,277.00	$46,245.25
08	Foster	Richard	6621 Eastern	Stockton	IN	47962	$71,245.00	$65,121.33
14	Galvez	Juanita	684 Valley	Leland	MI	47205	$34,252.50	$22,645.90

FIGURE 1-45

Steps To Create an Additional Table

① **Make sure the Mason Clinic database is open. Point to the New button.**

The Mason Clinic : Database window displays (Figure 1-46). If you recently maximized another window, this window also will be maximized as shown in the figure. If not, it will appear in its normal size.

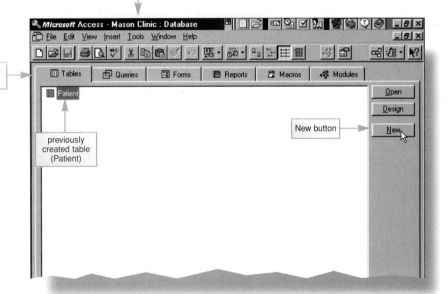

FIGURE 1-46

2 Click the New button, click Design View in the New Table dialog box, click the OK button, and then enter the data for the fields for the Therapist table from Figure 1-45 on page A 1.33. Be sure to click the Primary Key button when you enter the Ther Number field. Point to the Save button on the toolbar.

The entries display (Figure 1-47).

3 Click the Save button, type Therapist as the name of the table, and click the OK button.

4 Click the Close button to close the Table window.

The table is saved in the Mason Clinic database. The Table window no longer displays.

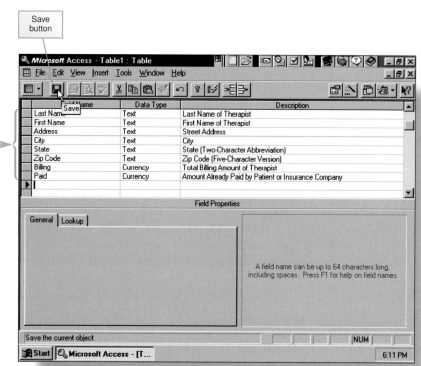

FIGURE 1-47

Adding Records to the Therapist Table

Now that you have created the Therapist table, use the following steps to add records to it.

 Steps To Add Records to the Additional Table

1 Click the Therapist table in the Database window.

The Therapist table is selected (Figure 1-48).

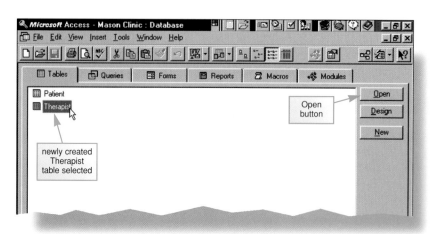

FIGURE 1-48

2 Click the Open button and then enter the Therapist data from Figure 1-45 into the Therapist table.

The datasheet displays with three records entered (Figure 1-49).

3 Click the Close button for the Therapist : Table window to close the table.

Access closes the table and removes the datasheet from the screen.

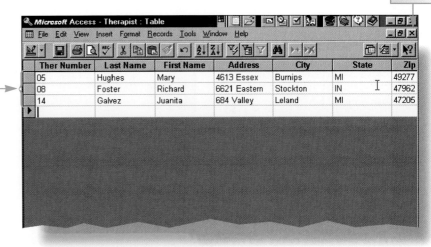

FIGURE 1-49

Using a Form to View Data

In creating tables, you have used Datasheet view; that is, the data on the screen displayed as a table. You also can use **Form view**, in which you see a single record at a time.

The advantage with Datasheet view is you can see multiple records at once. It has the disadvantage that, unless you have few fields in the table, you cannot see all the fields at the same time. With Form view you see only a single record, but you can see all the fields in the record. The view you click is a matter of personal preference.

To use Form view, you first must **create a form**. The simplest way to create a form is to use the New Object button on the toolbar. To do so, first select the table for which the form is to be created in the Database window, and then click the New Object button. A list of available objects displays. Select AutoForm from the list by clicking it in the list.

Perform the following steps using the New Object button to create a form for the Patient table.

More *About* **Forms**

Forms are very powerful tools in database management systems. Forms can incorporate data from multiple tables in the same form. They also can include special types of data such as pictures and sounds.

 To Use the New Object Button to Create the Form

1 Make sure the Mason Clinic database is open, the Database window displays, and the Patient table is selected. Point to the New Object button down arrow on the toolbar (Figure 1-50).

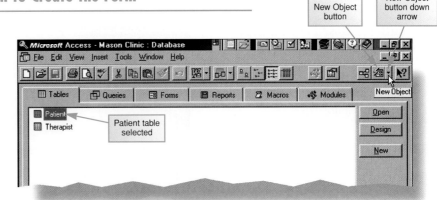

FIGURE 1-50

2 **Click the New Object button down arrow and then point to AutoForm.**

A list of objects that can be created displays (Figure 1-51).

FIGURE 1-51

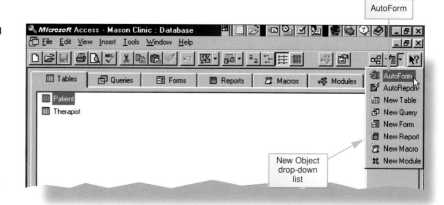

3 **Click AutoForm in the New Object drop-down list.**

The form displays (Figure 1-52).

FIGURE 1-52

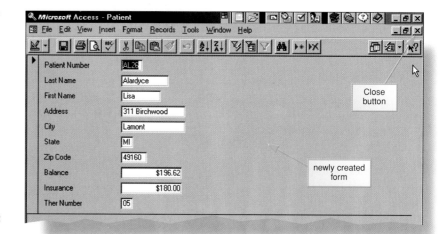

Closing and Saving the Form

Closing a form is similar to closing a table. The only difference is that you will be asked if you want to **save the form** unless you have previously saved it. Perform the following steps to close the form and save it as Patient form.

Steps To Close and Save the Form

1 **Click the Close button for the Patient window (see Figure 1-52).**

The Microsoft Access dialog box displays (Figure 1-53).

FIGURE 1-53

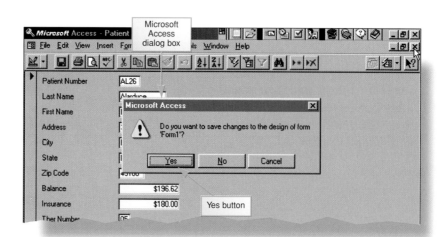

2 Click the Yes button and then point to the OK button.

The Save As dialog box displays (Figure 1-54). The name of the table (Patient) has been automatically entered as the name of the form. If you wished, you could replace it with another name.

3 Click the OK button in the Save As dialog box.

The form is saved as part of the database and is removed from the screen. The Mason Clinic : Database window again displays.

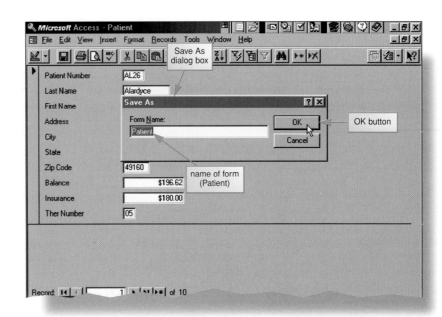

FIGURE 1-54

Opening the Saved Form

Once you have saved a form, you can use it at any time in the future by opening it. **Opening a form** is similar to opening a table; that is, make sure the form to be opened is selected and then click the Open button. Before opening the form, however, the Forms tab, rather than the Tables tab, must be selected.

Perform the following steps to open the Patient form.

 To Open the Form

1 With the Mason Clinic database open and the Database window on the screen, point to the Forms tab (Figure 1-55).

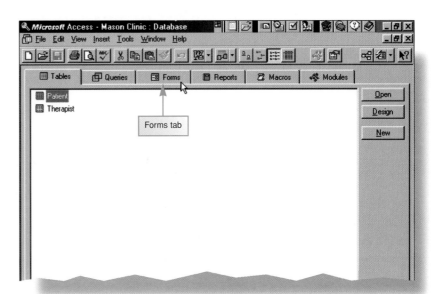

FIGURE 1-55

2 **Click the Forms tab.**

The Forms tab is selected and the list of available forms displays (Figure 1-56). Currently, the Patient form is the only form.

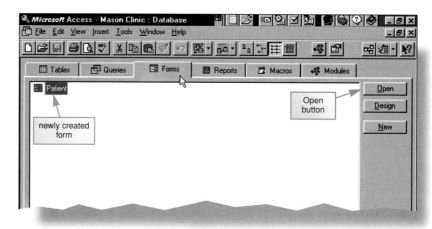

FIGURE 1-56

3 **Click the Open button.**

The Patient form displays (Figure 1-57).

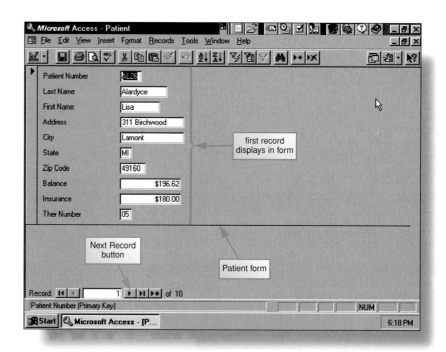

FIGURE 1-57

Using the Form

You can **use the form** just as you used Datasheet view. You use the Navigation buttons to move between records. You can add new records or change existing ones. Press the DELETE key to delete the record displayed on the screen after selecting the record by clicking its row selector. In other words, you can perform database operations using either Form view or Datasheet view.

Because you can see only one record at a time in Form view, to see a different record, such as the fifth record, use the Navigation buttons to move to it. To move from record to record in Form view, perform the following step.

Steps To Use the Form

1 Click the Next Record button (Figure 1-57) four times.

The fifth record displays on the form (Figure 1-58).

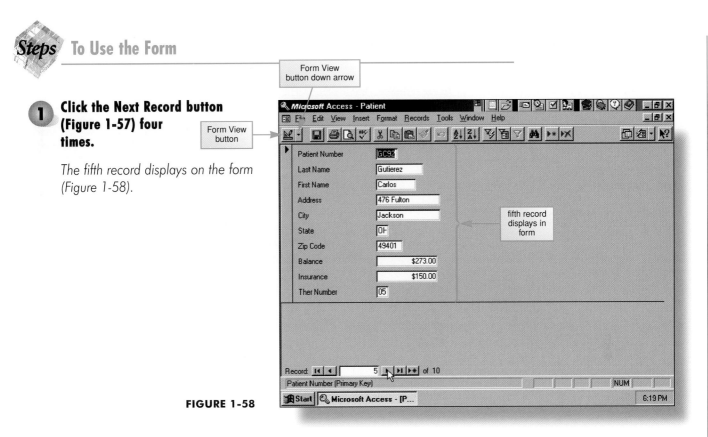

FIGURE 1-58

Switching Between Form View and Datasheet View

In some cases, once you have seen a record in Form view, you will want to move to Datasheet view to once again see a collection of records. To do so, click the Form View button down arrow on the toolbar and then click Datasheet View in the drop-down list that displays.

Perform the following steps to transfer from Form view to Datasheet view.

More *About* **Reports**

The capability to create sophisti-cated custom reports is one of the major benefits of a data-base management system. Reports can incorporate data from multiple tables. They also can be formatted in a wide vari-ety of ways.

Steps To Switch from Form View to Datasheet View

1 Click the Form View button down arrow on the toolbar (see Figure 1-58).

The drop-down list of available views displays (Figure 1-59).

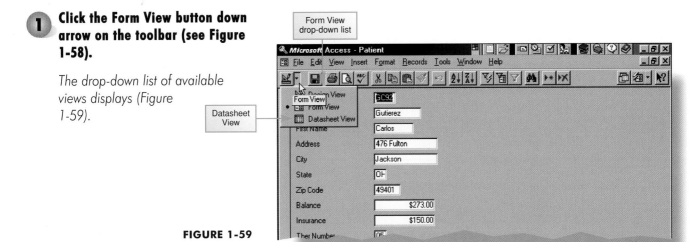

FIGURE 1-59

2 **Click Datasheet View.**

The table displays in Datasheet view (Figure 1-60). The highlight is positioned on the fifth record.

3 **Close the Patient window by clicking its Close button.**

The datasheet no longer displays.

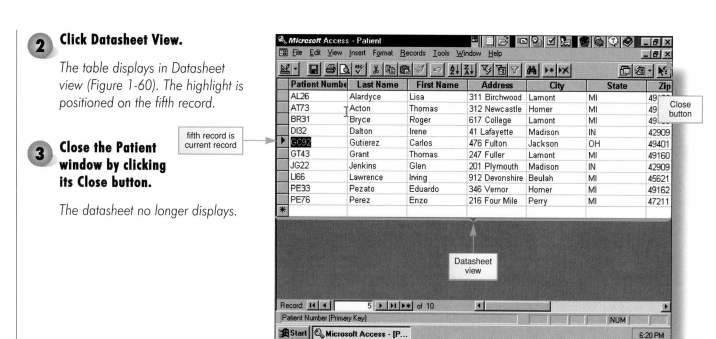

FIGURE 1-60

Creating a Report

Earlier in this project, you printed a table using the Print button. The report you produced was shown in Figure 1-36 on page A 1.29. While this type of report presented the data in an organized manner, it was not very flexible. It included all fields, in precisely the same order in which they occurred in the table. A way to change the title was not presented. It was simply Patient, whether or not you wanted that title.

In this section, you will **create the report** shown in Figure 1-61. This report features significant differences from the one in Figure 1-36. The portion at the top of the report in Figure 1-61, called a **page header**, contains a custom title. The contents of this page header appear at the top of each page. The **detail lines**, the lines that are printed for each record, contain only those fields you specify.

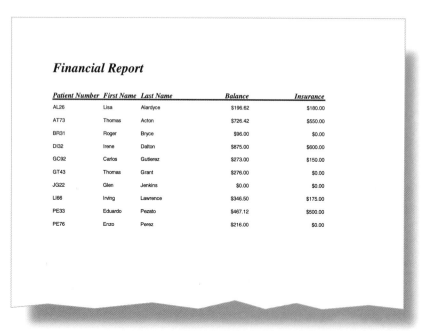

FIGURE 1-61

Perform the following steps to create the report in Figure 1-61.

Steps | **To Create the Report**

1 Click the Tables tab. Make sure the Patient table is selected. Click the New Object button down arrow on the toolbar.

The drop-down list of available objects displays (Figure 1-62).

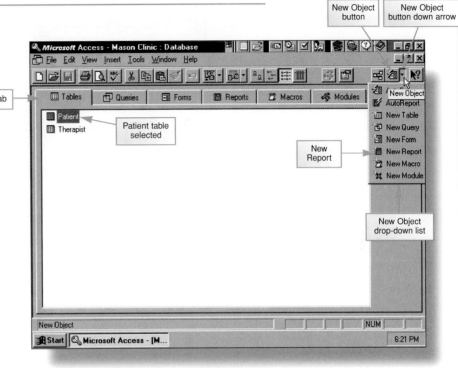

FIGURE 1-62

2 Click New Report and then point to Report Wizard.

The New Report dialog box displays (Figure 1-63).

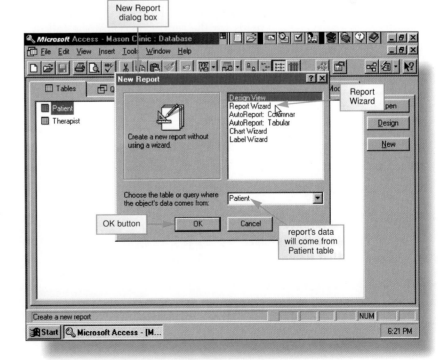

FIGURE 1-63

3 **Click Report Wizard and then click the OK button. Point to the Add Field button.**

The Report Wizard dialog box displays (Figure 1-64).

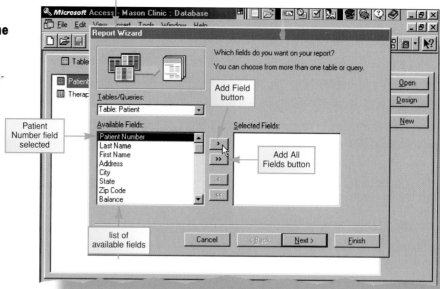

FIGURE 1-64

Selecting the Fields for the Report

To **select a field** for the report; that is, to indicate the field that is to be included in the report, click the field in the Available Fields list box. Next, click the Add Field button. This will move the field from the Available Fields list box to the Selected Fields list box, thus including the field in the report. If you wanted to select all fields, a shortcut is available by simply clicking the Add All Fields button.

To select the Patient Number, First Name, Last Name, Balance, and Insurance fields for the report, perform the following steps.

Steps **To Select the Fields for the Report**

1 **Click the Add Field button to add the Patient Number field. Add the First Name field by clicking it, and then clicking the Add Field button. Add the Last Name, Balance, and Insurance fields just as you added the Patient Number and First Name fields.**

The fields for the report display in the Selected Fields list box (Figure 1-65).

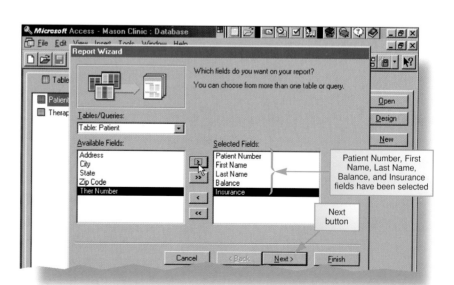

FIGURE 1-65

Report Wizard
dialog box

2 **Click the Next button.**

The Report Wizard dialog box displays (Figure 1-66).

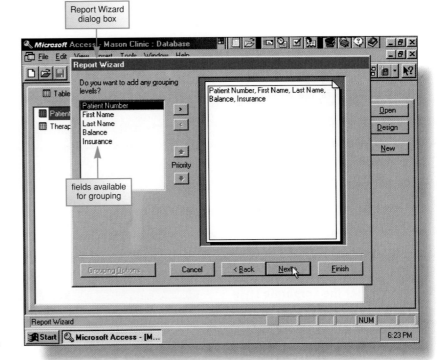

fields available
for grouping

FIGURE 1-66

Completing the Report

Several additional steps are involved in **completing the report**. With the exception of changing the title, the selections Access has already made in these other steps are acceptable, so you will simply click the Next button.

Perform the following steps to complete the report.

 To Complete the Report

Report Wizard
dialog box

1 **Because you will not specify any grouping, click the Next button in the Report Wizard dialog box (see Figure 1-66). Click the Next button a second time because you will not need to make changes on the screen that follows.**

The Report Wizard dialog box displays (Figure 1-67). Use this dialog box to change the layout or orientation of the report.

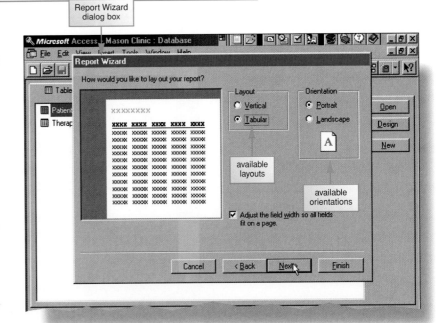

available
layouts

available
orientations

FIGURE 1-67

2 **Because the options currently selected in the dialog box in Figure 1-67 on page A 1.43 are acceptable, click the Next button.**

The Report Wizard dialog box displays (Figure 1-68). Use this dialog box to select a style for the report.

FIGURE 1-68

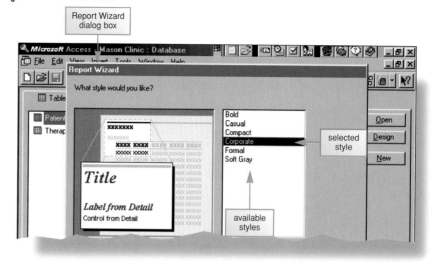

3 **Be sure that the Corporate style is selected and then click the Next button.**

The Report Wizard dialog box displays (Figure 1-69). Use this dialog box to specify a title for the report.

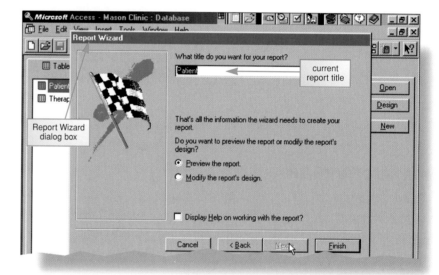

FIGURE 1-69

4 **Type** Financial Report **as the new title, and then click the Finish button.**

A preview of the report displays (Figure 1-70). Yours may look slightly different, depending on your printer.

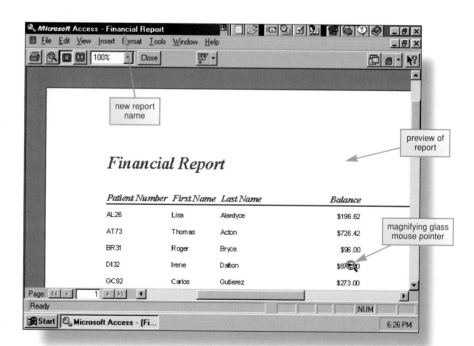

FIGURE 1-70

5 To see the entire report, click the magnifying glass mouse pointer somewhere within the report.

The entire report displays (Figure 1-71).

6 Close the report by clicking the Close button for the Financial Report window.

The report no longer displays. It has been saved automatically using the name Financial Report.

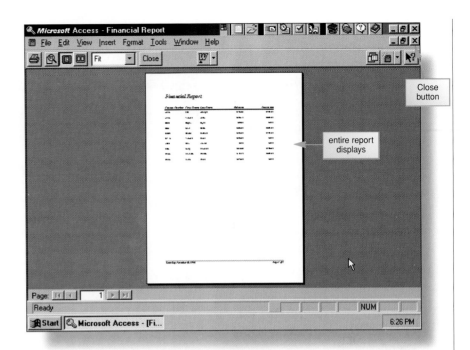

FIGURE 1-71

Printing the Report

To **print a report** from the Database window, first make sure that the reports display. If they do not, click the Reports tab. Next, make sure the report you want to print is selected, and then click the Preview button. After the preview displays and you have verified it is the correct report, click the Print button on the toolbar just as you did earlier.

Perform the following steps to print the report.

 To Print the Report

1 Click the Reports tab in the Database window.

The list of reports displays (Figure 1-72). Currently, the only report is the Financial Report.

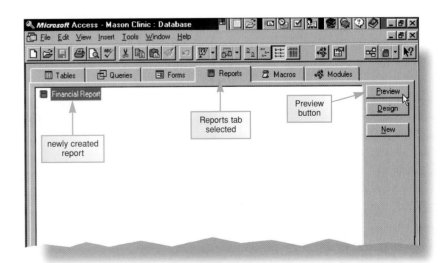

FIGURE 1-72

2 **Because the desired report is already selected, click the Preview button. Point to the Print button on the toolbar.**

A preview of the report displays (Figure 1-73).

3 **Click the Print button on the toolbar.**

The report prints. It looks similar to the one in Figure 1-61 on page A 1.40.

4 **Close the report by clicking the Close button for the Financial Report window.**

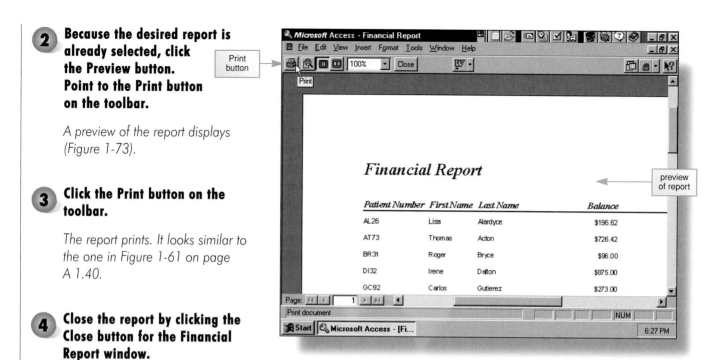

FIGURE 1-73

OtherWays

1. On File menu click Print Preview to preview; on File menu click Print to print
2. Press CTRL+P to print

Closing the Database

Once you have finished working with a database, you should close it. The following step closes the database by closing its Database window.

TO CLOSE A DATABASE

Step 1: Click the Close button for the Mason Clinic : Database window.

Access Online Help

At any time while you are using Access, you can answer your Access questions by using **online Help.** Used properly, this form of online assistance can increase your productivity and reduce your frustrations by minimizing the time you spend learning how to use Access.

Using the Contents Sheet to Obtain Help

The **Contents sheet** in the Help Topics dialog box offers you assistance when you know the general category of the topic in question, but not the specifics. Use the Contents sheet in the same manner you would use a table of contents at the front of a textbook.

The following steps show how to use the Contents sheet tab to obtain information on adding or editing data.

Steps To Obtain Help Using the Contents Sheet

1 **Double-click the Help button on the toolbar (the button containing an arrowhead and question mark).**

The Help Topics: Microsoft Access for Windows 95 dialog box displays (Figure 1-74).

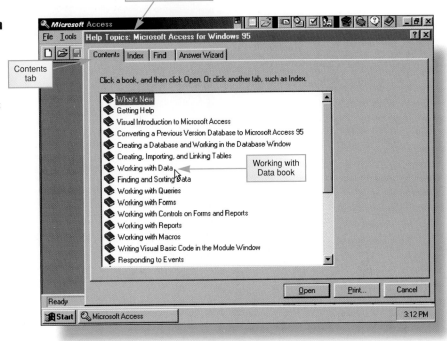

FIGURE 1-74

2 **If necessary, click the Contents tab to make the Contents sheet active. In the list box, double-click the Working with Data book.**

*Each topic on the Contents sheet is preceded by a book or question mark icon. A **book icon** means there are subtopics. A **question mark icon** means information will display on the topic if the title is double-clicked. Notice how the book icon opens when the book (or its title) is double-clicked (Figure 1-75).*

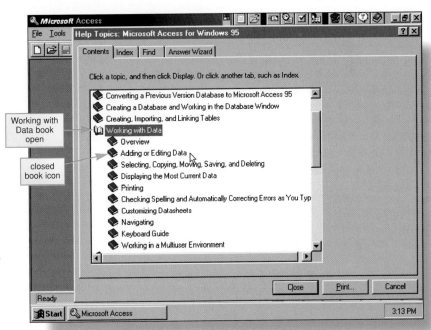

FIGURE 1-75

3 **Double-click the book Adding or Editing Data listed below the open book Working with Data.**

The Adding or Editing Data book is open with a list of topics (Figure 1-76).

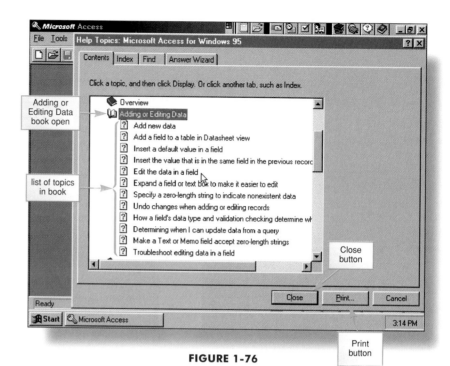

FIGURE 1-76

4 **Double-click the topic, Edit the data in a field, listed below the open book Adding or Editing Data.**

A Microsoft Access for Win Help window displays describing the steps for editing the data in a field (Figure 1-77).

5 **After reading the information, click the Close button in the Microsoft Access for Win Help window.**

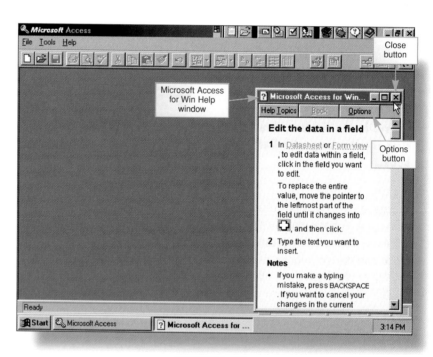

FIGURE 1-77

OtherWays

1. On Help menu, click either Microsoft Access Help Topics or Answer Wizard
2. Press F1

Rather than double-clicking a topic in the list box, you can click it and then use the buttons at the bottom of the Help Topics dialog box to open a book, display information on a topic, or print information on a topic (Figure 1-76).

You also can print the information in the Help window by right-clicking in the window (Figure 1-77) or clicking the Options button and then clicking Print Topic. To close the Help window, click its Close button to return to Access or click the Help Topics button to return to the Contents sheet.

Using the Index Sheet to Obtain Help

The next sheet in the Help Topics: Microsoft Access for Windows 95 dialog box is the Index sheet. Use the **Index sheet** when you know the term you are after or at least the first few letters of the term. Use the Index sheet in the same manner you would an index at the back of a textbook.

The following steps show how to obtain information on primary keys by using the Index sheet and entering the letters, pri, the first three letters of primary.

 Steps To Obtain Help Using the Index Sheet

① Double-click the Help button on the toolbar.

The Help Topics: Microsoft Access for Windows 95 dialog box displays.

② If necessary, click the Index tab. Type pri **in the top box labeled 1.**

The term primary keys displays in the lower box labeled 2 (Figure 1-78). Several index entries relating to primary keys are in the list.

FIGURE 1-78

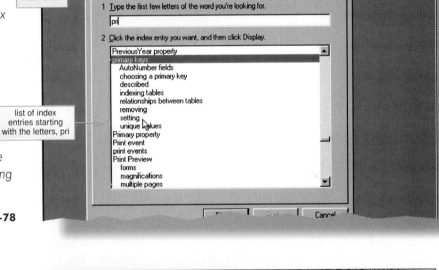

③ Double-click the index entry, setting, under primary keys. Double-click Set or change the primary key in the Topics Found dialog box.

Information on setting, or changing the primary key displays in the Microsoft Access for Win Help window (Figure 1-79).

FIGURE 1-79

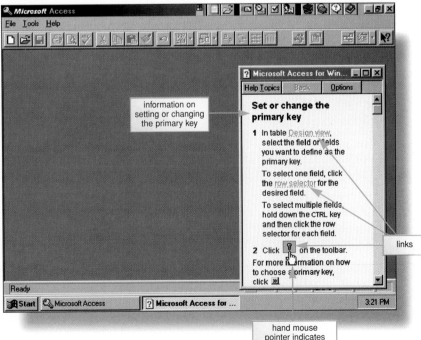

4 **Point to the Primary Key button link. Click the mouse pointer when it changes to a hand.**

The information on the Primary Key button displays above the Primary Key button link (Figure 1-80). When you click a link, *a picture, or phrase, Access displays further Help information.*

5 **Click anywhere in the Primary Key button information box to close it, and then click the Close button in the upper right corner of the Microsoft Access for Win Help window to close it.**

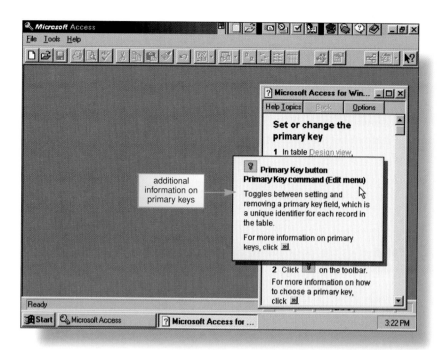

FIGURE 1-80

Not all information you look up through online Help is printable. Generally speaking if the Help window contains an Options button, then you can print the information.

Using the Find Sheet to Obtain Help

The third sheet in the Help Topics: Microsoft Access for Windows 95 dialog box is the Find sheet. Use the **Find sheet** when you know a word that is located *anywhere* in the term or phrase. The Find sheet will return a list of all topics pertaining to the word. You then can further select words to narrow your search.

The following steps show how to obtain information on adding a field to a table structure.

Steps **To Obtain Help Using the Find Sheet**

1 **Double-click the Help button on the toolbar.**

The Help Topics: Microsoft Access for Windows 95 dialog box displays.

2 **If necessary, click the Find tab. Type** add **in the top box labeled 1.**

Matching words display in the middle box labeled 2, and 714 topics relating to the term add are accessible in the lower box labeled 3 (Figure 1-81). Your computer may contain fewer or more topics found.

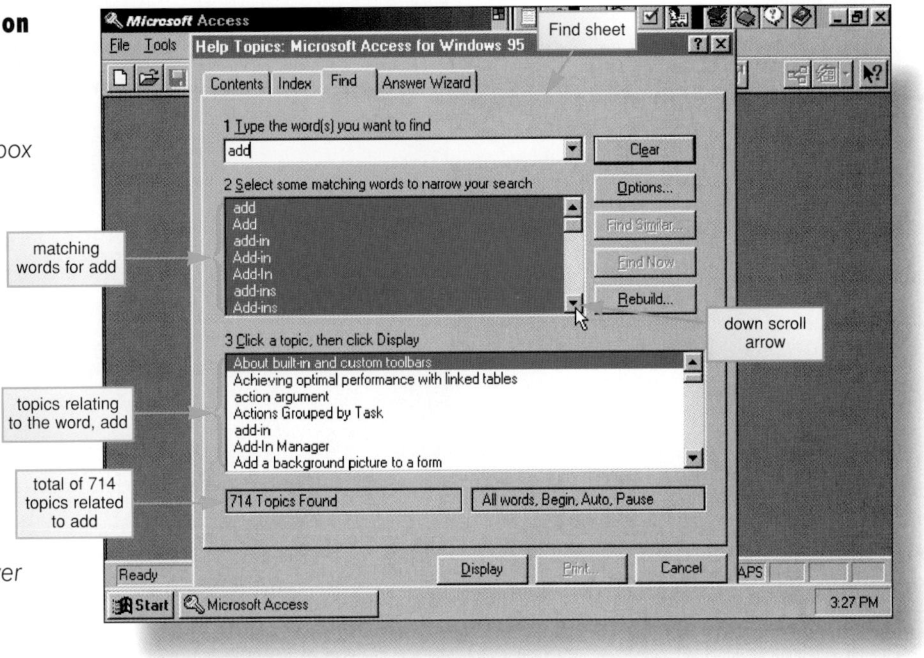

FIGURE 1-81

3 **Click the down scroll arrow to display the word, adding. Click the word, adding, in the middle box labeled 2.**

The number of topics found changes from 714 to 74 in the lower box labeled 3 (Figure 1-82). The number may be different on your computer.

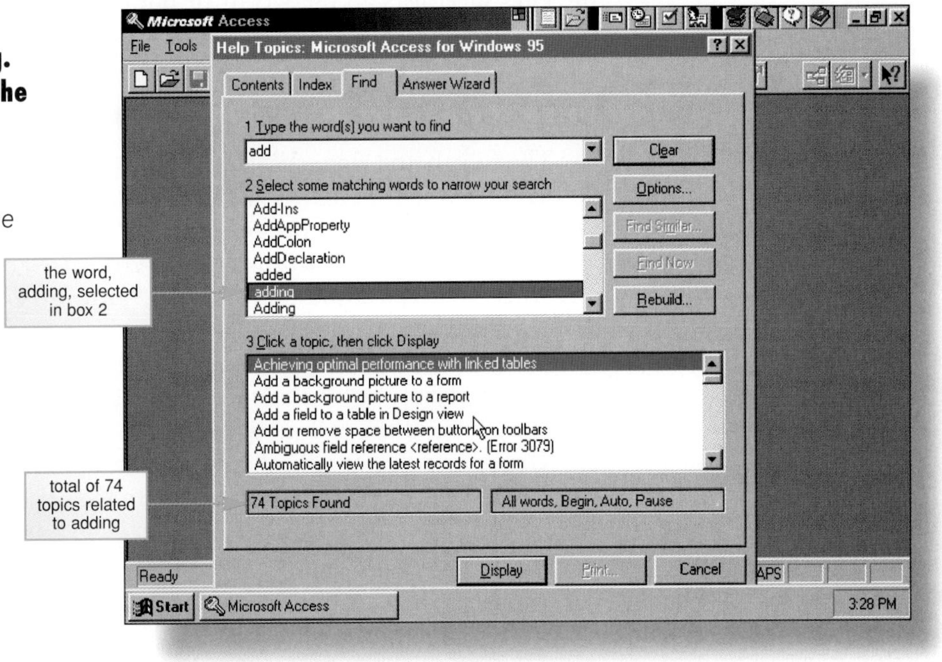

FIGURE 1-82

4 **Double-click the topic, Add a field to a table in Design view, in the lower box labeled 3 on the Find sheet.**

The information regarding adding a field to a table in Design view displays as shown in Figure 1-83. To display more information click the Insert Row button link.

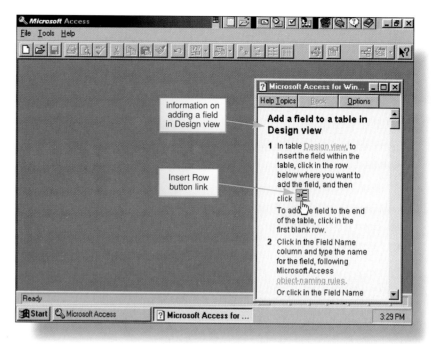

FIGURE 1-83

You can see from the previous steps that the Find sheet allows you to enter a word similar to the Index sheet, but instead of displaying an alphabetical listing, the Find sheet lists all the words or phrases that include the word you entered. You then can click the appropriate words or phrases to narrow your search.

Using the Answer Wizard to Obtain Help

The fourth and final sheet in the Help Topics: Microsoft Access for Windows 95 dialog box is the Answer Wizard sheet. Use the **Answer Wizard** sheet when you know what you want to do, but have no idea what the task is called. Simply type a question in your own words and the Answer Wizard will assist you. For example, when you type a question such as, "How do I create a table?" on the Answer Wizard sheet, it responds by displaying two categories of topics - *How Do I* and *Tell Me About*. The *How Do I* topics show how to complete a task, listing a step-by-step procedure or by example. The *Tell Me About* topics give you a better understanding of the task in question.

The following steps show how to obtain information on creating a table by entering the question, "How do I create a table?"

Steps To Obtain Help Using the Answer Wizard

1 **Double-click the Help button on the toolbar.**

The Help Topics: Microsoft Access for Windows 95 dialog box displays.

2 **If necessary, click the Answer Wizard tab. Type** how do i create a table **in the box labeled 1. Click the Search button.**

The Answer Wizard responds by displaying two categories (How Do I and Tell Me About) of topics in the lower box labeled 2 (Figure 1-84).

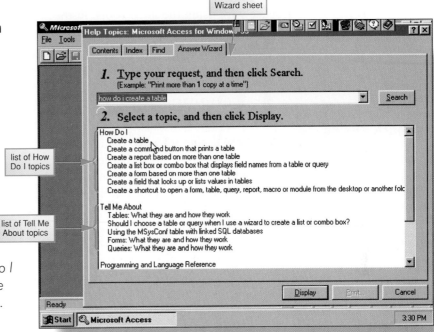

FIGURE 1-84

3 **Double-click the topic Create a table in the lower box labeled 2.**

A Microsoft Access for Windows 95 Help window displays describing the various ways you can create a table (Figure 1-85).

4 **After reviewing the information, click the Close button in the upper right corner of the Help window to close it.**

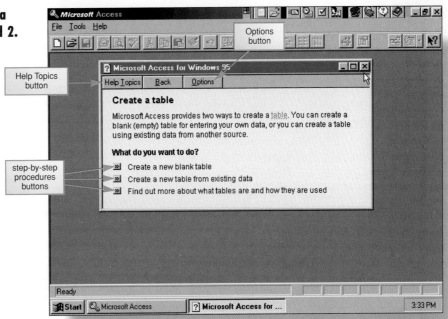

FIGURE 1-85

OtherWays

1. On Help menu, click either Microsoft Access Help Topics or Answer Wizard
2. Press F1

Here again, you can print the information in Figure 1-85 by right-clicking in the Help window or by clicking the Options button. Instead of quitting online Help by clicking the Close button in Step 4, you can click the Help Topics button (Figure 1-85) to return to the Answer Wizard sheet shown in Figure 1-84.

The four online Help features (Contents, Index, Find, and Answer Wizard) of Access presented thus far are powerful and easy to use. The best way to familiarize yourself with these Help tools is to use them. Also to give you more experience with using the Help tools, in the Student Assignments at the end of each project is a section titled Use Help. It is recommended that you step through these Help exercises to gain a better understanding of Access online Help.

Designing a Database

Database design refers to the arrangement of data into tables and fields. In the example in this project, the design is specified, but in many cases, you will have to determine the design based on what you want the system to accomplish.

With large, complex databases, the database design process can be extensive. Major sections of advanced database textbooks are devoted to this topic. Often, however, you should be able to design a database effectively by keeping one simple principle in mind: *Design to remove redundancy*. **Redundancy** means storing the same fact in more than one place.

To illustrate, you need to maintain the following information shown in Figure 1-86. In the figure, all the data is contained in a single table. Notice that the data for a given therapist (number, name, address, and so on) occurs on more than one record.

Patient Table

PATIENT NUMBER	LAST NAME	FIRST NAME	ADDRESS	CITY	STATE	ZIP CODE	BALANCE	INSURANCE	THER NUMBER	LAST NAME	FIRST NAME
AL26	Alardyce	Lisa	311 Birchwood	Lamont	MI	49160	$196.62	$180.00	05	Hughes	Mary
AT73	Acton	Thomas	312 Newcastle	Homer	MI	49162	$726.42	$550.00	08	Foster	Richard
BR31	Bryce	Roger	617 College	Lamont	MI	49160	$96.00	$5,000.00	08	Foster	Richard
DI32	Dalton	Irene	41 Lafayette	Madison	IN	42909	$875.00	$600.00	14	Galvez	Maria
GC92	Gutierez	Carlos	476 Fulton	Jackson	OH	49401	$273.00	$150.00	05	Hughes	Mary
GT43	Grant	Thomas	247 Fuller	Lamont	MI	49160	$276.00	$0.00	08	Foster	Richard
JG22	Jenkins	Glen	201 Plymouth	Madison	IN	42909	$0.00	$0.00	08	Foster	Richard
LI66	Lawrence	Irving	912 Devonshire	Beulah	MI	45621	$346.50	$175.00	05	Hughes	Mary
PE33	Pezato	Eduardo	346 Vernor	Homer	MI	49162	$467.12	$500.00	14	Galvez	Maria
PE76	Perez	Enzo	216 Four Mile	Perry	MI	47211	$216.00	$0.00	08	Foster	Richard

duplicate therapist names

FIGURE 1-86

ADDRESS	CITY	STATE	ZIP CODE	BILLING	PAID
4613 Essex	Burnips	MI	49277	$62,277.00	$46,245.25
6621 Eastern	Stockton	IN	47962	$71,245.00	$65,121.33
6621 Eastern	Stockton	IN	47962	$71,245.00	$65,121.33
684 Valley	Leland	MI	47205	$34,252.50	$22,645.90
4613 Essex	Burnips	MI	49277	$62,277.00	$46,245.25
6621 Eastern	Stockton	IN	47962	$71,245.00	$65,121.33
6621 Eastern	Stockton	IN	47962	$71,245.00	$65,121.33
4613 Essex	Burnips	MI	49277	$62,277.00	$46,245.25
684 Valley	Leland	MI	47205	$34,252.50	$22,645.90
6621 Eastern	Stockton	IN	47962	$71,245.00	$65,121.33

Storing this data on multiple records is an example of redundancy, which causes several problems:

1. Redundancy wastes space on the disk. The address of therapist 05 (Mary Hughes), for example, should be stored only once. Storing this fact several times is wasteful.
2. Redundancy makes updating the database more difficult. If, for example, Mary Hughes moves, her address would need to be changed in several different places.
3. A possibility of inconsistent data exists. Suppose, for example, that you change the address of Mary Hughes on patient GC92's record to 146 Valley, but do not change it on patient AL26's record. In both cases, the Ther Number is 05, but the addresses are different. In other words, the data is *inconsistent*.

The solution to the problem is to place the redundant data in a separate table, one in which the data will no longer be redundant. If, for example, you place the data for therapists in a separate table (Figure 1-87), the data for each therapist will appear only once.

therapist data in separate table

Therapist Table

THER NUMBER	LAST NAME	FIRST NAME	ADDRESS	CITY	STATE	ZIP CODE	BILLING	PAID
05	Hughes	Mary	4613 Essex	Burnips	MI	49277	$62,277.00	$46,245.25
08	Foster	Richard	6621 Eastern	Stockton	IN	47962	$71,245.00	$65,121.33
14	Galvez	Juanita	684 Valley	Leland	MI	47205	$34,252.50	$22,645.90

Patient Table

PATIENT NUMBER	LAST NAME	FIRST NAME	ADDRESS	CITY	STATE	ZIP CODE	BALANCE	INSURANCE	THER NUMBER
AL26	Alardyce	Lisa	311 Birchwood	Lamont	MI	49160	$196.62	$180.00	05
AT73	Acton	Thomas	312 Newcastle	Homer	MI	49162	$726.42	$550.00	08
BR31	Bryce	Roger	617 College	Lamont	MI	49160	$96.00	$0.00	08
DI32	Dalton	Irene	41 Lafayette	Madison	IN	42909	$875.00	$600.00	14
GC92	Gutierez	Carlos	476 Fulton	Jackson	OH	49401	$273.00	$150.00	05
GT43	Grant	Thomas	247 Fuller	Lamont	MI	49160	$276.00	$0.00	08
JG22	Jenkins	Glen	201 Plymouth	Madison	IN	42909	$0.00	$0.00	08
LI66	Lawrence	Irving	912 Devonshire	Beulah	MI	45621	$346.50	$175.00	05
PE33	Pezato	Eduardo	346 Vernor	Homer	MI	49162	$467.12	$500.00	14
PE76	Perez	Enzo	216 Four Mile	Perry	MI	47211	$216.00	$0.00	08

FIGURE 1-87

Notice that you need to have the Ther Number in both tables. Without it, there would be no way to tell which therapist was associated with which patient. All the other therapist data, however, was removed from the Patient table and placed in the Therapist table. This new arrangement corrects the problems:

1. Because the data for each therapist is stored only once, space is not wasted.
2. Changing the address of a therapist is easy. You have only to change one row in the Therapist table.
3. Because the data for a therapist is stored only once, inconsistent data cannot occur.

Designing to omit redundancy will help you to produce good and valid database designs.

Project Summary

Project 1 introduced you to starting Access and creating a database. You created the database that will be used by Mason Clinic. Within the Mason Clinic database, you created the Patient and Therapist tables by defining the fields within them. You then added records to these tables. Once you created the tables, you printed the contents of the tables. You also used a form to view the data in the table. Finally, you used the Report Wizard to create a report containing the patient number, first name, last name, balance, and insurance amount fields for each patient of Mason Clinic.

What You Should Know

Having completed this project, you should now be able to perform the following tasks:

▸ Add Additional Records to the Table   *(A 1.26)*
▸ Add Records to the Additional Table   *(A 1.34)*
▸ Add Records to the Table   *(A 1.21)*
▸ Begin Creating the Table   *(A 1.15)*
▸ Create a New Database   *(A 1.10)*
▸ Create an Additional Table   *(A 1.33)*
▸ Create the Report   *(A 1.41)*
▸ Close and Save the Form   *(A 1.36)*
▸ Close the Table and the Database   *(A 1.24)*
▸ Complete the Report   *(A 1.43)*
▸ Define the Fields in the Table   *(A 1.16)*
▸ Exit Access   *(A 1.23)*
▸ Obtain Help Using the Answer Wizard   *(A 1.53)*
▸ Obtain Help Using the Contents Sheet   *(A 1.47)*
▸ Obtain Help Using the Find Sheet   *(A 1.51)*
▸ Obtain Help Using the Index Sheet   *(A 1.49)*
▸ Open a Database   *(A 1.25)*
▸ Open the Form   *(A 1.37)*
▸ Preview and Print the Contents of the Table   *(A 1.29)*
▸ Print the Report   *(A 1.45)*
▸ Save the Table   *(A 1.19)*
▸ Select the Fields for the Report   *(A 1.42)*
▸ Start Access   *(A 1.10)*
▸ Switch from Form View to Datasheet View   *(A 1.39)*
▸ Use the Form   *(A 1.39)*
▸ Use the New Object Button to Create the Form   *(A 1.35)*

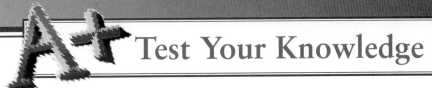 Test Your Knowledge

1 True/False

Instructions: Circle T if the statement is true or F if the statement is false.

T F 1. The term database describes a collection of data organized in a manner that allows access, retrieval, and use of that data.

T F 2. Table names can be from one to 64 characters in length and can include blank spaces.

T F 3. If you do not assign a width to a text field, Access assumes the width is 50.

T F 4. You can use the TAB key to move to the next field in a record in Datasheet view.

T F 5. Field names can be no more than 64 characters in length and cannot include numeric digits.

T F 6. The only field type available for fields that must be used in arithmetic operations is Number.

T F 7. If you enter 10000 in a field that has been defined as a currency field type, then the value will display as $10,000.00.

T F 8. To delete a record from a table, select the record and then press CTRL+DELETE.

T F 9. To add a field to a table structure, select the field that will follow the field you wish to add, click Edit on the menu bar, and then click Insert Row.

T F 10. Controlling redundancy results in an increase in consistency.

2 Multiple Choice

Instructions: Circle the correct response.

1. A database is _____.
   a. the same as a file
   b. a software product
   c. a collection of data organized in a manner that allows access, retrieval, and use of that data
   d. none of the above

2. Which of the following is not a benefit of controlling redundancy?
   a. greater consistency is maintained
   b. less space is occupied
   c. update is easier
   d. all of the above are benefits

3. A field that uniquely identifies a particular record in a table is called a _____.
   a. foreign key
   b. secondary key
   c. primary key
   d. principal key

4. Access is a(n) _____.
   a. applications software package
   b. DBMS
   c. database
   d. both a and b

(continued)

 Test Your Knowledge

Multiple Choice *(continued)*

5. To change to landscape orientation to print a table, click _____ on the File menu.
   a. Print Settings
   b. Page Setup
   c. Print Preview
   d. Print

6. A record in Access is composed of a _____.
   a. series of databases
   b. series of files
   c. series of records
   d. series of fields

7. To make a field the primary key for a table, select the field and then click the _____ button on the toolbar.
   a. Unique Key
   b. Single Key
   c. First Key
   d. Primary Key

8. To remove a field from a table structure, select the field and then press the _____ key(s).
   a. DELETE
   b. CTRL+D
   c. CTRL+DELETE
   d. CTRL+Y

9. To create a form for a table, highlight the table and click the _____ button down arrow on the toolbar, and then click AutoForm on the drop-down list.
   a. New Form
   b. New Object
   c. Create Form
   d. Create Object

10. To move from the upper pane, the one where you define fields, in the Table window to the lower pane, the one where you define field properties, press the _____ key.
    a. F3
    b. F4
    c. F6
    d. F7

3 Understanding Access Windows

Instructions: In Figure 1-88, arrows point to the major components of an Access window. Identify the various parts of the window in the spaces provided.

Test Your Knowledge

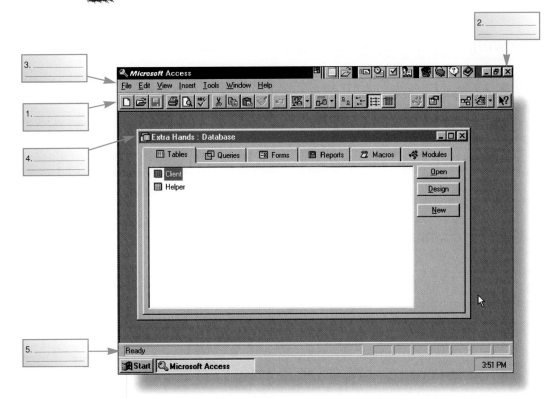

3. _____

2. _____

1. _____

4. _____

5. _____

FIGURE 1-88

4 Understanding the Table Window in Form View

Instructions: On the form in Figure 1-89, arrows point to several of the buttons on the toolbar and status bar. In the spaces provided, identify each button.

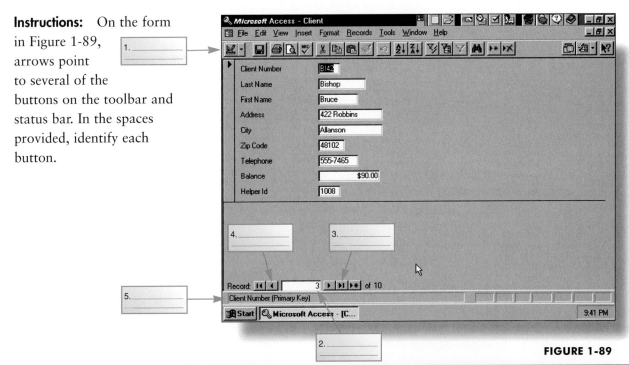

1. _____
4. _____
3. _____
5. _____
2. _____

FIGURE 1-89

Use Help

1 Reviewing Project Activities

Instructions: Perform the following tasks using a computer.

1. Start Access.
2. Double-click the Help button on the toolbar to display the Help Topics: Microsoft Access for Windows 95 dialog box.
3. Click the Index tab. Type Datasheet in box 1, and then double-click editing records under Datasheet view in box 2. Double-click Delete a record in Datasheet or Form view in the Topics Found dialog box. When the Help information displays, read it. Next, right-click within the window, and then click Print Topic. Hand in the printout to your instructor. Click the Help Topics button to return to the Help Topics: Microsoft Access for Windows 95 dialog box.
4. Click the Find tab. Type preview in box 1. Click Previewing in box 2. Double-click Preview a report in box 3. When the Microsoft Access for Windows 95 Help window displays, read it, ready the printer, right-click in the window, and click Print Topic. Click the Preview all the data in the report page by page button in the Help window. Print the Help information. Hand in the printouts to your instructor. Click the Help Topics button to return to the Help Topics: Microsoft Access for Windows 95 dialog box.
5. Click the Answer Wizard tab. Type how do i use data types in box 1. Click the Search button. Double-click What data type should I use for a field in my table? in box 2 under Tell Me About. Read and print the Help information. Hand in the printout to your instructor.

2 Expanding on the Basics

Instructions: Use Access online Help to better understand the topics listed below. Begin each of the following by double-clicking the Help button on the toolbar. If you are unable to print the Help information, then answer the question on your own paper.

1. Using the Working with Data book on the Contents sheet in the Help Topics: Microsoft Access for Windows 95 dialog box, answer the following questions:
   a. When does Access save the data in a record?
   b. How can you save the data in a record while you are editing it?
2. Using the key term, *shortcut keys*, and the Index tab in the Help Topics: Microsoft Access for Windows 95 dialog box, display and print the shortcut keys to use in Datasheet view and Form view. Then, answer the following questions:
   a. Which key or combination keys add a new record?
   b. Which key or combination keys delete a record?
   c. Which key or combination keys save changes to the current record?
   d. Which key or combination keys undo changes in the current field?
   e. Which key or combination keys check spelling?
3. Use the Find sheet in the Help Topics: Microsoft Access for Windows 95 dialog box to display and print information about correcting two capital letters in a row automatically.
4. Use the Answer Wizard in the Help Topics: Microsoft Access for Windows 95 dialog box to display and print information about backing up a database.

Apply Your Knowledge

1 Changing Data and Creating Reports

Instructions: Read the Caution box. Start Access and open the Extra Hands document from the Access folder on the Student Floppy Disk that accompanies this book. Extra Hands is a local company that provides various services to individuals in the community. Helpers run errands, clean houses, drive people to appointments, and assist with other chores. Extra Hands has a database that keeps track of their clients and their helpers. The database has two tables. The Client table contains data on the clients who use the Extra Hands service. The Helper table contains data on individuals employed by Extra Hands. The data and structure are shown for the Client table in Figure 1-90 and for the Helper table in Figure 1-91 on the next page.

Structure of Client Table

FIELD NAME	DATA TYPE	FIELD SIZE	PRIMARY KEY?	DESCRIPTION
Client Number	Text	4	Yes	Client Number (Primary Key)
Last Name	Text	10		Last Name of Client
First Name	Text	8		First Name of Client
Address	Text	15		Street Address
City	Text	15		City
Zip Code	Text	5		Zip Code (Five-Character Version)
Telephone	Text	8		Telephone Number (999-9999 Version)
Balance	Currency			Amount Owed by Client
Helper Id	Text	4		Id of Client's Helper

Data for Client Table

CLIENT NUMBER	LAST NAME	FIRST NAME	ADDRESS	CITY	ZIP CODE	TELEPHONE	BALANCE	HELPER ID
AR86	Arends	Carolyn	268 Getty	Allanson	48102	555-9523	$35.00	1001
AT24	Atwater	Shelly	542 Dune	Allanson	48103	555-1354	$0.00	1008
BI42	Bishop	Bruce	422 Robbins	Allanson	48102	555-7465	$90.00	1008
CH26	Chiang	Doi	62 Stryker	Oakdale	48101	555-2018	$0.00	1012
CH66	Chown	Douglas	266 Norton	Oakdale	48101	555-4890	$55.00	1001
JO12	Johns	Patricia	420 Robbins	Allanson	48102	555-9182	$24.00	1008
KI15	Kirk	Robert	12 Hellerman	Oakdale	48101	555-8273	$65.00	1008
MA21	Martinez	Marie	215 Glen	Allanson	48102	555-1234	$0.00	1001
MO31	Morton	Julie	557 Dune	Allanson	48103	555-5361	$78.00	1012
RO92	Robertson	Mary	345 Magee	Oakdale	48101	555-2056	$43.00	1008

FIGURE 1-90

(continued)

Apply Your Knowledge

Changing Data and Creating Reports *(continued)*

Structure of Helper Table

FIELD NAME	DATA TYPE	FIELD SIZE	PRIMARY KEY?	DESCRIPTION
Helper Id	Text	4	Yes	Helper Identification Number (Primary Key)
Last Name	Text	10		Last Name of Helper
First Name	Text	8		First Name of Helper
Address	Text	15		Street Address
City	Text	15		City
Zip Code	Text	5		Zip Code (Five-Character Version)
Telephone	Text	8		Telephone Number (999-9999 Version)
Pay Rate	Currency			Hourly Pay Rate

Data for Helper Table

HELPER ID	LAST NAME	FIRST NAME	ADDRESS	CITY	ZIP CODE	TELEPHONE	PAY RATE
1001	Carson	Helen	872 Devon	Allanson	48102	555-7980	$7.25
1008	Ortez	Julia	96 Pierce	Oakdale	48101	555-2395	$6.95
1012	Zwieback	Robert	35 Henry	Allanson	48103	555-2040	$6.35

FIGURE 1-91

Perform the following tasks:

1. Open the Helper table in Datasheet view and add the following record to the table:

1010	Rassler	John	12 Seminole	Oakdale	48101	555-4112	$6.75

To add the record, move past the first three records and then type the data for the new record. Close the Helper table.

2. Open the Helper table again. Notice that the record you just added has been moved. It is no longer at the end of the table. The records are in order by the primary key, Helper Id.
3. Print the Helper table.
4. Open the Client table.
5. Change the Helper Id for client KI15 to 1010.
6. Print the Client table.
7. Create the report shown in Figure 1-92 for the Client table.

Apply Your Knowledge

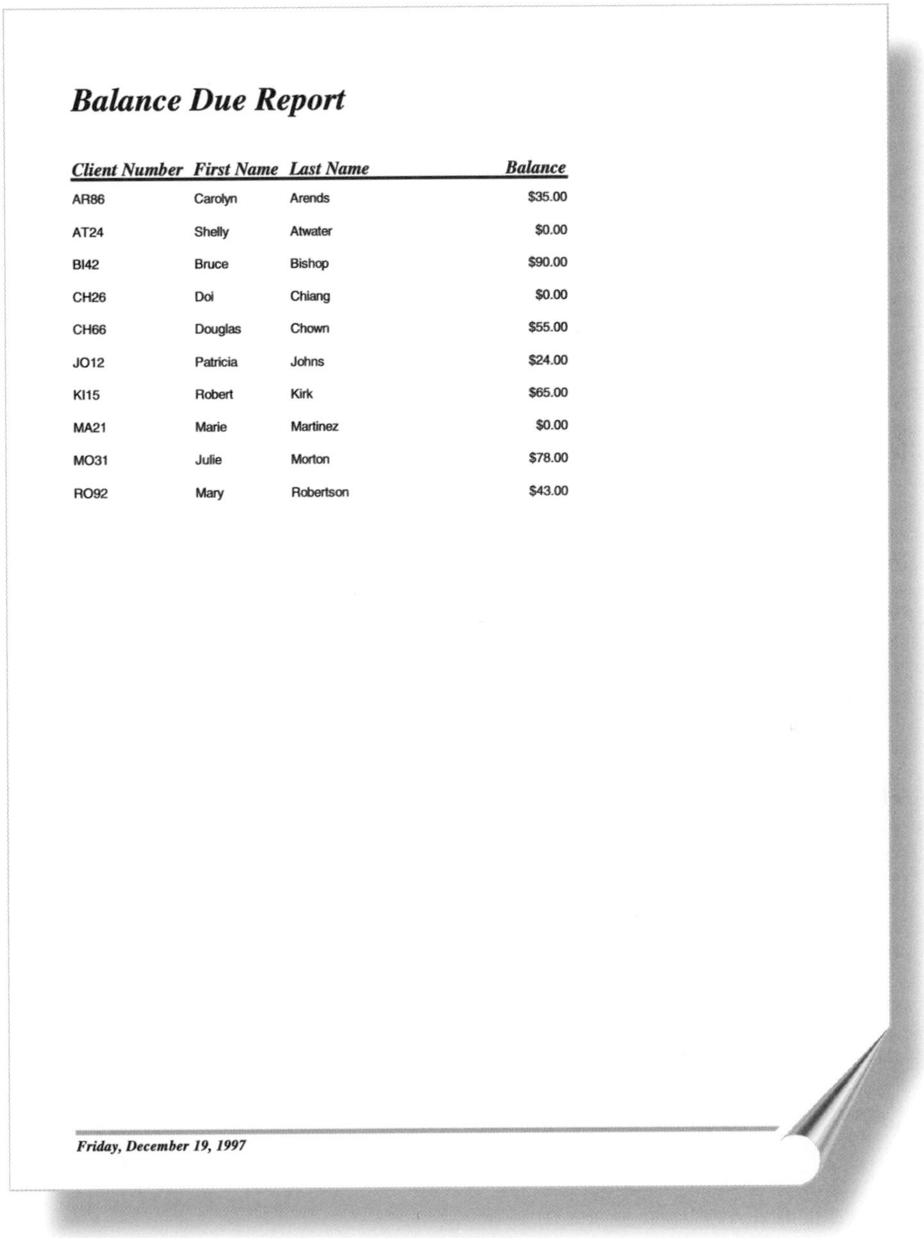

Balance Due Report

Client Number	*First Name*	*Last Name*	*Balance*
AR86	Carolyn	Arends	$35.00
AT24	Shelly	Atwater	$0.00
BI42	Bruce	Bishop	$90.00
CH26	Doi	Chiang	$0.00
CH66	Douglas	Chown	$55.00
JO12	Patricia	Johns	$24.00
KI15	Robert	Kirk	$65.00
MA21	Marie	Martinez	$0.00
MO31	Julie	Morton	$78.00
RO92	Mary	Robertson	$43.00

Friday, December 19, 1997

FIGURE 1-92

8. Print the report.

In the Lab

1 Creating the Symphony Shop Database

Problem: The local symphony raises money by selling musical novelties during concerts. Volunteers purchase novelty items from distributors that specialize in musical products. The president of the symphony board has asked you to create and update a database that volunteers can use. The database consists of two tables. The Novelty table contains information on items available for sale. The Distributor table contains information on the distributors.

Instructions: Perform the following tasks:

1. Create a new database in which to store all the objects related to the musical novelty data. Call the database Symphony Shop.
2. Create the Novelty table using the structure shown in Figure 1-93. Use the name Novelty for the table.

Structure of Novelty Table

FIELD NAME	DATA TYPE	FIELD SIZE	PRIMARY KEY?	DESCRIPTION
Novelty Id	Text	3	Yes	Novelty Id Number (Primary Key)
Description	Text	15		Description of Novelty Item
Units On Hand	Number	Long Integer		Number of Units On Hand
Cost	Currency			Unit Cost of Novelty Item
Selling Price	Currency			Selling Price of Novelty Item
Dist Code	Text	2		Code of Distributor of Novelty Item

Data for Novelty Table

NOVELTY ID	DESCRIPTION	UNITS ON HAND	COST	SELLING PRICE	DIST CODE
E01	Erasers	35	$0.15	$0.25	MM
G05	Gloves	10	$2.95	$4.00	CC
K03	Key Chains	25	$0.95	$1.20	AD
N01	Note Pads	20	$1.00	$1.50	AD
P02	Pencils	70	$0.10	$0.25	MM
P03	Pens	50	$0.75	$1.00	MM
S10	Scarves	5	$4.95	$6.50	CC
S12	Socks	15	$1.95	$3.00	CC
S25	Stationery	8	$3.95	$5.00	AD
U10	Umbrellas	12	$6.95	$8.00	CC

FIGURE 1-93

In the Lab

3. Add the data shown in Figure 1-93 to the Novelty table.
4. Print the Novelty table.
5. Create the Distributor table using the structure shown in Figure 1-94. Use the name Distributor for the table.
6. Add the data shown in Figure 1-94 to the Distributor table.

Structure of Distributor Table

FIELD NAME	DATA TYPE	FIELD SIZE	PRIMARY KEY?	DESCRIPTION
Dist Code	Text	2	Yes	Distributor Code (Primary Key)
Name	Text	18		Name of Distributor
Address	Text	15		Street Address
City	Text	15		City
State	Text	2		State (Two-Character Abbreviation)
Zip Code	Text	5		Zip Code (Five-Character Version)
Telephone	Text	12		Telephone Number (999-999-9999 Version)

Data for Distributor Table

DIST CODE	NAME	ADDRESS	CITY	STATE	ZIP CODE	TELEPHONE
AD	AAA Distributor	9661 King	Nova	MI	49401	517-555-3953
CC	Cook's Catalog	1625 Brook	Adelaide	MI	49441	616-555-8292
MM	Music Makers	145 Oak	Grand Fork	IL	49302	317-555-4477

FIGURE 1-94

7. Print the Distributor table.
8. Create a form for the Novelty table. Use the name Novelty for the form.
9. Create the report shown in Figure 1-95 on the next page for the Novelty table.

(continued)

In the Lab

Creating the Symphony Shop Database *(continued)*

Inventory Report

Novelty Id	Description	Units On Hand	Cost
E01	Erasers	35	$0.15
G05	Gloves	10	$2.95
K03	Key Chains	25	$0.95
N01	Note Pads	20	$1.00
P02	Pencils	70	$0.10
P03	Pens	50	$0.75
S10	Scarves	5	$4.95
S12	Socks	15	$1.95
S25	Stationery	8	$3.95
U10	Umbrellas	12	$6.95

FIGURE 1-95

2 Creating the College Telephone System Database

Problem: The Telecommunications group at your school operates the school telephone system. Each user is billed separately for monthly charges and all the bills for a department are sent to the department chair. The telephone manager has asked you to create and update a database that the school can use as a telephone tracking system. The database consists of two tables. The User table contains information on the individuals with telephone accounts. The Department table contains information on the department to which the individual is assigned.

Instructions: Perform the following tasks:

1. Create a new database in which to store all the objects related to the telephone system data. Call the database College Telephone System.
2. Create the User table using the structure shown in Figure 1-96. Use the name User for the table.
3. Add the data shown in Figure 1-96 to the User table.

In the Lab

Structure of User Table

FIELD NAME	DATA TYPE	FIELD SIZE	PRIMARY KEY?	DESCRIPTION
User Id	Text	5	Yes	User Id Number (Primary Key)
Last Name	Text	14		Last Name of User
First Name	Text	10		First Name of User
Phone Ext	Text	4		Telephone Extension (9999 Version)
Office	Text	6		Office Location (Room Number and Building Code)
Basic Charge	Currency			Basic Service Charge (per Month)
Extra Charges	Currency			Extra Charges for Special Services and Long Distance Calls (per Month)
Dept Code	Text	3		Code of User's Department

Data for User Table

USER ID	LAST NAME	FIRST NAME	PHONE EXT	OFFICE	BASIC CHARGE	EXTRA CHARGES	DEPT CODE
T1290	Chou	Tanya	2383	112ABH	$15.00	$27.00	ACC
T2389	Cookson	Christin	2495	120EMH	$18.00	$34.95	BIO
T3487	Hoveman	Benjamin	3267	223SHH	$15.00	$12.75	ENG
T4521	Janson	Catherine	2156	244ABH	$22.00	$57.85	MTH
T5364	Keatty	Richard	2578	116ABH	$18.00	$23.75	ACC
T6457	Medlar	Michelle	3445	212SHH	$26.00	$7.75	ENG
T7579	Nadzia	Rodean	2068	268SHH	$15.00	$18.55	HIS
T7890	Richardson	Maria	2418	122EMH	$22.00	$78.95	BIO
T8521	Sanchez	Javier	2134	248ABH	$16.00	$11.25	MTH
T8883	TenHoopen	Adrian	2414	134EMH	$15.00	$42.45	BIO

FIGURE 1-96

4. Print the User table.
5. Create the Department table using the structure shown in Figure 1-97. Use the name Department for the table.
6. Add the data shown in Figure 1-97 on the next page to the Department table.

(continued)

In the Lab

Creating the College Telephone System Database *(continued)*

Structure of Department Table

FIELD NAME	DATA TYPE	FIELD SIZE	PRIMARY KEY?	DESCRIPTION
Dept Code	Text	3	Yes	Department Code (Primary Key)
Name	Text	14		Name of Department
Location	Text	6		Location of Departmental Office (Room Number and Building Code)
First Name	Text	8		First Name of Department Chair
Last Name	Text	12		Last Name of Department Chair

Data for Department Table

DEPT CODE	NAME	LOCATION	FIRST NAME	LAST NAME
ACC	Accounting	100ABH	Leslie	Anderson
BIO	Biology	110EMH	Donald	Kleinfelter
ENG	English	200SHH	Louisa	Fernandez
HIS	History	260SHH	Peter	Chou
MTH	Mathematics	210ABH	Phyllis	Patterson

FIGURE 1-97

7. Print the Department table.
8. Create a form for the User table. Use the name User for the form.
9. Use the form you created to add the following two new faculty members to the User table.

T6503	Myrich	Bruce	2038	132ABH	$15.00	$0.00	ACC
T7654	Rabon	Claudia	2239	268ABH	$18.00	$0.00	MTH

10. Create the report shown in Figure 1-98 for the User table. When the Report Wizard asks What Sort Order do you want for your records, click the Last Name field.

In the Lab

Telephone List

Last Name	First Name	Phone Ext	Office	Dept Code
Chou	Tanya	2383	112ABH	ACC
Cookson	Christin	2495	120EM	BIO
Hoveman	Benjamin	3267	223SHH	ENG
Janson	Catherine	2156	244ABH	MTH
Keatty	Richard	2578	116ABH	ACC
Medlar	Michelle	3445	212SHH	ENG
Myrich	Bruce	2038	132ABH	ACC
Nadzia	Rodean	2068	268SHH	HIS
Rabon	Claudia	2239	268ABH	MTH
Richardson	Maria	2418	122EM	BIO
Sanchez	Javier	2134	248ABH	MTH
TenHoopen	Adrian	2414	134EM	BIO

FIGURE 1-98

3 Creating the WWWW Radio Station Database

Problem: The WWWW Radio Station relies on advertising to help finance its operations. Local firms buy advertising from account representatives that work for the radio station. Account representatives are paid a base salary and receive a commission based on the advertising revenues that they generate. The manager of the radio station has asked you to create and update a database that will keep track of the advertising accounts and account representatives. The database consists of two tables. The Accounts table contains information on the organizations that advertise on the radio station. The Account Reps table contains information on the representative assigned to the account.

Instructions: Perform the following tasks:

1. Create a new database in which to store all the objects related to the advertising data. Call the database WWWW Radio Station.
2. Create the Accounts table using the structure shown in Figure 1-99. Use the name Accounts for the table.
3. Add the data shown in Figure 1-99 on the next page to the Accounts table.

(continued)

In the Lab

Creating the WWWW Radio Station Database (continued)

Structure of Accounts Table

FIELD NAME	DATA TYPE	FIELD SIZE	PRIMARY KEY?	DESCRIPTION
Account Number	Text	4	Yes	Account Number (Primary Key)
Name	Text	20		Name of Account
Address	Text	15		Street Address
City	Text	15		City
State	Text	2		State (Two-Character Abbreviation)
Zip Code	Text	5		Zip Code (Five-Character Version)
Balance	Currency			Amount Currently Owed
Amount Paid	Currency			Amount Paid Year-to-Date
Acc Rep Number	Text	2		Number of Account Representative

Data for Accounts Table

ACCOUNT NUMBER	NAME	ADDRESS	CITY	STATE	ZIP CODE	BALANCE	AMOUNT PAID	ACC REP NUMBER
A125	Allen Cleaners	24 Ryan	Kensington	PA	19117	$50.00	$525.00	15
B099	Bea's Bakery	234 Tyson	Mayfair	PA	19111	$0.00	$785.00	18
B133	Bob the Barber	12 Adams	Lawndale	NJ	18923	$145.00	$335.00	18
C046	Carter Shoes	65 Reisling	Mayfair	PA	19111	$90.00	$1,025.00	21
D205	Dennis & Son	457 Oakley	Roxborough	NJ	18919	$250.00	$475.00	15
F304	Fred's Pet Shop	34 Passmore	Kensington	PA	19117	$0.00	$1,275.00	18
G075	Geo's Tires	569 Brea	Kensington	PA	19117	$175.00	$950.00	18
H001	Howard Toys	78 Leland	Roxborough	NJ	18919	$25.00	$650.00	15
M012	Mary's Marina	97 Ada	Lawndale	NJ	18923	$425.00	$1,100.00	21
R111	Ruth's Diner	102 Main	Mayfair	PA	19111	$75.00	$575.00	15

FIGURE 1-99

4. Print the Accounts table.
5. Create the Account Reps table using the structure shown in Figure 1-100. Use the name Account Reps for the table. Be sure to change the field size for the Comm Rate field to Double.
6. Add the data shown in Figure 1-100 to the Account Reps table.

In the Lab

Structure of Account Reps Table

FIELD NAME	DATA TYPE	FIELD SIZE	PRIMARY KEY?	DESCRIPTION
Acc Rep Number	Text	2	Yes	Account Rep Number (Primary Key)
Last Name	Text	10		Last Name of Account Representative
First Name	Text	8		First Name of Account Representative
Address	Text	15		Street Address
City	Text	15		City
State	Text	2		State (Two-Character Abbreviation)
Zip Code	Text	5		Zip Code (Five-Character Version)
Salary	Currency			Base Salary
Comm Rate	Number	Double		Commission Rate on Advertising Sales

Data for Account Reps Table

ACC REP NUMBER	LAST NAME	FIRST NAME	ADDRESS	CITY	STATE	ZIP CODE	SALARY	COMM RATE
15	Glynn	Nancy	26 Barton	Mayfair	PA	19111	$12,000.00	0.08
18	Helko	Brian	12 Shaw	Lawndale	NJ	18923	$11,500.00	0.07
21	Rogers	Helen	34 Manly	Kensington	PA	19117	$13,000.00	0.08

FIGURE 1-100

7. Print the Account Reps table.
8. Create a form for the Accounts table. Use the name Accounts for the form.
9. Open the form you created and change the address for Account Number G075 to 569 Breame.
10. Change to Datasheet view and delete the record for Account Number F304.
11. Print the Accounts table.
12. Create the report shown in Figure 1-101 on the next page for the Accounts table.

(continued)

In the Lab

Creating the WWWW Radio Station Database *(continued)*

Status Report

Account Number	Name	Balance	Amount Paid
A125	Allen Cleaners	$50.00	$525.00
B099	Bea's Bakery	$0.00	$785.00
B133	Bob the Barber	$145.00	$335.00
C046	Carter Shoes	$90.00	$1,025.00
D205	Dennis & Son	$250.00	$475.00
G075	Geo's Tires	$175.00	$950.00
H001	Howard Toys	$25.00	$650.00
M012	Mary's Marina	$425.00	$1,100.00
R111	Ruth's Diner	$75.00	$575.00

Friday, December 19, 1997   *Par*

FIGURE 1-101

Cases and Places

The difficulty of these case studies varies:

▶ Case studies preceded by a single half moon are the least difficult. You are asked to create the required database based on information that has already been placed in an organized form.

▶▶ Case studies preceded by two half moons are more difficult. You must organize the information presented before using it to create the desired database.

▶▶▶ Case studies preceded by three half moons are the most difficult. You must choose a specific topic, and then obtain and organize the necessary information before using it to create the required database.

1 ▶ You often consult the telephone directory for the numbers of local restaurants to make reservations and to order food for carry out and delivery. You have decided to create a database to store these numbers, along with other pertinent data about the establishment such as address, hours of operation, type of food, and days when specials are offered. You gather the information shown in Figure 1-102.

Create a database to store the file related to the restaurants. Then create a table, enter the data from Figure 1-102, and print the table.

NAME	PHONE	ADDRESS	OPEN	CLOSE	FOOD TYPE	SPECIALS	CARRYOUT	DELIVERY
Pablo's Tacos	(714) 555-2339	223 N. Jackson	11:00 a.m.	11:00 p.m.	Mexican	Wednesday	Yes	No
Italian Villages	(714) 555-5444	3294 E. Devon	4:00 p.m.	10:00 p.m.	Italian	Monday	Yes	Yes
Madras Ovens	(714) 555-8001	1632 W. Clark	3:00 p.m.	1:00 a.m.	Indian	Friday	No	No
Parthenon	(714) 555-2470	3140 W. Halsted	11:00 a.m.	4:00 a.m.	Greek	Thursday	Yes	No
New Orient	(714) 555-9337	1805 W. Broadway	3:30 p.m.	10:00 p.m.	Chinese	Monday	Yes	No
Pizza Mia	(714) 555-1673	2200 E. Lawrence	4:30 p.m.	1:00 a.m.	Italian	Thursday	Yes	Yes
Hat Dancers	(714) 555-8632	13 N. Devon	11:30 a.m.	2:00 a.m.	Mexican	Wednesday	Yes	No
Bukhara Bar	(714) 555-3377	1027 E. Wells	5:00 p.m.	2:00 a.m.	Indian	Thursday	Yes	No
Taranio's	(714) 555-6168	787 N. Monroe	10:30 a.m.	3:00 a.m.	Italian	Tuesday	Yes	Yes
Mr. Ming's	(714) 555-7373	1939 W. Michigan	11:00 a.m.	11:00 p.m.	Chinese	Wednesday	Yes	No

FIGURE 1-102

Cases and Places

2 ▶ Book prices increase every semester, so you want to devise a system to curb these expenses. You organize a system whereby students can locate other students who have used a particular book in a previous semester and want to sell it to another student. You advertise your plan in the campus newspaper and receive the responses shown in Figure 1-103

Create a database to store the file related to the textbooks. Then create a table, enter the data from Figure 1-103, and print the table.

BOOK TITLE	AUTHOR	COURSE USED	PRICE	SELLER'S NAME	SELLER'S PHONE NUMBER	CONDITION (E=Excellent, G=Good, P=Poor)
Psychology Today	Murrow	Psy 101	$15	Joe Tran	555-7632	G
Rhetoric for Writers	Swan & Stuart	Eng 101	$19	Mary Nord	555-9421	E
Reach for the Stars	Alvarez	Ast 210	$24	John Mote	555-9981	E
Rhetoric for Writers	Swan & Stuart	Eng 101	$16	Peter Rodgers	555-9156	E
History for Today's Society	Garrison & Pierce	Hst 310	$20	Sandi Radleman	555-7636	P
Psychology Today	Murrow	Psy 101	$18	Daniel Lewis	555-0873	E
Understanding Sociology	Navarre	Soc 101	$23	Karen Sim	555-9802	P
Electronic Circuitry	Carlson	Egr 255	$37	Karen Sim	555-9802	G
Nutrition for Our Souls	Francis	Nrs 320	$18	Dave Corsi	555-2384	E
Pediatric Nursing	Dyer	Nrs 253	$36	Margaret Healy	555-9932	E

FIGURE 1-103

3 ▶▶ Heart disease is one of the leading killers of adults in this country. With this knowledge the meat industry has aggressively tried to deliver products that are low in fat and yet high in nutrients. The American Heart Association states that lean meat can be part of a healthy diet, as long as the meat is served in moderation. Three cooked ounces of lean cuts of beef have various nutritional contents. Eye of round has 140 calories, top round steak has 150 calories, tip round roast has 160 calories, sirloin steak has 170 calories, and top loin and tenderloin steaks both have 180 calories. Regarding fat content, eye of round and top round steak have four fat grams in three ounces, tip round roast and sirloin both have six grams, top loin steak has eight grams, and tenderloin steak has the most with nine grams. Cholesterol also varies, with eye of round the lowest at 60 milligrams in three ounces, top loin with 65 mg, top round, tip round, and tenderloin with 70 mg, and sirloin the highest with 75 mg. Create a database to store the file related to the nutritional content of meat. Then create a table, enter the data, and print the table.

Cases and Places

4 ▶▶ You have a variety of classic movies on videocassette, and you want to make an inventory of your favorite films in the collection. One rainy afternoon you sort through your boxes and list each movie's name, leading actors, year produced, original running time, and your rating system of one to four stars. You create the following list: *The Little Princess*, starring Shirley Temple and Richard Greene, 1939, 94 minutes, three stars; *North by Northwest*, Cary Grant and Eva Marie Saint, 1959, 136 minutes, four stars; *Of Mice and Men*, Burgess Meredith and Lon Chaney Jr., 1939, 107 minutes, four stars; *The Quiet Man*, John Wayne and Maureen O'Hara, 1952, 129 minutes, four stars; *On the Waterfront*, Marlon Brando and Eva Marie Saint, 1954, 108 minutes, four stars; *Pardon My Sarong*, Bud Abbott and Lou Costello, 1942, 84 minutes, three stars; *Ride 'em Cowboy*, Bud Abbott and Lou Costello, 1942, 82 minutes, two stars; *You Can't Take It With You*, Jean Arthur and Lionel Barrymore, 1938, 127 minutes, three stars; *The Undefeated*, John Wayne and Rock Hudson, 1969, 119 minutes, two stars; and *Operation Pacific*, John Wayne and Patricia Neal, 1951, 109 minutes, three stars. Using this information, create a database to store the file related to these movies. Then create a table, enter the data, and print the table.

5 ▶▶▶ You do not participate in a retirement plan at work, so your tax preparer advises you to open an Individual Retirement Account (IRA). You analyze your financial situation and estimate you could afford to invest $1,000 now to open the account. Visit or call a total of five local banks, credit unions, or savings and loan associations. Make a list of the current interest rates for an IRA opened with $1,000, minimum investment amount, total amount earned by the time you turn age 65, annual fees, and amount you would be penalized if you withdrew the money in two years. Using this information, create a database and enter the data showing the types of financial institutions (bank, savings and loan, or credit union), names of the financial institutions, their addresses and telephone numbers, interest rates, annual fees, total values of the IRAs by age 65, amount of interest earned in this time, and amount you would be penalized if you withdrew the money in two years. Print this table, and then create and print a bar graph indicating the amount of interest you would earn and the total value of your IRA at age 65 for each financial institution.

6 ▶▶▶ You often have difficulty finding your campus directory to get the telephone numbers of campus personnel and offices. When you do locate the book, usually you cannot find the information you need. Consequently, you have decided to create your own database containing this pertinent information. Obtain important names, phone numbers, and office room numbers of campus offices that you frequent. Start by organizing the data in the categories of faculty, administration, and services. In the faculty category, list your adviser and your instructors from this semester. In the administration category, list the registrar, the dean of your area, and the financial aid director. In the services category, list the bookstore, campus police station, baby-sitting services, and library reference desk. Add other pertinent data to any of the categories. Then create a table, enter the data you obtained, and print the table.

Cases and Places

7 ▶▶▶ Food and drug store prices can vary dramatically from one store to another. Make a list of five specific items you purchase frequently from area stores in the four categories of dairy (for example, milk, yogurt, butter, sour cream, cottage cheese), snacks (for example, pretzels, soda, granola bars, raisins, rice cakes), cosmetics/toiletries (for example, deodorant, bath soap, toothpaste, shampoo, contact lens solution), and kitchen supplies (for example, paper towels, dish washing detergent, scouring pads, trash bags, sandwich bags). List the size or weight of each item. Then, visit a local convenience store, grocery store, and discount store to compare prices. Be certain you obtain prices on identical products. Then create a table, enter the data you obtained in each category, and print the table.

Microsoft Access 7

Windows 95

Querying a Database Using the Select Query Window

Objectives:

You will have mastered the material in this project when you can:

▶ State the purpose of queries
▶ Create a new query
▶ Use a query to display all records and all fields
▶ Run a query
▶ Print the answer to a query
▶ Close a query
▶ Clear a query
▶ Use a query to display selected fields
▶ Use character data in criteria in a query
▶ Use wildcards in criteria
▶ Use numeric data in criteria
▶ Use comparison operators
▶ Use compound criteria involving AND
▶ Use compound criteria involving OR
▶ Sort the answer to a query
▶ Join tables in a query
▶ Restrict the records in a join
▶ Use computed fields in a query
▶ Calculate statistics in a query
▶ Use grouping with statistics
▶ Save a query
▶ Use a saved query

Kick Up Your Feet and Go Grocery Shopping

Grocery shopping is a chore 60 percent of us dislike. From hunting for a parking space to waiting in long checkout lines, the entire experience, which on average requires 66 minutes, often is tiring and frustrating.

But this task does not have to be so taxing. In fact, it can be quick and efficient by using a computer. Microsoft Chairman Bill Gates predicts one-third of all grocery shopping will be done with interactive devices such as computers and televisions by the year 2005. Consumers in Chicago and San Francisco already are shopping online with a service called Peapod.

Here's how Peapod works. A shopper uses custom software to select from more than 25,000 items, ranging from apples to zinnias, available in a local grocery or drug store. The customer can shop by product category (e.g., produce, deli, meat/poultry), aisle (e.g., cereal and breakfast, ethnic foods), or specific item (e.g, reduced fat chocolate chip cookies).

Details such as the price and nutritional content of each item are kept in a database that is integrated with a billing system and a customer database. The products database is updated daily as prices change, new items are added to the stores' shelves, and unpopular items are removed. Produce prices change weekly.

A nutrition-conscious shopper can query, or question, the database to display a picture of the product, view its nutritional label, and sort items by nutritional content. A price-conscious shopper can instantly compare prices in the database to find the best deals. Buyers can create personal shopping lists of items frequently ordered, view previous orders, check subtotals at any time to stay within budget, redeem manufacturer and electronic coupons, and choose a delivery time.

Shoppers "go to the store" and select items on their computers. Drivers then bring the groceries to the consumer's door. The driver accepts payment by check, credit card, or automatic debit from a checking account and even will return bags for recycling. An average order exceeds $100, which is more than five times larger than the typical $18 spent by a walk-in customer.

One-half of the 20,000 Peapod customers say that by being able to comparison shop easily, to use coupons, and to take advantage of sales and specials, they can defray the charges for the service. The software costs $29.95, and typical shopping and delivery costs average $35 a month for a shopper who runs up a $100 grocery bill shopping three times a month.

The software runs on IBM-compatible and Macintosh computers. Minimum configurations for PC users are a 386 and Windows 3.1, and Mac users need System 7 or later. Both need at least 4 MB RAM and a 9600 bps modem.

The service is marketed to three types of people: upscale two-income families with children, individuals with disabilities, and the elderly. Peapod users are unusually loyal, as nearly 80 percent of the consumers who have tried the service keep using it.

Through the use of a virtual supermarket contained in a computer database, armchair shoppers have traded their squeaky shopping carts and frazzled nerves for the comfort of shopping in cyberspace.

Microsoft
Access 7
Windows 95

Querying a Database Using the Select Query Window

Case Perspective

Now that Mason Clinic has created a database with patient and therapist data, the management and staff of the clinic hope to gain the benefits they expected when they set up the database. One of the more important benefits is the capability to easily ask questions concerning the data in the database and rapidly obtain the answers. Among the questions they want answered are the following:

1. What is the balance of patient DI32?

2. Which patients' last names begin with the letters, Pe?

3. Which patients are located in Lamont?

4. What is the patient portion of the amount each patient owes (the balance minus the expected insurance payment)?

5. Which patients of therapist 08 currently do not have any money due to be paid by their insurance companies?

Introduction

A database management system like Access offers many useful features, among them the capability to answer questions such as those posed by the management of Mason Clinic (Figure 2-1). The answers to these questions, and many more, are found in the database, and Access can quickly find the answers. When you pose a question to Access, or any other database management system, the question is called a query. A **query** is simply a question represented in a way that Access can understand.

Thus, to find the answer to a question, you first create a corresponding query using the techniques illustrated in this project. Once you have created the query, you instruct Access to **run the query**; that is, to perform the steps necessary to obtain the answer. When finished, Access will display the answer to your question in the format shown at the bottom of Figure 2-1.

Project Two – Mason Clinic

You must obtain answers to the questions posed by the management of Mason Clinic. These include the questions shown in Figure 2-1, as well as any other questions management deems important.

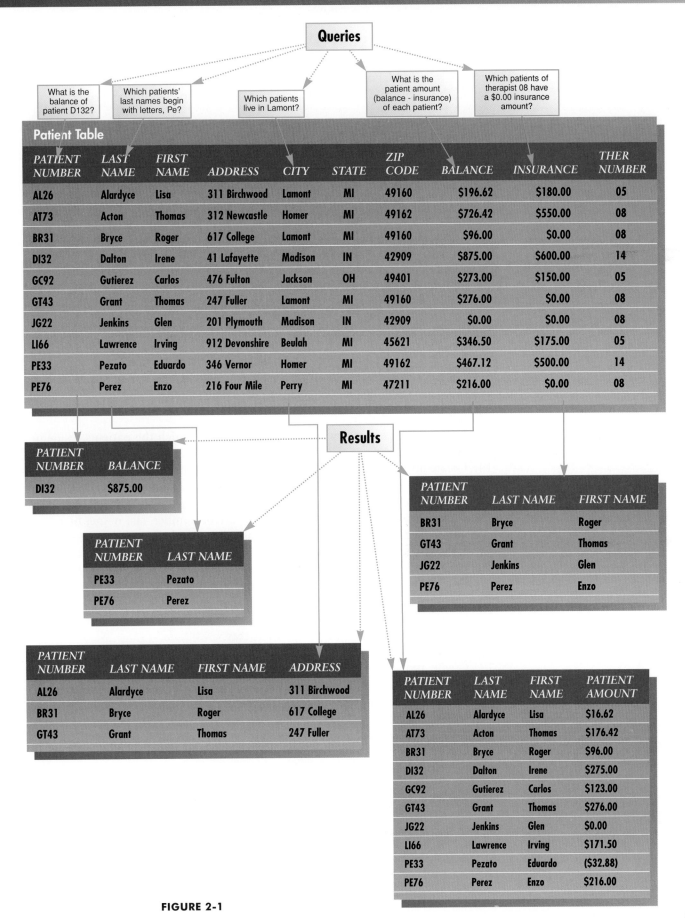

FIGURE 2-1

Overview of Project Steps

The project steps give you an overview of how the Mason Clinic database will be queried in this project. The following tasks will be completed in this project.

1. Start Access and open the Mason Clinic database.
2. Create a new query
3. Create and run a query to display all records and all fields.
4. Print the results of a query; that is, print the answer to the question.
5. Create and run a query to display the patient number, last name, first name, and balance of patient DI32.
6. Create and run a query to display only selected fields.
7. Create and run a query to display the number, name, and address of those patients whose names begin with the letters, Pe.
8. Create and run a query to display the number, last name, first name, and address for patients living in Lamont.
9. Create and run a query to display all patients whose insurance amount is $0.00.
10. Create and run a query to display all patients whose balance is more than $500.
11. Create and run a query to display all patients whose insurance amount is $0.00 and whose therapist is therapist 08.
12. Create and run a query to display all patients whose balance is more than $500 or whose therapist is therapist 08.
13. Create and run a query to display the cities in which the patients reside in alphabetical order.
14. Create and run a query to display the number, name, therapist number, and insurance amount for all patients sorted by insurance amount within therapist number.
15. Create and run a query to display the patient number, last name, first name, therapist number, therapist's last name, and therapist's first name for all patients.
16. Create and run a query to display the patient number, last name, first name, therapist number, therapist's last name, and therapist's first name for all patients whose balance is more than $200.
17. Create and run a query to display the number, name, and patient amount (balance minus insurance) for all patients.
18. Create and run a query to calculate the average balance for all patients.
19. Create and run a query to calculate the average balance for patients of therapist 08.
20. Create and run a query to calculate the average balance for patients of each therapist.
21. Create and save a query that will display, for each therapist, the therapist's number and last name as well as the number, last name, and first name of each of the therapist's patients.

The following pages contain a detailed explanation of each of these steps.

Opening the Database

Before creating queries, first you must open the database. Perform the following steps to complete this task.

TO OPEN A DATABASE

Step 1: Click the Start button.
Step 2: Click Open Office Document, and then click 3½ Floppy [A:] in the Look in text box. Make sure the database called Mason Clinic is selected.
Step 3: Click the Open button. If the Tables tab is not already selected, click the Tables tab.

The database is open and the Mason Clinic : Database window displays.

Creating a New Query

You **create a query** by making entries in a special window called a **Select Query window**. Once the database is open, the first step in creating a query is to select the table for which you are creating a query in the Database window. Next, click the New Object button down arrow, click New Query, and select Design View. The Select Query window will then display. It is typically easier to work with the Select Query window if it is maximized. Thus, as a standard practice, maximize the Select Query window as soon as you have created it.

Perform the following steps to begin the creation of a query.

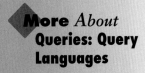

More *About*
Queries: Query Languages

Query languages, which are languages that made it easy to obtain answers to questions concerning data in a database, first appeared in the early 1970s. Prior to that time, obtaining such answers required having someone write lengthy (several hundred line) programs in languages such as COBOL.

 Steps **To Create a Query**

1 With the Mason Clinic database open, the Tables tab selected, and the Patient table selected, click the New Object button down arrow on the toolbar.

The list of available objects displays (Figure 2-2).

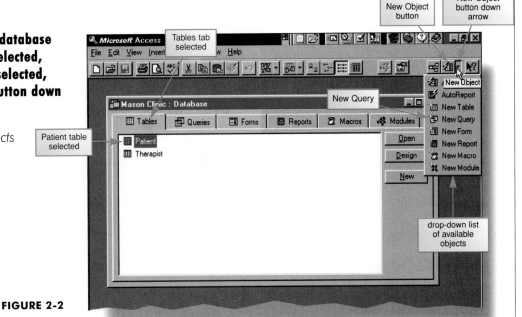

FIGURE 2-2

2 **Click New Query.**

The New Query dialog box displays (Figure 2-3).

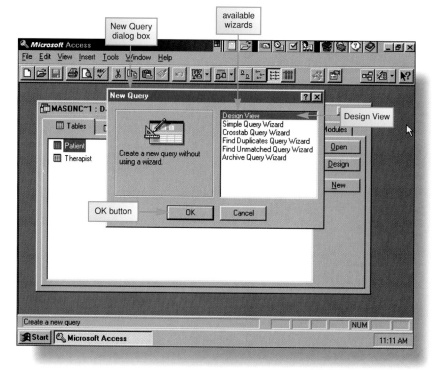

FIGURE 2-3

3 **With Design View highlighted, click the OK button.**

The Query1 : Select Query window displays (Figure 2-4).

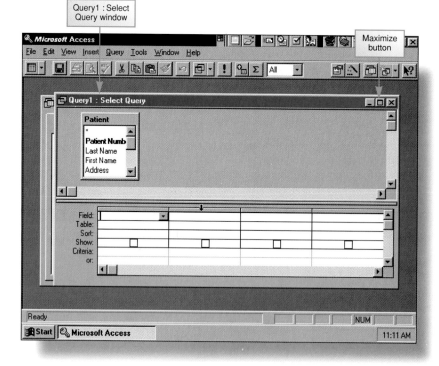

FIGURE 2-4

4 **Maximize the Query1 : Select Query window by clicking its Maximize button, and then point to the line that separates the upper and lower panes of the window. The mouse pointer will change shape to a double-headed arrow with a horizontal bar.**

*The Select Query window is maximized (Figure 2-5). The upper pane of the window contains a field list for the Patient table. The lower pane contains the **design grid**, the area where you specify fields to be included, sort order, and the criteria the records you are looking for must satisfy.*

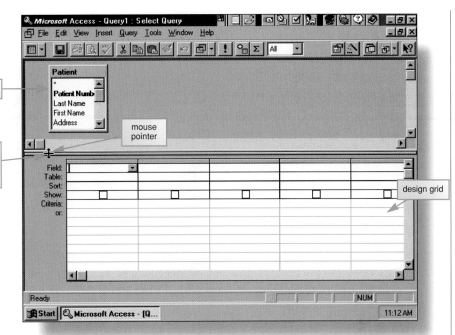

FIGURE 2-5

5 **Drag the line down to the approximate position shown in Figure 2-6 and then move the mouse pointer to the lower edge of the field list box so it changes shape to a double-headed arrow as shown in the figure.**

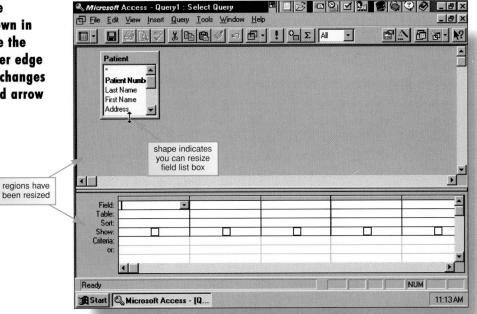

FIGURE 2-6

6 Drag the lower edge of the box down far enough so that all fields in the Patient table are visible.

All fields in the Patient table display (Figure 2-7).

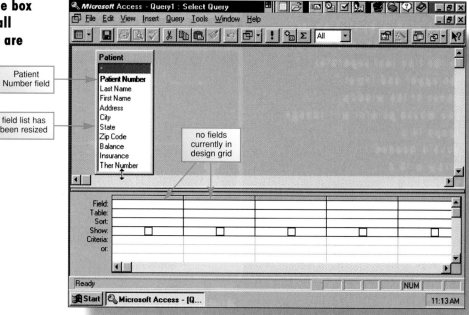

FIGURE 2-7

Using the Select Query Window

Once you have created a new Select Query window, you are ready to create the actual query by making entries in the design grid that appears in the lower portion of the window. You enter the names of the fields you want included in the Field row in the grid. You also can enter criteria, such as the patient number must be DI32, in the Criteria row of the grid. When you do so, only the record or records that match the criterion will be included in the answer.

Displaying Selected Fields in a Query

Only the fields that appear in the design grid will be included in the results of the query. Thus, to display only certain fields, place only these fields in the grid, and no others. If you inadvertently place the wrong field in the grid, click Edit on the menu bar and then click Delete to remove it. Alternatively, you could click Clear Grid to clear the entire design grid and then start over.

The following steps create a query to show the patient number, last name, first name, and therapist number for all patients by including only those fields in the design grid.

More About Queries: Query-by-Example

One of the early approaches to querying a database was called Query-by-Example, often referred to as QBE. In this approach, users asked questions by filling in a table on the screen. The approach taken in Access, as well as several other database management systems, is based on Query-by-Example.

Steps To Include Fields in the Design Grid

1 **Make sure you have a maximized Select Query window containing a field list for the Patient table in the upper pane of the window and an empty design grid in the lower pane (see Figure 2-7).**

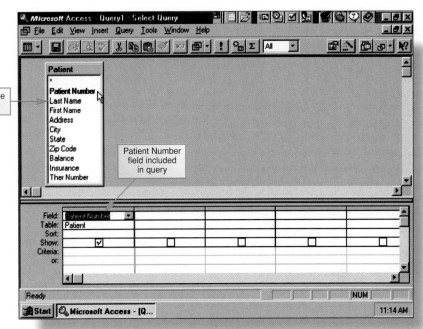

FIGURE 2-8

2 **Double-click the Patient Number field to include the Patient Number field in the query.**

The Patient Number is included as the first field in the design grid (Figure 2-8).

3 **Double-click the Last Name field to include it in the query. Include both the First Name and Ther Number fields using the same technique.**

The Patient Number, Last Name, First Name, and Ther Number fields are included in the query (Figure 2-9).

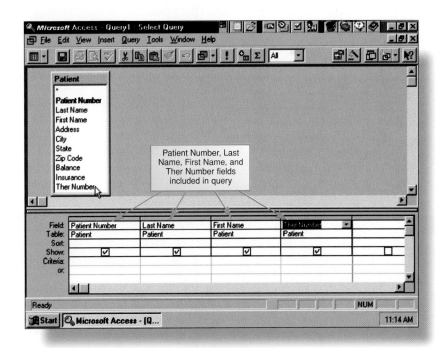

FIGURE 2-9

More *About*
Queries: SQL

Another major approach to querying a database is a language called SQL. In SQL, users type commands such as SELECT BALANCE FROM PATIENT WHERE CITY = "LAMONT" to find the balances of all patients who live in Lamont. Many database management systems, including Access, offer SQL as one option for querying databases.

Running a Query

Once you have created the query, you need to **run the query** to produce the results. To do so, click the Run button. Access will then perform the steps necessary to obtain and display the answer. The set of records that make up the answer will be displayed in Datasheet view. Although it looks like a table that is stored on your disk, it really is not. The records are constructed from data in the existing Patient table. If you were to change the data in the Patient table and then rerun this same query, the results would reflect the changes.

Steps **To Run the Query**

① **Point to the Run button on the toolbar (Figure 2-10).**

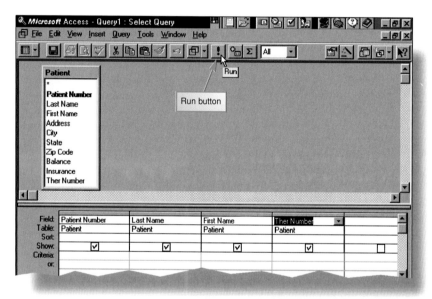

FIGURE 2-10

② **Click the Run button.**

The query is executed and the results display (Figure 2-11). If the mouse pointer points to the Filter by Selection button, the description of the button may obscure a portion of the first record.

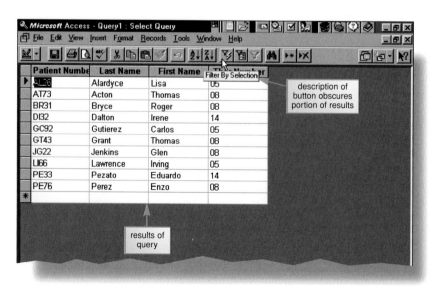

FIGURE 2-11

3 **Move the mouse pointer to a position that is outside of the data and is not on the toolbar.**

The data displays without obstruction (Figure 2-12). Notice that an extra blank row, marking the end of the table, displays at the end of the results. This will always be the case.

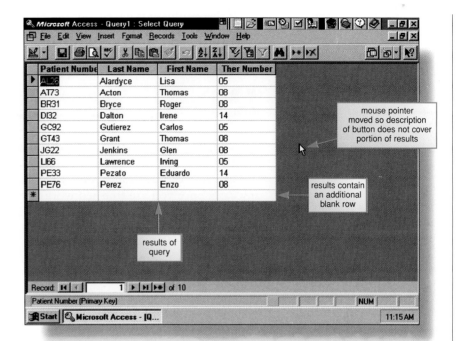

FIGURE 2-12

Other Ways
1. On Query menu click Run

In all future examples, after running a query, move the mouse pointer so the table displays without obstruction.

Printing the Results of a Query

To print the results of a query, use the same techniques you learned in Project 1 to print the data in the table. Complete the following step to print the query results that currently display on the screen.

Steps To Print the Results of a Query

1 **Click the Print button on the toolbar (Figure 2-13).**

The results print.

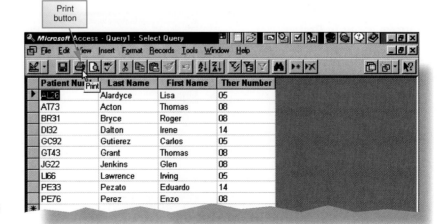

FIGURE 2-13

If the results of a query require landscape orientation, switch to landscape orientation before you click the Print button as indicated in Project 1 on page A1.31.

Returning to the Select Query Window

You can examine the results of a query on your screen to see the answer to your question. You can scroll through the records, if necessary, just as you scroll through the records of any other table. You also can print a copy of the table. In any case, once you are finished working with the results, you can return to the Select Query window to ask another question. To do so, click the Query View button down arrow as shown in the following steps.

Steps **To Return to the Select Query Window**

1 **Point to the Query View button down arrow on the toolbar (Figure 2-14).**

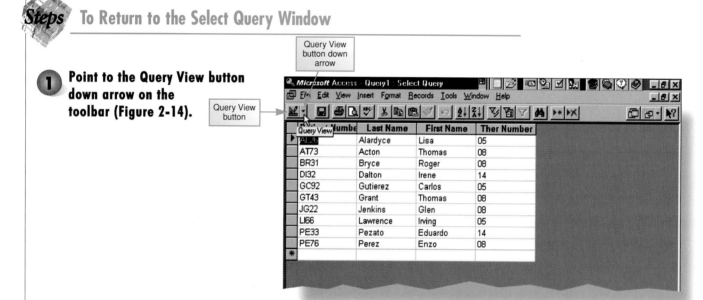

FIGURE 2-14

2 **Click the Query View button down arrow. Point to Design View.**

The Query View drop-down list displays (Figure 2-15).

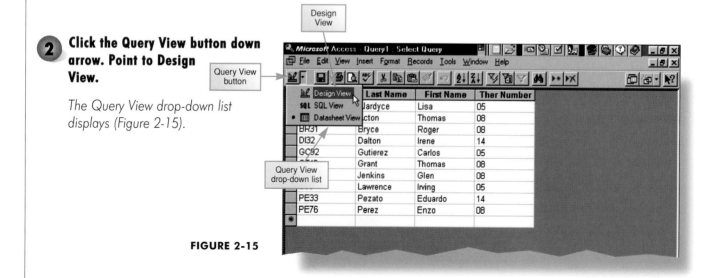

FIGURE 2-15

3 **Click Design View.**

The Select Query window displays once again (Figure 2-16).

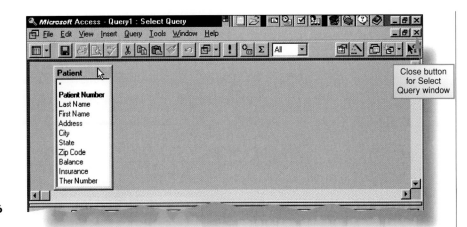

FIGURE 2-16

Closing a Query

To **close a query**, close the Select Query window. When you do so, Access asks if you want to save your query for future use. If you expect you will need to create the same exact query often, you should save the query. For now, you will not save any queries. You will see how to save them later in the project. The following steps close a query without saving it.

Steps To Close the Query

1 **Click the Close button for the Select Query window (see Figure 2-16).**

The Microsoft Access dialog box displays (Figure 2-17). Click the Yes button to save the query or click the No button to close the query without saving.

2 **Click the No button in the Microsoft Access dialog box.**

The Select Query window is removed from the desktop.

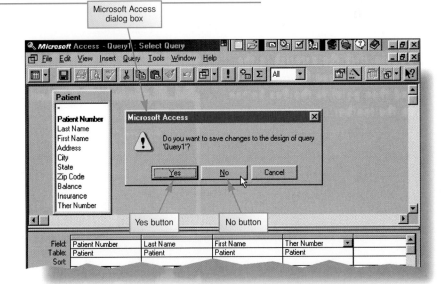

FIGURE 2-17

Including All Fields in a Query

If you want to **include all fields** in a query, you could select each field individually. There is a simpler way, however. By selecting the asterisk (*) that appears in the field list, you are indicating that all fields are to be included. Complete the following steps to use the asterisk to include all fields.

Steps To Include All Fields in a Query

1 **Be sure you have a maximized Select Query window containing a field list for the Patient table in the upper pane of the window and an empty design grid in the lower pane. (See Steps 1 through 6 on pages A 2.7 through A 2.10.) Point to the asterisk at the top of the field list box.**

A maximized Select Query window displays (Figure 2-18). The two panes of the window have been resized.

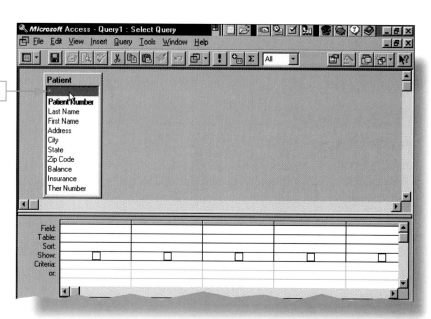

FIGURE 2-18

2 **Double-click the asterisk in the field list box (see Figure 2-18) and then point to the Run button on the toolbar.**

The table name, Patient, followed by an asterisk is added to the design grid (Figure 2-19), indicating all fields are included.

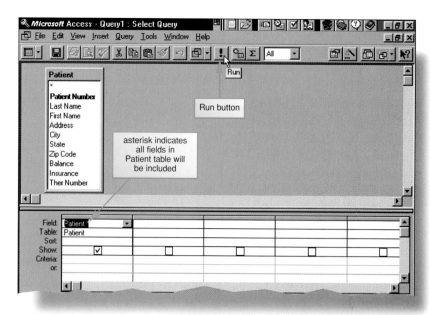

FIGURE 2-19

3 **Click the Run button.**

The results display and all fields in the Patient table are included (Figure 2-20).

Query View button

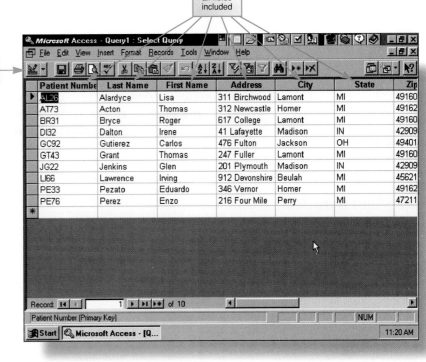

all fields included

4 **Click the Query View button down arrow on the toolbar to return to the Select Query window. Click Design View.**

The datasheet is replaced by the Select Query window.

FIGURE 2-20

Clearing the Design Grid

If you make mistakes as you are creating a query, you can fix them individually. Alternatively, you simply may want to **clear the query**; that is, clear out the entries in the design grid and start over. One way to clear out the entries is to close the Select Query window and then start a new query just as you did earlier. A simpler approach, however, is to click Clear Grid on the Edit menu.

 To Clear a Query

1 **Click Edit on the menu bar.**

The Edit menu displays (Figure 2-21).

2 **Click Clear Grid.**

Access clears the design grid so you can enter your next query.

Edit menu

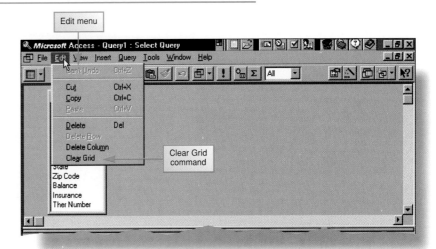

Clear Grid command

FIGURE 2-21

Entering Criteria

When you use queries, usually you are looking for those records that satisfy some criterion. You might want the name of the patient whose number is DI32, for example, or the numbers, names, and addresses of those patients whose names start with the letters, Pe. To enter criteria, enter them on the Criteria row in the design grid underneath the field name to which the criterion applies. For example, to indicate that the patient number must be DI32, type DI32 in the Criteria row underneath the Patient Number field. You first must add the Patient Number field to the design grid before you can enter the criterion.

The next examples illustrate the types of criteria that are available.

More *About*
Using Text Data in Criteria

In many database management systems, text data must be enclosed in quotation marks. For example, to find customers in Michigan, "MI" would be entered as the criterion for the State field. In Access this is not necessary, since Access will insert the quotation marks automatically.

Using Text Data in Criteria

To use **text data** (data in a field whose type is text) in criteria, simply type the text in the Criteria row below the corresponding field name. The following steps query the Patient table and display the patient number, last name, first name, and balance of patient DI32.

Steps **To Use Text Data in a Criterion**

1 **One-by-one, double-click the Patient Number, Last Name, First Name, and Balance fields to add them to the query. Then point to the Criteria entry for the first field in the design grid.**

The Patient Number, Last Name, First Name, and Balance fields are added to the design grid (Figure 2-22). The mouse pointer on the Criteria entry for the first field (Patient Number) has changed shape to an I-beam.

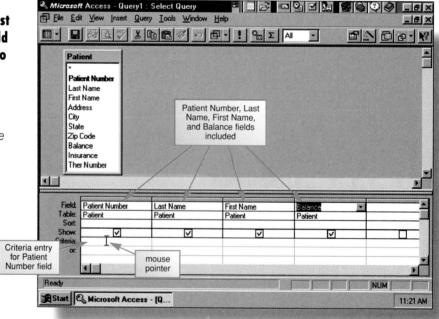

FIGURE 2-22

2 Click the criteria entry, type
DI32 **as the criteria for the
Patient Number field, and then
point to the Run button on the
toolbar. (Be sure you type the
letter I and not the number 1.)**

The criteria is entered (Figure 2-23).

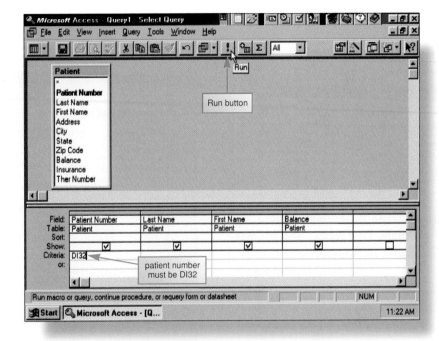

FIGURE 2-23

3 Run the query by clicking the Run
button.

The results display (Figure 2-24).
Only patient DI32 is included. (The
extra blank row contains $0.00 in
the Balance field. Unlike text fields,
which are left blank, number and
currency fields in the extra row contain 0. Because Balance is a currency field, the value displays as
$0.00.)

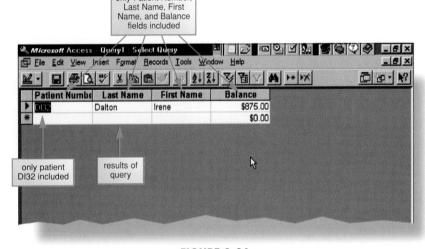

FIGURE 2-24

Using Wildcards

Two special **wildcards** are available in Microsoft Access. Wildcards are symbols
that represent any character or combination of characters.

The first of the two wildcards, the asterisk (*), represents any collection of
characters. Thus pe* represents the letters, Pe, followed by any collection of characters. The other wildcard symbol is the question mark (?), which represents any
individual character. Thus t?m represents the letter, T, followed by any single
character followed by the letter, m, such as Tim or Tom.

The steps on the next page use a wildcard to find the number, name, and
address of those patients whose names begin with Pe. Because you do not know
how many characters will follow the Pe, the asterisk is appropriate.

Steps **To Use a Wildcard**

① **Use the Query View button on the toolbar to return to the Select Query window. On the Edit menu, click Clear Grid.**

Access clears the design grid so you can enter the next query.

② **Include the Patient Number, Last Name, First Name, and Address fields in the query and then click the Criteria entry for the second field. Type** LIKE PE* **as the entry.**

The fields are selected and LIKE PE is entered as the criterion (Figure 2-25).*

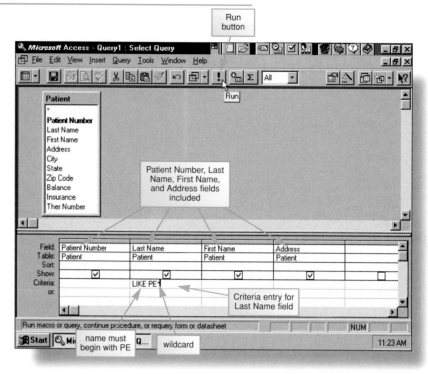

FIGURE 2-25

③ **Click the Run button on the toolbar.**

The results display (Figure 2-26). Only the patients whose names start with "Pe" are included.

FIGURE 2-26

Criteria for a Field Not in the Result

In some cases, you may have criteria for a particular field that should not appear in the results of the query. For example, you may wish to see the patient number, last name, first name, and address for all patients who live in Lamont. The criteria involves the City field, which is not one of the fields to be included in the results.

To enter a criterion for the City field, it must be included in the design grid. Normally, this also would mean it would appear in the results. To prevent this from happening, remove the check mark from its **Show check box**, the box in the Show row of the grid. The following steps illustrate the process by displaying the patient number, last name, first name, and address for patients living in Lamont.

Steps To Use Criteria for a Field Not Included in the Results

1 **Use the Query View button on the toolbar to return to the Select Query window. On the Edit menu, click Clear Grid.**

Access clears the design grid so you can enter next query.

2 **Include the Patient Number, Last Name, First Name, Address, and City fields in the query. Type** Lamont **as the criteria for the City field and then point to the City field's Show check box.**

The fields are included in the grid, and the criteria for the City field is entered (Figure 2-27). The gap between the left scroll arrow and the scroll box indicates that fields are off the leftmost edge of the grid. In this case, the first field, Patient Number, currently does not display. Clicking the left scroll arrow will move the scroll box to the left, shift the fields currently in the grid to the right, and cause the Patient Number field to display.

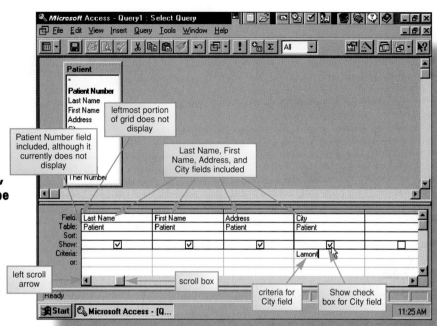

FIGURE 2-27

3 **Click the Show check box to remove the check mark (✓).**

The check mark is removed from the Show check box for the City field (Figure 2-28), indicating it will not show in the result. Access has automatically added quotation marks before and after Lamont.

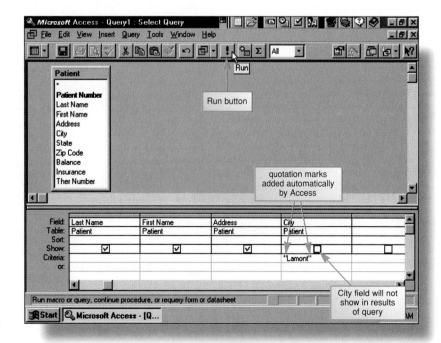

FIGURE 2-28

4 **Click the Run button on the toolbar.**

The results display (Figure 2-29). The City field does not appear. The only patients included are those who live in Lamont.

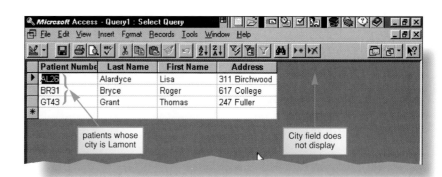

FIGURE 2-29

Using Numeric Data in Criteria

To enter a number in a criterion, type the number without any dollar signs or commas. Complete the following steps to display all patients whose insurance amount is $0.00 To do so, you will need to type 0 as criteria for the Insurance field.

 Steps **To Use a Number in a Criterion**

1 **Use the Query View button on the toolbar to return to the Select Query window. On the Edit menu, click Clear Grid. Click the left scroll arrow so no space exists between the scroll arrow and the scroll box.**

Access clears the design grid so you can enter the next query.

2 **Include the Patient Number, Last Name, First Name, Balance, and Insurance fields, in the query. Type 0 as the criterion for the Insurance field. You need not enter a dollar sign or decimal point in the criterion.**

The fields are selected and the criterion is entered (Figure 2-30).

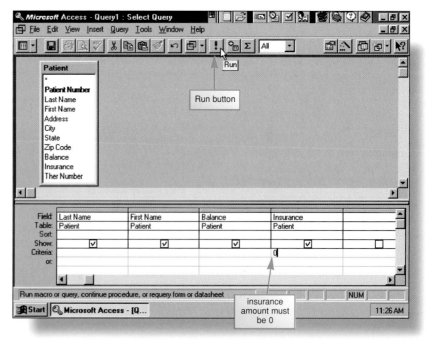

FIGURE 2-30

3 **Click the Run button on the toolbar.**

The results display (Figure 2-31). Only those patients who have an insurance amount of $0.00 are included.

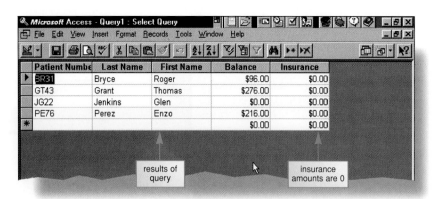

FIGURE 2-31

Using Comparison Operators

Unless you specify otherwise, Access assumes that the criteria you enter involve equality (exact matches). In the last query, for example, you were requesting those patients whose insurance amount is *equal to* 0. If you want something other than an exact match, you must enter the appropriate **comparison operator**. The comparison operators are > (greater than), < (less than), >= (greater than or equal to), <= (less than or equal to), and NOT (not equal to).

Perform the following steps to use the > operator to find all patients whose balance is more than $500.

 Steps To Use a Comparison Operator in a Criterion

1 **Use the Query View button on the toolbar to return to the Select Query window. On the Edit menu, click Clear Grid. Click the left scroll arrow so no space exists between the scroll arrow and the scroll box.**

Access clears the design grid so you can enter the next query.

2 **Include the Patient Number, Last Name, First Name, Balance, and Insurance fields in the query. Type >500 as the criterion for the Balance field.**

The fields are selected and the criterion is entered (Figure 2-32).

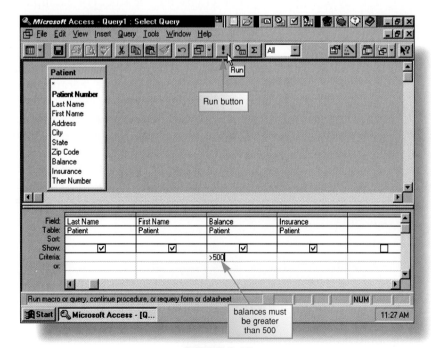

FIGURE 2-32

3 **Click the Run button on the toolbar.**

The results display (Figure 2-33). Only those patients who have a balance more than $500 are included.

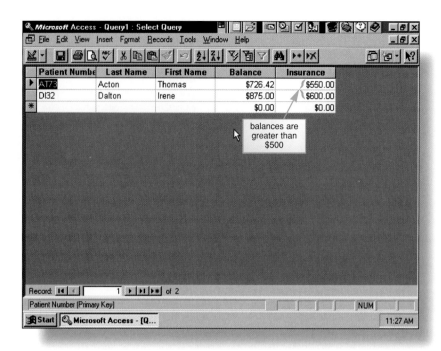

FIGURE 2-33

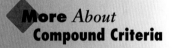

More *About*
Compound Criteria

The approach taken by Access to compound criteria is precisely the approach that was proposed for Query-by-Example. (Placing criteria on the same lines indicates they are connected by the word AND. Placing them on separate lines indicates they are connected by the word OR.)

Using Compound Criteria

Often you will have more than one criterion that the data for which you are searching must satisfy. This type of criterion is called a **compound criterion**. There are two types of compound criteria.

In **AND criterion**, each individual criterion must be true in order for the compound criterion to be true. For example, an AND criterion would allow you to find those patients who have an insurance amount of $0.00 *and* whose therapist is therapist 08.

OR criterion, on the other hand, are true provided either individual criterion is true. An OR criterion would allow you to find those patients who have a balance greater than $500 *or* whose therapist is therapist 08. In this case, any patient whose balance is greater than $500 would be included in the answer whether or not the patient's therapist is therapist 08. Likewise, any patient whose therapist is therapist 08 would be included whether or not the patient had a balance more than $500.

To combine criteria with AND, place the criteria on the same line. Perform the following steps to use an AND criterion to find those patients whose insurance amount is $0.00 and whose therapist is therapist 08.

Steps To Use a Compound Criterion Involving AND

1 Use the Query View button on the toolbar to return to the Select Query window. On the Edit menu, click Clear Grid.

Access clears the design grid so you can enter the next query.

2 Include the Patient Number, Last Name, First Name, Balance, Insurance, and Ther Number fields in the query.

3 Click the Criteria entry for the Insurance field, and then type 0 as a criterion for the Insurance field. Click the Criteria entry for the Ther Number field and then type 08 as the criterion for the Ther Number field.

The fields shift to the left (Figure 2-34). Criteria have been entered for the Insurance and Ther Number fields.

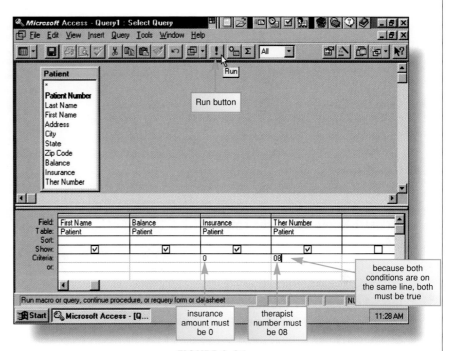

FIGURE 2-34

4 Click the Run button on the toolbar.

The results display (Figure 2-35). Only those patients whose insurance is $0.00 and whose therapist number is 08 are included.

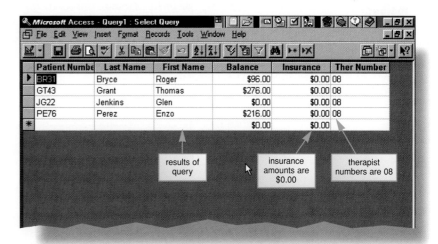

FIGURE 2-35

To combine criteria with OR, the criteria must go on separate lines in the Criteria area of the grid. The steps on the next page use an OR criterion to find those patients whose balance is more than $500 or whose therapist is therapist 08 (or both).

Steps To Use a Compound Criterion Involving OR

1 Use the Query View button on the toolbar to return to the Select Query window.

2 Click the Criteria entry for the Insurance field. Use the BACKSPACE key to delete the entry (0). Click the Criteria entry for the Balance field. Type >500 as the criterion. Click the Criteria entry for the Ther Number field. Use the BACKSPACE key to delete the entry ("08").

3 Click the or entry (the second line of Criteria) for the Ther Number field and then type 08 as the entry.

The criteria are entered for the Insurance and Ther Number fields on different lines (Figure 2-36).

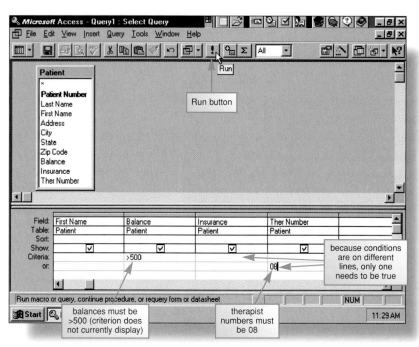

FIGURE 2-36

4 Click the Run button on the toolbar.

The results display (Figure 2-37). Only those patients whose balance is more than $500 or whose therapist number is 08 are included.

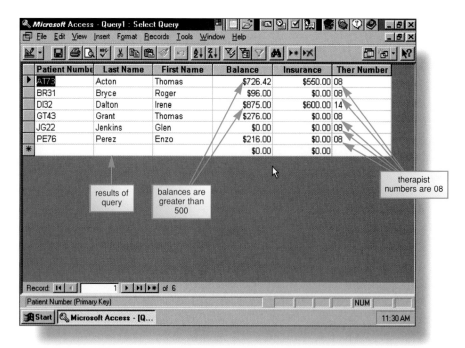

FIGURE 2-37

Sorting Data in a Query

In some queries, the order in which the records are displayed really does not matter. All you need be concerned about are the records that appear in the results. It does not matter which one is first or which one is last.

In other queries, however, the order can be very important. You may want to see the cities in which patients are located and would like them arranged alphabetically. Perhaps you want to see the patients listed by therapist number. Further, within all the patients of any given therapist, you would like them to be listed by insurance amount.

To order the records in the answer to a query in a particular way, you **sort** the records. The field or fields on which the records are sorted is called the **sort key**. If you are sorting on more than one field (such as sorting by insurance amount within therapist number), the more important field (Ther Number) is called the **major key** and the less important field (Insurance) is called the **minor key**.

To sort in Microsoft Access, specify the sort order in the Sort line of the design grid underneath the field that is the sort key. If you specify more than one sort key, the sort key on the left will be the major sort key and the one on the right will be the minor key.

The following steps sort the cities in the Patient table.

More *About*

Sorting Data in a Query

When a query involves sorting, the records in the underlying tables (the tables on which the query is based) are not actually rearranged. Instead, Access will determine the most efficient method of simply displaying the records in the requested order. The records in the underlying tables remain in their original order.

 To Sort Data in a Query

1 Use the Query View button on the toolbar to return to the Select Query window. On the Edit menu, click Clear Grid. Click the left scroll arrow so no space exists between the scroll arrow and the scroll box.

2 Include the City field in the design grid. Click the Sort entry under the City field, and then click the down arrow that appears.

The City field is included (Figure 2-38). A list of available sort orders displays.

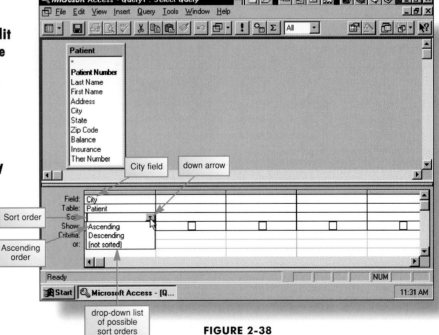

FIGURE 2-38

3 **Click Ascending.**

Ascending is selected as the order (Figure 2-39).

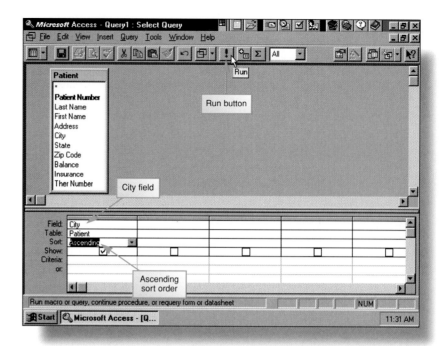

FIGURE 2-39

4 **Run the query by clicking the Run button on the toolbar.**

The results contain the cities from the Patient table (Figure 2-40). The cities display in alphabetical order. **Duplicates,** *that is, identical rows, are included.*

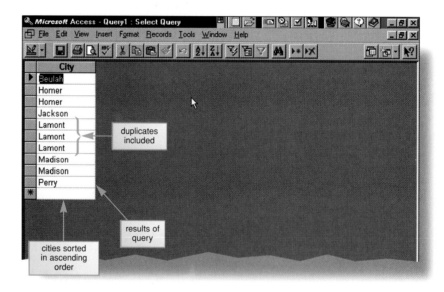

FIGURE 2-40

Sorting on Multiple Keys

The next example lists the number, name, therapist number, and insurance amount for all patients. The data is to be sorted by descending insurance amount *within* therapist number, which means that the Ther Number field is the major key and the Insurance field is the minor key. It also means that the Insurance field should be sorted in descending order.

The following steps accomplish this sorting by specifying the Ther Number and Insurance fields as sort keys and by selecting Descending as the sort order for the Insurance field.

Steps To Sort on Multiple Keys

1 Use the Query View button on the toolbar to return to the Select Query window. On the Edit menu, click Clear Grid.

2 Include the Patient Number, Last Name, First Name, Ther Number, and Insurance fields in the query *in this order*. Select Ascending as the sort order for the Ther Number field and Descending as the sort order for the Insurance field (Figure 2-41).

FIGURE 2-41

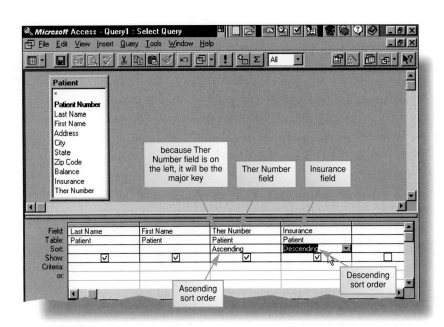

3 Run the query.

The results display (Figure 2-42). The patients are sorted by therapist number. Within the collection of patients having the same therapist, the patients are sorted by descending insurance amount.

FIGURE 2-42

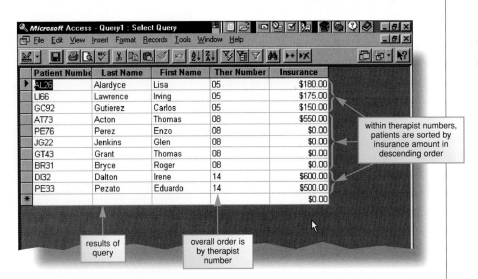

It is important to remember that the major sort key must appear to the left of the minor sort key in the design grid. If you attempted to sort the patient data by insurance amount within therapist number, for example, but placed the Insurance field to the left of the Ther Number field, your results would be incorrect.

Omitting Duplicates

As you saw earlier, when you sort data, duplicates are included. In Figure 2-40 on page A 2.28, for example, Homer appeared two times, Lamont appeared three times, and Madison appeared twice. If you do not want duplicates included, use the Query Properties command and specify Unique Values Only. Perform the following steps to produce a sorted list of the cities in the Patient table in which each city is listed only once.

Steps To Omit Duplicates

1 Use the Query View button on the toolbar to return to the Select Query window. On the Edit menu, click Clear Grid. Click the left scroll arrow so no space exists between the scroll arrow and the scroll box.

2 Include the City field, click Ascending as the sort order, and click the *second* field in the design grid (the empty field following City). Then right-click.

The shortcut menu displays (Figure 2-43).

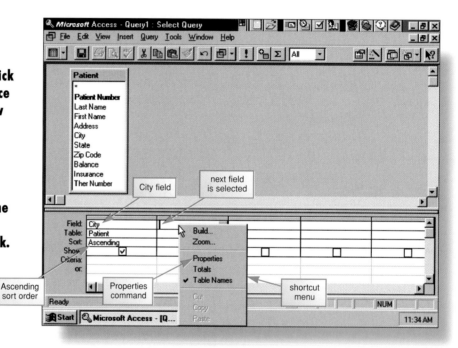

FIGURE 2-43

3 Click Properties.

The Query Properties dialog box displays (Figure 2-44).

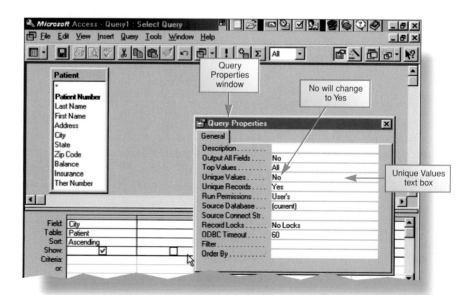

FIGURE 2-44

4 Click the Unique Values text box, and then click the down arrow that displays to produce a list of available choices for Unique Values (Figure 2-45).

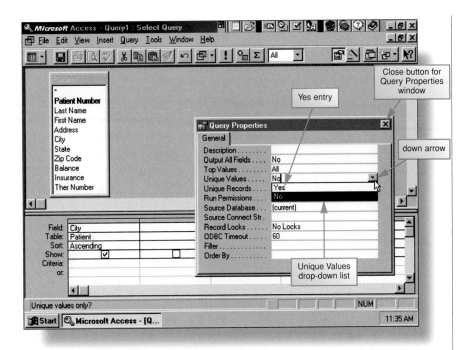

FIGURE 2-45

5 Click Yes, and then click the Close button for the Query Properties dialog box to close the dialog box. Run the query by clicking the Run button on the toolbar.

The results display (Figure 2-46). The cities are sorted alphabetically. Each city is included only once.

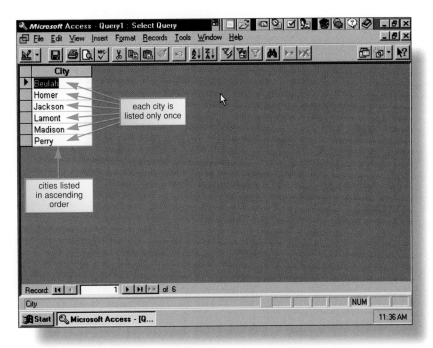

FIGURE 2-46

Other Ways

1. Right click, in upper pane of window, click Properties on shortcut menu

2. Click Properties button on toolbar

3. On View menu click Properties

More *About*
Joining Tables

The ability to join tables, that is, to create queries that draw data from multiple tables is a key feature that has always distinguished database management systems from file systems. Several types of joins are available. The most common type, the one illustrated in the text, is formally called the natural join.

Joining Tables

Mason Clinic needs to list the number and name of each patient along with the number and name of the patient's therapist. The patient's name is in the Patient table, whereas the therapist's name is in the Therapist table. Thus, this query cannot be satisfied using a single table. You need to **join** the tables; that is, to find records in the two tables that have identical values in matching fields (Figure 2-47). In this example, you need to find records in the Patient table and the Therapist table that have the same value in the Ther Number fields.

give the number and name of each patient along with the number and name of the patient's therapist

Patient Table

PATIENT NAME	LAST NAME	FIRST NAME	...	THER NUMBER
AL26	Alardyce	Lisa	...	05
AT73	Acton	Thomas	...	08
BR31	Bryce	Roger	...	08
DI32	Dalton	Irene	...	14
GC92	Gutierez	Carlos	...	05
GT43	Grant	Thomas	...	08
JG22	Jenkins	Glen	...	08
LI66	Lawrence	Irving	...	05
PE33	Pezato	Eduardo	...	14
PE76	Perez	Enzo	...	08

Therapist Table

THER NUMBER	LAST NAME	FIRST NAME	...
05	Hughes	Mary	...
08	Foster	Richard	...
14	Galvez	Maria	...

PATIENT NUMBER	LAST NAME	FIRST NAME	THER NUMBER	LAST NAME	FIRST NAME
AL26	Alardyce	Lisa	05	Hughes	Mary
AT73	Acton	Thomas	08	Foster	Richard
BR31	Bryce	Roger	08	Foster	Richard
DI32	Dalton	Irene	14	Galvez	Maria
GC92	Gutierez	Carlos	05	Hughes	Mary
GT43	Grant	Thomas	08	Foster	Richard
JG22	Jenkins	Glen	08	Foster	Richard
LI66	Lawrence	Irving	05	Hughes	Mary
PE33	Pezato	Eduardo	14	Galvez	Maria
PE76	Perez	Enzo	08	Foster	Richard

FIGURE 2-47

To join tables in Access, first you bring field lists for both tables to the upper pane of the Select Query window. Access will draw a line between matching fields in the two tables indicating that the tables are related. You then can select fields from either table. Access will join the tables automatically.

The first step is to add an additional table to the query as illustrated in the following steps, which add the Therapist table.

Steps To Join Tables

1 Use the Query View button on the toolbar to return to the Select Query window. On the Edit menu, click Clear Grid.

2 Right-click any open area in the upper pane of the Select Query window.

The shortcut menu displays (Figure 2-48).

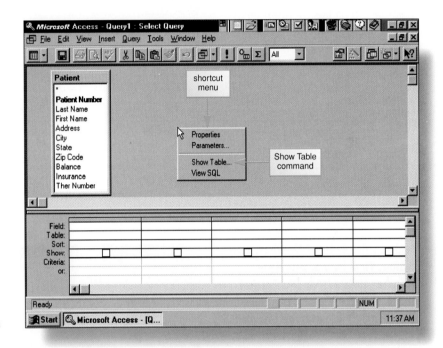

FIGURE 2-48

3 Click Show Table on the shortcut menu.

The Show Table dialog box displays (Figure 2-49).

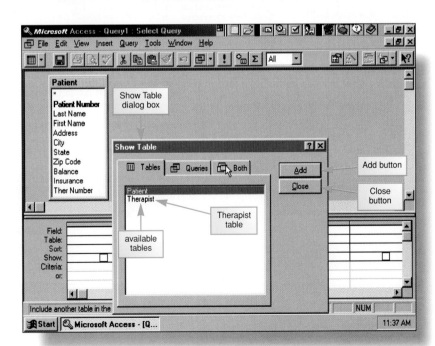

FIGURE 2-49

4 **Click Therapist to select the Therapist table, and then click the Add button. Close the Show Table dialog box by clicking its Close button. Expand the size of the field list so all the fields in the Therapist table display.**

A field list for the Therapist table displays (Figure 2-50). It has been enlarged so all the Therapist fields are visible. A line appears joining the Ther Number fields in the two field lists. This line indicates how the tables are related; that is, linked through the matching fields. (If you did not give the matching fields the same name, Access will not insert the line. You can insert it manually by clicking one of the two matching fields and dragging the mouse pointer to the other matching field.)

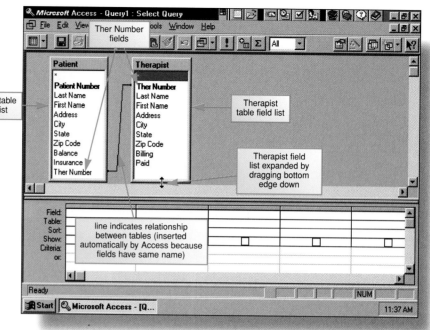

FIGURE 2-50

5 **Include the Patient Number, Last Name, First Name, and Ther Number fields from the Patient table and the Last Name and First Name fields in the Therapist table.**

The fields from both tables are selected (Figure 2-51). Notice that you do not have to click the Ther Number from both tables for the join to work.

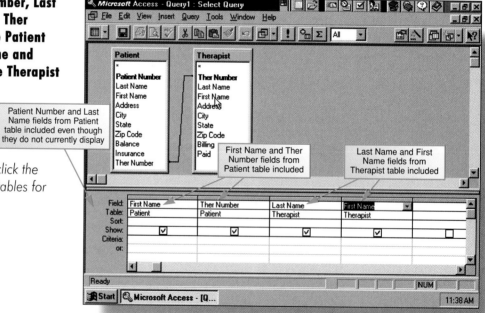

FIGURE 2-51

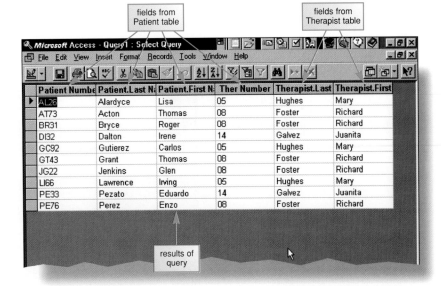

fields from Patient table

fields from Therapist table

6 **Run the query.**

The results display (Figure 2-52). They contain data from the Patient table as well as data from the Therapist table.

results of query

FIGURE 2-52

Restricting Records in a Join

Sometimes you will want to join tables, but you will not want to include all possible records. In such cases, you will relate the tables and include fields just as you did before. You also will include criteria. For example, to include the same fields as in the previous query, but only those patients whose balance is more than $200, you will make the same entries as before and then also type the number >200 as a criterion for the Balance field.

The following steps modify the query from the previous example to restrict the records that will be included in the join.

 To Restrict the Records in a Join

1 **Use the Query View button on the toolbar to return to the Select Query window. Add the Balance field to the query. Type >200 as the criterion for the Balance field and then click the Show check box for the Balance field to remove the check mark.**

The Balance field displays in the design grid (Figure 2-53). A criterion is entered for the Balance field and the Show check box is empty, indicating that the field will not display in the results of the query.

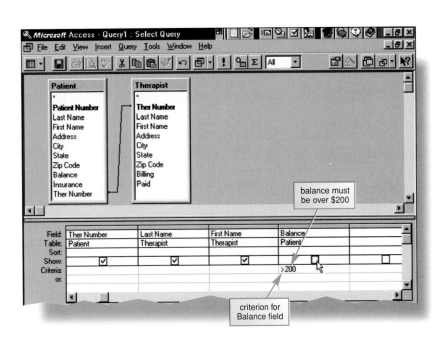

balance must be over $200

criterion for Balance field

FIGURE 2-53

2 **Run the query.**

The results display (Figure 2-54). Only those patients with a balance more than $200 appear in the result. The Balance field does not display.

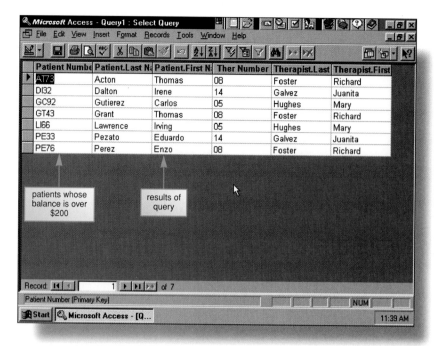

FIGURE 2-54

Using Computed Fields in a Query

It is important to the Mason Clinic to know the amount expected to be paid by each patient; that is, the amount owed by the patient minus the amount expected to be paid by the patient's insurance. This poses a problem because there is no such field in the Patient table. You can compute it, however, because the expected amount is equal to the balance minus the insurance amount. Such a field is called a **computed field**.

To include computed fields in queries, you enter a name for the computed field, a colon, and then the expression in one of the columns in the Field row. For the patient amount, for example, you will type Patient Amount:[Balance]-[Insurance]. You can type this directly into the Field row. You will not be able to see the entire entry, however, because not enough room is available for it. A better way is to select the column in the Field row, right-click to display the shortcut menu, and then click Zoom. The Zoom dialog box will display. You then can type the expression in the dialog box.

You are not restricted to subtraction in computations. You can use addition (+), multiplication (*), or division (/). Also, you can include parentheses in your computations to indicate which computations should be done first.

Perform the following steps to use a computed field to display the number, name, and patient amount of all patients.

Steps To Use a Computed Field in a Query

1 **Use the Query View button on the toolbar to return to the Select Query window. Right-click any field in the list of fields in the Therapist table.**

The shortcut menu displays (Figure 2-55).

2 **Click Remove Table to remove the Therapist table from the Select Query window. On the Edit menu, click Clear Grid. Click the left scroll arrow so no space exists between the scroll arrow and the scroll box.**

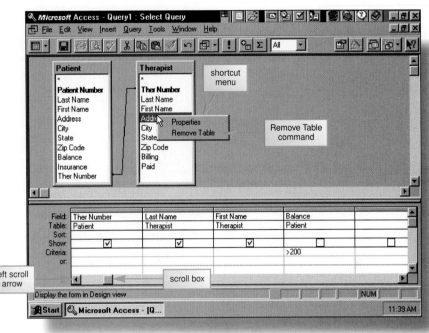

FIGURE 2-55

3 **Include the Patient Number, Last Name, and First Name fields. Click the Field entry in the fourth column in the design grid to select the field. Right-click and then click Zoom on the shortcut menu. Type** Patient Amount:[Balance]-[Insurance] **in the Zoom dialog box that displays.**

The Zoom dialog box displays (Figure 2-56). The expression you typed displays within the dialog box.

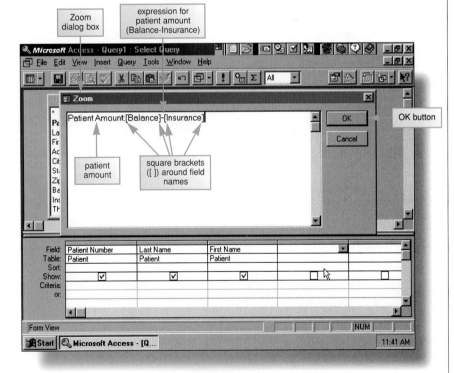

FIGURE 2-56

Click the OK button.

The Zoom dialog box no longer displays (Figure 2-57). A portion of the expression you entered displays in the fourth field within the design grid.

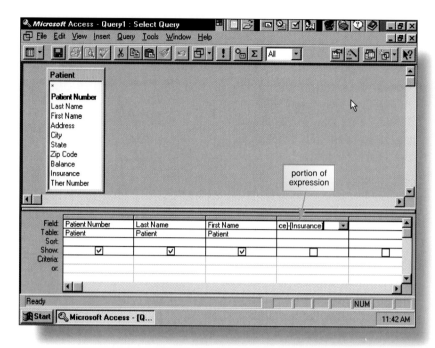

FIGURE 2-57

Run the query.

The results display (Figure 2-58). Microsoft Access has calculated and displayed the patient amounts. The parentheses around the $32.88 indicate it is a negative number; that is, the patient evidently has already paid more than the patient portion.

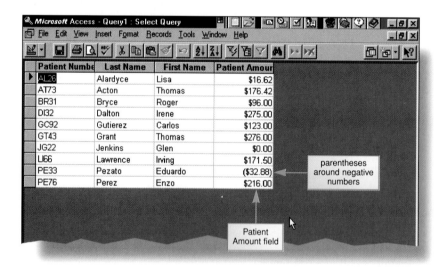

FIGURE 2-58

OtherWays
1. Press SHIFT+F2

More *About*
Calculating Statistics

Virtually all database management systems support the basic set of statistical calculations: sum, average, count, maximum, and minimum as part of their query feature. Some systems, including Access, add several more, such as standard deviation, variance, first, and last.

Calculating Statistics

Microsoft Access supports the built-in **statistics**: COUNT, SUM, AVG (average), MAX (largest value), MIN (smallest value), STD (standard deviation), VAR (variance), FIRST, and LAST. To use any of these in a query, you include it in the Total row in the design grid. The Total row routinely does not appear in the grid. To include it, right-click the grid, and then click Totals on the shortcut menu.

The following example illustrates how you use these functions by calculating the average balance for all patients.

Steps To Calculate Statistics

1 Use the Query View button on the toolbar to return to the Select Query window. On the Edit menu, click Clear Grid.

2 Right-click the grid.

The shortcut menu displays (see Figure 2-59).

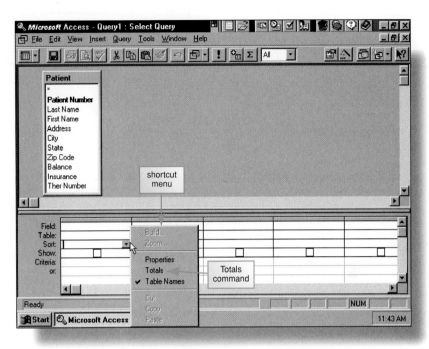

FIGURE 2-59

3 Click Totals on the shortcut menu and then include the Balance field. Point to the Totals line for the Balance field.

The Total row is now included in the design grid (Figure 2-60). The Balance field is included, and the entry in the Total row is Group By. The mouse pointer, which has changed shape to an I-beam, is positioned on the Total row under the Balance field.

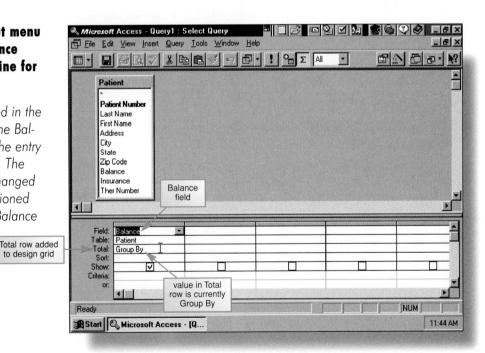

FIGURE 2-60

④ Click the Total row under the Balance field, and then click the arrow that appears.

The list of available selections displays (Figure 2-61).

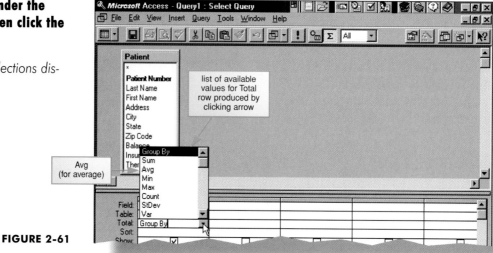

FIGURE 2-61

⑤ Click Avg.

Avg is selected (Figure 2-62).

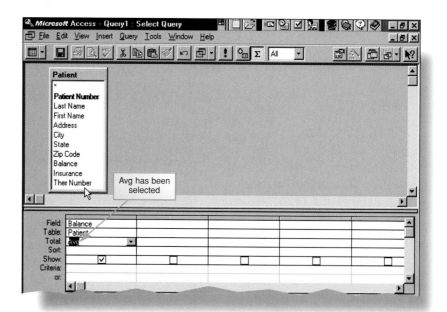

FIGURE 2-62

⑥ Run the query.

The result displays (Figure 2-63), showing the average balance for all patients.

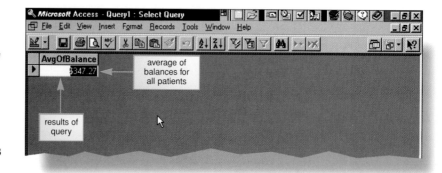

FIGURE 2-63

OtherWays

1. Click Totals button on toolbar
2. On View menu click Totals

Using Criteria in Calculating Statistics

Sometimes calculating statistics for all the records in the table is appropriate. In other cases, however, you will need to calculate the statistics for only those records that satisfy certain criteria. To enter a criterion in a field, first you select Where as the entry in the Total row for the field and then enter the criterion in the Criteria row. The following steps use this technique to calculate the average balance for patients of therapist 08.

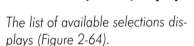

Steps   To Use Criteria in Calculating Statistics

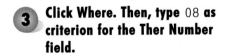

1 Use the Query View button on the toolbar to return to the Select Query window.

2 Be sure totals are included in the query just as you did in the previous example. (If they are not, click the Totals button.) Include the Ther Number field in the second column of the Total row on the design grid. Next, produce the list of available options for the Total entry just as you did when you selected Avg for the Balance field. Use the vertical scroll bar to move through the options until the word, Where, displays.

The list of available selections displays (Figure 2-64).

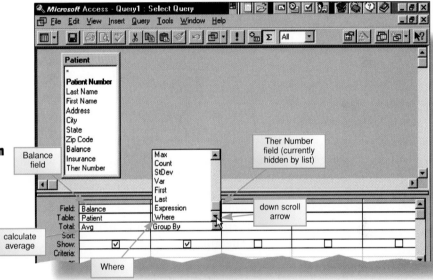

FIGURE 2-64

3 Click Where. Then, type 08 as criterion for the Ther Number field.

Where is selected as the entry in the Total row for the Ther Number field (Figure 2-65) and 08 is entered as the Criteria.

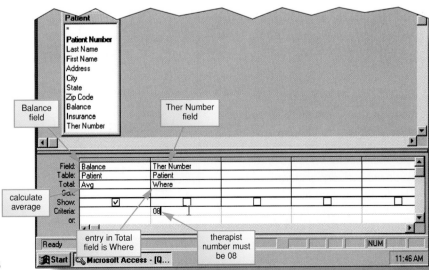

FIGURE 2-65

4 **Run the query.**

The result displays (Figure 2-66), giving the average balance for patients of therapist 08.

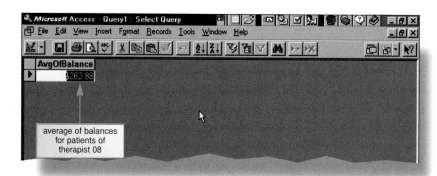

FIGURE 2-66

Grouping

Another way statistics are often used is in combination with grouping. The statistics are then calculated for groups of records. You may, for example, need to calculate the average balance for the patients of each therapist. You will want the average for the patients of therapist 05, the average for patients of therapist 08, and so on.

This type of calculation involves **grouping**, which simply means creating groups of records that share some common characteristic. In grouping by Ther Number, the patients of therapist 05 would form one group, the patients of therapist 08 would be a second, and the patients of therapist 14 form a third. The calculations are then made for each group. To indicate grouping in Access, select Group By as the entry in the Total row for the field to be used for grouping.

Perform the following steps to calculate the average balance for patients of each therapist.

 To Use Grouping

1 **Use the Query View button on the toolbar to return to the Select Query window. On the Edit menu, click Clear Grid.**

2 **Include the Ther Number field. Include the Balance field, and then click Avg as the calculation.**

The Ther Number and Balance fields are included (Figure 2-67). The Totals entry for the Ther Number field currently is Group By, which is correct, so it did not need to be changed.

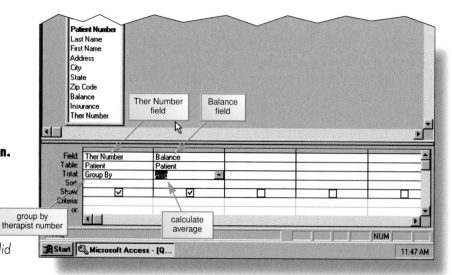

FIGURE 2-67

3 **Run the query.**

The result displays (Figure 2-68), showing each therapist's number along with the average balance of the patients of that therapist.

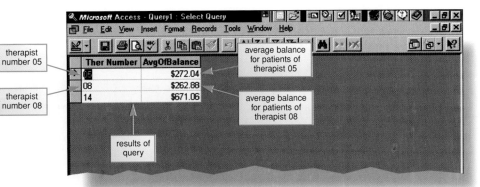

FIGURE 2-68

Saving a Query

In some cases, you will construct a query that you think you will want to use again. You can avoid having to repeat all your entries by **saving the query**. To do so, click the Save button on the toolbar after you have created the query and then assign a name to the query. The following steps illustrate the process by creating and saving a query and calling it Therapists and Patients.

More *About*
Saved Queries

Saved queries can be used in forms and reports just as tables are used. To create a report or form for the query, click the Query tab, select the query, click the New Object button, and then click the appropriate command (New Report or New Form).

Steps **To Save a Query**

1 **Return to the Select Query screen and clear the grid. Right-click the design grid.**

The shortcut menu displays (Figure 2-69).

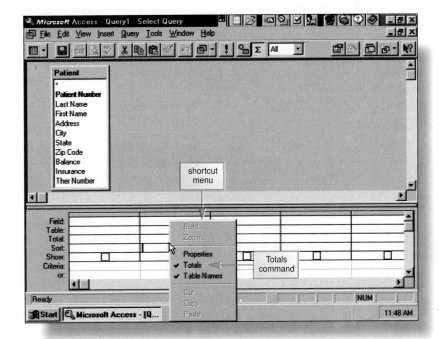

FIGURE 2-69

2 **Click Totals on the shortcut menu to remove the Total row. (It is not used in this query.) Right-click the upper pane of the Select Query window.**

The shortcut menu displays (Figure 2-70).

FIGURE 2-70

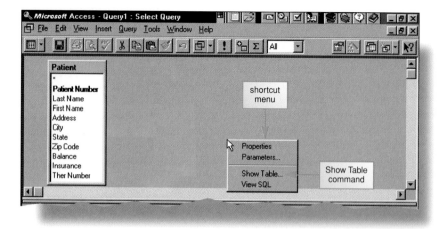

3 **Click Show Table on the shortcut menu. Click Therapist in the Show Table dialog box, and then click the Add button. Close the dialog box. Expand the Therapist field list so all fields display. To the query, add the Ther Number field and the Last Name field from the Therapist table; and add the Patient Number field, the Last Name field, the First Name field, and the Balance field from the Patient table. Point to the Save button on the toolbar.**

The query design is complete (Figure 2-71).

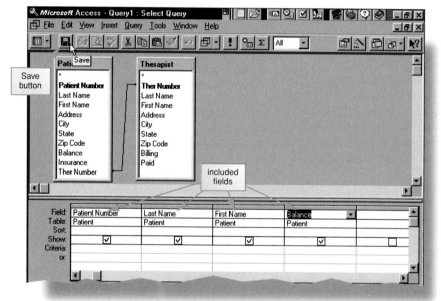

FIGURE 2-71

4 **Click the Save button and then type** Therapists and Patients **as the name of the query.**

The Save As dialog box displays (Figure 2-72). The name of the query has been entered.

5 **Click the OK button to save the query, and then close the query by clicking its window's Close button.**

Access saves the query and closes the Select Query window.

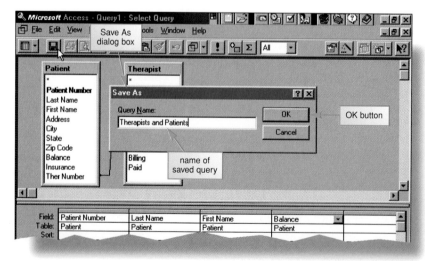

FIGURE 2-72

OtherWays

1. On File menu click Save As
2. Press CTRL+S

Once you have saved a query, you can use it at any time in the future by *opening* it. To open a saved query, click the Queries tab in the Database window, right-click the query, and then click Open.

The query is run against the current database. Thus, if changes have been made to the data since the last time you ran it, the results of the query may be different.

Closing the Database

The following step closes the database by closing its Database window.

TO CLOSE A DATABASE

Step 1: Click the Close button for the Mason Clinic : Database window.

Project Summary

Project 2 introduced you to querying a database using Access. You created and ran queries for Mason Clinic. You used various types of criteria in these queries. You joined tables in some of the queries. Some Mason Clinic queries used calculated fields and statistics. Finally, you saved one of the queries for future use.

What You Should Know

Having completed this project, you should now be able to perform the following tasks:

- Calculate Statistics (*A 2.39*)
- Clear a Query (*A 2.17*)
- Close a Database (*A 2.45*)
- Close the Query (*A 2.15*)
- Create a Query (*A 2.7*)
- Include All Fields in a Query (*A 2.16*)
- Include Fields in the Design Grid (*A 2.11*)
- Join Tables (*A 2.33*)
- Omit Duplicates (*A 2.30*)
- Open a Database (*A 2.7*)
- Print the Results of a Query (*A 2.13*)
- Restrict the Records in a Join (*A 2.35*)
- Return to the Select Query Window (*A 2.14*)
- Run the Query (*A 2.12*)
- Save a Query (*A 2.43*)
- Sort Data in a Query (*A 2.27*)
- Sort on Multiple Keys (*A 2.29*)
- Use a Comparison Operator in a Criterion (*A 2.23*)
- Use a Compound Criterion Involving AND (*A 2.25*)
- Use a Compound Criterion Involving OR (*A 2.26*)
- Use a Computed Field in a Query (*A 2.37*)
- Use a Number in a Criterion (*A 2.22*)
- Use a Wildcard (*A 2.20*)
- Use Criteria for a Field Not Included in the Results (*A 2.21*)
- Use Criteria in Calculating Statistics (*A 2.41*)
- Use Grouping (*A 2.42*)
- Use Text Data in a Criterion (*A 2.18*)

Test Your Knowledge

1 True/False

Instructions: Circle T if the statement is true or F if the statement is false.

T F 1. To include all the fields in a record in a query, click the asterisk (*) that appears in the field list.

T F 2. To create a compound criterion using OR, type the word, UNION, before the second criterion.

T F 3. To create a compound criterion using AND, enter all criteria on the same line.

T F 4. To create a criterion involving Equals, you must type the equal sign (=).

T F 5. When you enter a criteria for a particular field, that field must appear in the results of the query.

T F 6. To find all Patients whose balance is $100 or less, type <=$100.00 as the criterion for the Balance field.

T F 7. To clear all the entries in a design grid, from the Query menu, click Clear Grid.

T F 8. When you sort a query on more than one key, the major sort key must appear to the left of the minor sort key.

T F 9. To omit duplicates from a query, use the Query Properties command and specify Unique Values Only.

T F 10. The wildcard symbols available for use in a query are * and &.

2 Multiple Choice

Instructions: Circle the correct response.

1. To list only certain records in a table use a _____.
   a. list
   b. query
   c. question
   d. answer

2. To find all Patients whose balance is $100 or less, type _____ as the criteria for the Balance field.
   a. <= $100.00
   b. <=100
   c. =<$100.00
   d. =<100

3. To clear all the entries in a design grid, from the _____ menu, click Clear Grid.
   a. File
   b. Edit
   c. View
   d. Query

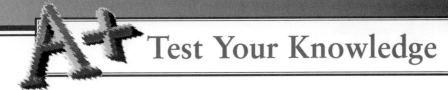

Test Your Knowledge

4. The wildcard symbols available for use in a query are the _____ and the _____.
   a. double period (..), asterisk (*)
   b. question mark (?), ampersand (&)
   c. double period (..), at symbol (@)
   d. question mark (?), asterisk (*)

5. Equal to (=), less than (<), and greater than (>) are examples of _____.
   a. criteria
   b. comparison operators
   c. values
   d. compound criteria

6. When two or more criteria are connected with AND or OR, the result is called a _____.
   a. compound criterion
   b. simple criterion
   c. character criterion
   d. pattern criterion

7. To add an additional table to a query, click _____ on the shortcut menu for the Select Query window.
   a. Show Table
   b. Join Table
   c. Include Table
   d. Add Table

8. Use a query to _____ tables; that is, find records in two tables that have identical values in matching fields.
   a. merge
   b. match
   c. join
   d. combine

9. To remove a table from a query, right-click any field in the field list for the table and click _____ on the shortcut menu.
   a. Delete Table
   b. Remove Table
   c. Erase Table
   d. Clear Table

10. To add a Total row to a design grid, click _____ on the shortcut menu for the Select Query window.
    a. Statistics
    b. Totals
    c. Aggregates
    d. Functions

Test Your Knowledge

3 Understanding the Select Query Window

Instructions: In Figure 2-73, arrows point to the major components of the Select Query window. Identify the various parts of the Query window in the spaces provided.

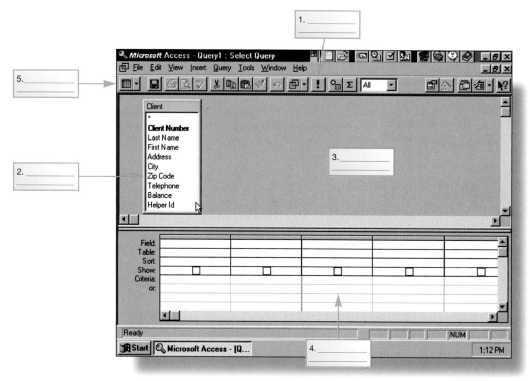

FIGURE 2-73

4 Understanding Statistics

Instructions: Figure 2-74 shows a created query using statistics for the Client table and Figure 2-75 lists the contents of the Client table. List the answer to this query in the spaces provided.

 Test Your Knowledge

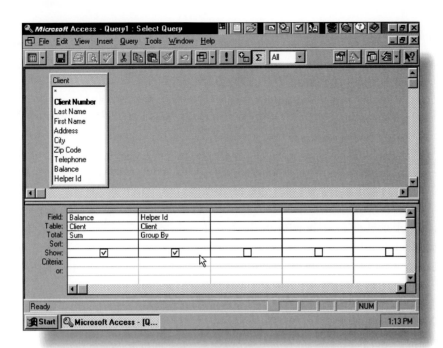

FIGURE 2-74

Data for Client Table

CLIENT NUMBER	LAST NAME	FIRST NAME	ADDRESS	CITY	ZIP CODE	TELEPHONE	BALANCE	HELPER ID
AR86	Arends	Carolyn	268 Getty	Allanson	48102	555-9523	$35.00	1001
AT24	Atwater	Shelly	542 Dune	Allanson	48103	555-1354	$0.00	1008
BI42	Bishop	Bruce	422 Robbins	Allanson	48102	555-7465	$90.00	1008
CH26	Chiang	Doi	62 Stryker	Oakdale	48101	555-2018	$0.00	1012
CH66	Chown	Douglas	266 Norton	Oakdale	48101	555-4890	$55.00	1001
JO12	Johns	Patricia	420 Robbins	Allanson	48102	555-9182	$24.00	1008
KI15	Kirk	Robert	12 Hellerman	Oakdale	48101	555-8273	$65.00	1010
MA21	Martinez	Marie	215 Glen	Allanson	48102	555-1234	$0.00	1001
MO31	Morton	Julie	557 Dune	Allanson	48103	555-5361	$78.00	1012
RO92	Robertson	Mary	345 Magee	Oakdale	48101	555-2056	$43.00	1008

FIGURE 2-75

Use Help

1 Reviewing Project Activities

Instructions: Perform the following tasks using a computer.

1. Start Access.
2. Double-click the Help button on the toolbar to display the Help Topics: Microsoft Access for Windows 95 dialog box.
3. Click the Contents tab. Double-click the Working with Queries book. Double-click the Creating a Query book. Double-click Queries: What they are and how they work.
4. Read the Help information. Use the Next button in the lower right corner of the screen to move to the next Help windows. A total of three Help windows will display. When you finish reading the Help information, click the Close button in the lower right corner of the third Help window.
5. Double-click the Help button on the toolbar to display the Help Topics: Microsoft Access for Windows 95 dialog box. Click the Index tab. Type sort in box 1, and then double-click sorting records in queries in box 2. When the Help information displays, read it. Next, right-click within the box, and then click Print Topic. Hand in the printout to your instructor. Click the Help Topics button to return to the Help Topics: Microsoft Access for Windows 95 dialog box.
6. Click the Find tab. Type wildcard in box 1. Double-click Criteria expressions that use wildcard characters in box 3. When the Help information displays, read it, ready the printer, right-click, and click Print Topic. Hand in the printout to your instructor. Click the Help Topics button to return to the Help Topics: Microsoft Access for Windows 95 dialog box.
7. Click the Answer Wizard tab. Type how do i add calculated fields to a query in box 1. Click the Search button. Double-click Create a calculated field for custom calculations in a query in box 2 under How Do I. Read and print the Help information. Hand in the printout to your instructor.

Use Help

2 Expanding on the Basics

Instructions: Use Access online Help to better understand the topics listed below. Begin each of the following by double-clicking the Help button on the toolbar. If you cannot print the Help information, then answer the question on your own paper.

1. Using the Working with Queries book on the Contents sheet in the Help Topics: Microsoft Access for Windows 95 dialog box, answer the following questions:
   a. How do you insert a field between other fields in the design grid of a query?
   b. How do you remove a field from the design grid?
   c. How do you change a field name in a query?
   d. When you use the asterisk (*) to select all fields, how do you specify criteria for fields?
   e. How do you insert a Criteria row in the design grid?

2. Using the key term *format* and the Index tab in the Help Topics: Microsoft Access for Windows 95 dialog box, display and print information on formatting data in a query's results. Then, answer the following questions:
   a. How can you display a field's property sheet using the menu bar?
   b. How do the Regional Settings on the Windows Control Panel affect the formats in a query?

3. Use the Find tab in the Help Topics: Microsoft Access for Windows 95 dialog box to display and then print information about using criteria to retrieve certain records. Then answer the following questions:
   a. How do you enter criteria to OR two values in one field?
   b. How do you enter criteria to AND two values in one field?
   c. How do you enter criteria to OR and AND in three fields?

4. Use the Answer Wizard in the Help Topics: Microsoft Access for Windows 95 dialog box to display and print information on searching for a range of values.

Apply Your Knowledge

1 Querying the Extra Hands Database

Instructions: Start Access. Open the Extra Hands database from the Access folder on the Student Floppy Disk that accompanies this book. Perform the following tasks:

1. Create a new query for the Client table.
2. Add the Client Number, Last Name, First Name, and Balance fields to the design grid as shown in Figure 2-76.
3. Restrict retrieval to only those records where the balance is greater than $50.00.
4. Run the query and print the results.
5. Return to the Select Query window and clear the grid.
6. Add the Client Number, Last Name, First Name, City, Balance, and Helper Id fields to the design grid.
7. Restrict retrieval to only those records where the Helper Id is either 1010 or 1012.
8. Sort the records in order by Balance (descending) within City (ascending).
9. Run the query and print the results.
10. Return to the Select Query window and clear the grid.
11. Join the Client and Helper tables. Add the Client Number, Last Name, First Name, and Helper Id fields from the Client table and the Last Name field from the Helper table.
12. Sort the records in ascending order by Helper Id.
13. Run the query and print the results.

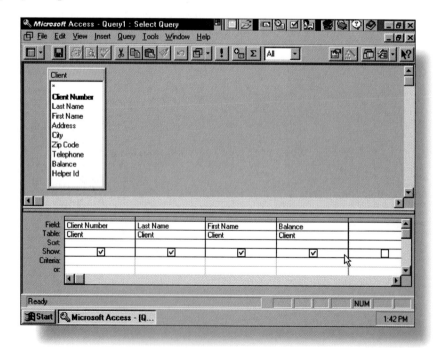

FIGURE 2-76

In the Lab

1 Querying the Symphony Shop Database

Problem: The Symphony Shop volunteers have determined a number of questions they want the database management system to answer. You must obtain answers to the questions posed by the volunteers.

Instructions: Use the database created in the In the Lab 1 of Project 1 for this assignment. Perform the following tasks:

1. Open the Symphony Shop database and create a new query for the Novelty table.
2. Display and print the Novelty Id, Description, and Selling Price for all records in the table as shown in Figure 2-77 on the next page.
3. Display all fields and print all the records in the table.
4. Display and print the Novelty Id, Description, Cost and Dist Code for all novelties where the Dist Code is MM.
5. Display and print the Novelty Id and Description for all novelties where the Description begins with the letters, Pe.
6. Display and print the Novelty Id, Description, and Dist Code for all novelties that cost more than $3.00.
7. Display and print the Novelty Id and Description for all novelties that have a Selling Price of $1.00 or less.
8. Display and print all fields for those novelties that cost more than $3.00 and where the number of units on hand is less than 10.
9. Display and print all fields for those novelties that have a Dist Code of AD or have a Selling Price greater than $4.00.
10. Join the Novelty table and the Distributor table. Display the Novelty Id, Description, Cost, Name, and Telephone fields. Run the query and print the results.
11. Restrict the records retrieved in task 10 above to only those novelties where the number of units on hand is less than 10. Display and print the results.
12. Remove the Distributor table and clear the design grid.
13. Include the Novelty Id and Description in the design grid. Compute the on-hand value (units on hand * cost) for all records in the table. Display and print the results.
14. Display and print the average selling price of all novelties.
15. Display and print the average selling price of novelties grouped by Dist Code.
16. Join the Novelty and Distributor tables. Include the Dist Code and Name fields from the Distributor table. Include the Novelty Id, Description, Cost, and Units On Hand fields from the Novelty table. Save the query as Distributors and Novelties.

(continued)

Querying the Symphony Shop Database *(continued)*

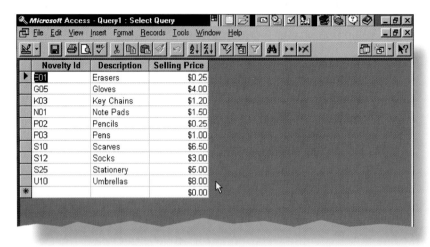

FIGURE 2-77

2 Querying the College Telephone System Database

Problem: The telephone manager has determined a number of questions that she wants the database management system to answer. You must obtain answers to the questions posed by the telephone manager.

Instructions: Use the database created in the In the Lab 2 of Project 1 for this assignment. Perform the following tasks:

1. Open the College Telephone System database and create a new query for the User table.
2. Display and print the User Id, Last Name, First Name, Phone Ext, and Office for all the records in the table as shown in Figure 2-78.
3. Display all fields and print all the records in the table.
4. Display and print the User Id, First Name, Last Name, Basic Charge, and Extra Charges for all users in the department with the code of MTH.
5. Display and print the User Id, First Name, Last Name, and Office of all users whose office is located in the ABH building.
6. Display and print the User Id, First Name, Last Name, and Phone Ext for all users whose basic charge is $15.00 per month.
7. Display and print the User Id, First Name, Last Name, and Extra Charges for all users in the department with a code BIO who have Extra Charges greater than $40.00. List the records in descending order by Extra Charges.
8. Display and print the User Id, First Name, Last Name, and Extra Charges for all users who have extra charges greater than $50.00 and are in either the Mathematics (MTH) or Biology (BIO) department. (Hint: Use information from Use Help Exercise 2 to solve this problem.)

In the Lab

9. Display and print the Basic Charge in ascending order. List each Basic Charge only once.

10. Join the User table and the Department table. Display and print the User Id, Last Name, First Name, Basic Charge, Extra Charges, Name of the department, and Location of the department.

11. Restrict the records retrieved in task 10 above to only those users who have extra charges greater than $20.00.

12. Remove the Department table and clear the design grid.

13. Include the User Id, First Name, Last Name, Basic Charge, and Extra Charges in the design grid. Compute the total bill for each user (Basic Charge + Extra Charges). Display and print the results.

14. Display and print the average extra charges.

15. Display and print the highest extra charge.

16. Display and print the average extra charges for each department.

17. Join the User and Department tables. Include the department Name, Location, User Id, Last Name, First Name, Phone Ext, Basic Charge, and Extra Charges. Save the query as Departments and Users.

User Id	Last Name	First Name	Phone Ext	Office
T1290	Chou	Tanya	2383	112ABH
T2389	Cookson	Christin	2495	120EMH
T3487	Hoveman	Benjamin	3267	223SHH
T4521	Janson	Catherine	2156	244ABH
T5364	Keatty	Richard	2578	116ABH
T6457	Medlar	Michelle	3445	212SHH
T6503	Myrich	Bruce	2038	132ABH
T7579	Nadzia	Rodean	2068	268SHH
T7654	Rabon	Claudia	2239	268ABH
T7890	Richardson	Maria	2418	122EMH
T8521	Sanchez	Javier	2134	248ABH
T8883	TenHoopen	Adrian	2414	134EMH

FIGURE 2-78

3 Querying the WWWW Radio Station Database

Problem: The manager of the radio station has determined a number of questions that he wants the database management system to answer. You must obtain answers to the questions posed by the radio station manager.

Instructions: Use the database created in the In the Lab 3 of Project 1 for this assignment. Perform the following tasks:

1. Open the WWWW Radio Station database and create a new query for the Accounts table.

2. Display and print the Account Number, Name, Balance, and Amount Paid for all the records in the table as shown in Figure 2-79 on the next page.

(continued)

In the Lab

Querying the WWWW Radio Station Database (*continued*)

3. Display and print the Account Number, Name, and Balance for all accounts where the Acc Rep Number is 18.

4. Display and print the Account Number, Name, and Balance for all accounts where the balance is greater than $100.00.

5. Display and print the Account Number, Name, and Amount Paid for all accounts where the Acc Rep Number is 15 and the Amount Paid is greater than $500.00.

6. Display and print the Account Number and Name of all accounts where the Name begins with B.

7. Display and print the Account Number, Name and Balance for all accounts where the Acc Rep Number is 18 or the Balance is less than $100.00.

8. Include the Account Number, Name, City, and State in the design grid. Sort the records in ascending order by City within State. Display and print the results. The City field should display in the result to the left of the State field. (Hint: Use information from Use Help Exercise 1.)

9. Display and print the cities in ascending order. Each city should display only once.

10. Join the Accounts table and the Account Reps table. Display and print the Account Number, Name, Balance, and Amount Paid from the Accounts table and the First Name, Last Name, and Comm Rate from the Account Reps table.

11. Restrict the records retrieved in task 10 above to only those accounts that are in NJ. Display and print the results.

12. Clear the design grid and add the Last Name, First Name, and Comm Rate from the Account Reps table to the grid. Add Amount Paid from the Accounts table. Compute the Commission (Amount Paid * Comm Rate) for the Account Rep. Sort the records in ascending order by Last Name and format Commission as currency. (Hint: Use information from Use Help Exercise 2 to solve this problem.)

13. Remove the Account Reps table and clear the design grid.

14. Display and print the total of all balances and amounts paid.

15. Display and print the total of all balances for Acc Rep Number 15.

16. Display and print the average amount paid by Acc Rep Number.

17. Join the Accounts and Account Reps tables. Display and print the Acc Rep Number, Last Name, Account Number, Name, Balance, and Amount Paid. Save the query as Account Reps and Accounts.

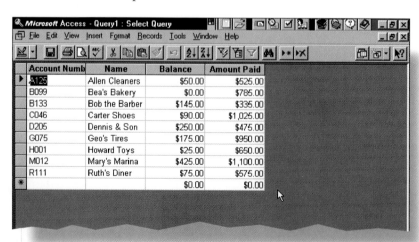

FIGURE 2-79

Cases and Places

The difficulty of these case studies varies:

▶ Case studies preceded by a single half moon are the least difficult. You are asked to create the required database based on information that has already been placed in an organized form.

▶▶ Case studies preceded by two half moons are more difficult. You must organize the information presented before using it to create the desired database.

▶▶▶ Case studies preceded by three half moons are the most difficult. You must choose a specific topic, and then obtain and organize the necessary information before using it to create the required database.

1 ▶ Use the restaurant database created in Case Study 1 of Project 1 for this assignment. Perform the following: (a) It is 10:30 p.m. and you have a craving for a pizza. Display and print the names and phone numbers of all Italian restaurants open that will deliver your order. (b) You are cramming for an exam at 2:00 a.m. and would settle for any type of food. Display and print the names, phone numbers, addresses, and closing times of all restaurants that are open. (c) Your last class on Wednesday ends at 3:50 p.m., and you want to pick up some food to take home to eat before you leave for work. Display and print the names, addresses, and opening times of all restaurants that open before 5:00 p.m. (d) Payday is Friday and you are short on cash at midweek. Display and print the names, addresses, phone numbers, and food types of all restaurants that have specials on Wednesday or Thursday. (e) You and a friend decide to meet for lunch. Display and print the names, addresses, phone numbers, and opening times of all restaurants that open before noon.

2 ▶ Use the textbook database created in Case Study 2 of Project 1 for this assignment. Perform the following: (a) You receive a call asking if anyone is selling a book for Eng 101. Display and print the sellers' names and phone numbers and their asking prices for books available for that course. (b) Karen Sim asks you which books she has submitted. Display and print the titles, authors, and courses of her books. (c) Several nursing students call to ask which textbooks from that department are available. Display and print the titles, authors, and courses of the nursing books. (d) Display and print the titles, authors, and prices of books listed for less than $20. (e) Display and print the titles and course numbers for books in excellent condition.

3 ▶▶ The American Heart Association recommends a maximum of two, three-ounce cooked servings of lean meat, or six ounces total daily. A three-ounce serving is the size of a woman's palm. Use the nutritional content database created in Case Study 3 of Project 1 for this assignment. Perform the following: (a) Display and print the cuts of beef with less than 70 milligrams of cholesterol in one, three-ounce serving. (b) Display and print the cuts of beef with more than 160 calories in a three-ounce serving. (c) Your nutritionist has told you to consume less than 20 grams of fat daily. During the day you have eaten food with a total fat gram content of 15. Display and print the cuts of beef that would be within the nutritionist's advice.

Cases and Places

4 ▶▶ Use the movie collection database created in Case Study 4 of Project 1 for this assignment. Perform the following: (a) Display and print the movie titles in ascending order, along with the two actors and year produced. (b) You have less than two hours to watch a movie tonight. Display and print the movie titles and running times that would fit this time constraint. (c) Display and print the movie titles starring John Wayne. (d) Display and print the movie titles starring Eva Marie Saint. (e) You are in the mood for a comedy. Display and print the movies starring Abbott and Costello. (f) Display and print the movie titles and leading actors of films rated more than two stars. (g) Display and print the movies produced before you were born.

5 ▶▶▶ Use the financial institutions database created in Case Study 5 of Project 1 for this assignment. Display and print the following: (a) The names of the financial institutions and total values of the IRAs at age 65 in descending order. (b) The names and phone numbers of the financial institutions and total amounts of interest earned at age 65 in descending order. (c) The average value of the IRAs at age 65. (d) The average interest rates for the banks, savings and loans, and credit unions. (e) The name, address, and interest rate of the financial institution with the highest interest rate. (f) The name, phone number, and interest rate of the financial institution with the lowest interest rate. (g) The names of the financial institutions and penalties for early withdrawal in two years in ascending order. (h) The names of the financial institutions and annual fees in descending order.

6 ▶▶▶ Use the campus directory database created in Case Study 6 of Project 1 for this assignment. Display and print the following: (a) The names of your instructors in ascending order, along with their phone numbers and room numbers. (b) The names of the administrators in ascending order, along with their phone numbers and room numbers. (c) The services in ascending order, including phone numbers and room numbers.

7 ▶▶▶ Use the product comparison database created in Case Study 7 of Project 1 for this assignment. Display and print the following: (a) The five specific items in ascending order, along with sizes and prices for the dairy items at the convenience, grocery, and discount stores. (b) The five specific items in ascending order, along with sizes and prices for the snack items at the convenience, grocery, and discount stores. (c) The five specific items in ascending order, along with sizes and prices for the cosmetics/toiletries items at the convenience, grocery, and discount stores. (d) The five specific items in ascending order, along with sizes and prices for the kitchen supplies items at the convenience, grocery, and discount stores.

Project

Microsoft Access 7

Windows 95

Maintaining a Database Using the Design and Update Features of Access

Objectives:

You will have mastered the material in this project when you can:

▶ Add records to a table
▶ Locate records
▶ Change the contents of records in a table
▶ Delete records from a table
▶ Restructure a table
▶ Change field characteristics
▶ Add a field
▶ Save the changes to the structure
▶ Update the contents of a single field
▶ Make changes to groups of records
▶ Delete groups of records
▶ Specify a required field
▶ Specify a range
▶ Specify a default value
▶ Specify legal values
▶ Specify a format
▶ Update a table with validation rules
▶ Specify referential integrity
▶ Order records
▶ Create single-field and multiple-field indexes

Project 3

Computer-Aided Dispatch System Makes Responding to EMERGENCIES a Real Gas

In its pure state, natural gas is odorless, colorless, and tasteless. To help keep their customers safe, natural gas utility companies add a distinctive odor that alerts customers to the presence of this gas. If this smell is present around a gas furnace, water heater, or other natural gas appliance, it is important to call the local gas utility company right away for help.

That is where Northern Illinois Gas's computer-aided dispatching system comes in.

No matter where the resident is calling from in the utility's 17,000 square mile territory, the call is received by a centralized customer service center. A customer service representative at the center queries a database containing hundreds of pieces of data for each of the 1.8 million residential, commercial, and industrial customers. The representative can locate this customer information by entering the customer's name, address, account number, or gas meter number on a computer.

DANGER

MOTOROLA MOBILE WORKSTATION 9100-386

The representative then asks the customer what work needs to be done, enters this information in a field on the screen, and transmits the updated record back to the database. If the customer service representative makes a service request, it is forwarded to the computer-aided dispatching system. The service request record generated by the system contains data such as trouble codes (for example, the customer smells gas or needs a meter changed), times when the customer plans to be home, and whether the customer has a dog, as well as information about the type of service required.

In a non-emergency situation, the service request is saved in the database and assigned to a mechanic at a later time. In an emergency, however, the call immediately is assigned to a dispatcher. The dispatcher can ask the system to analyze the address of the emergency and identify which mechanics are in the area. At all times, the system knows where each mechanic is working, the type of work being done, and when the job was started. This information is obtained from radio signals transmitted to and from the dispatch center and small computer terminals mounted in more than 260 mechanics' and supervisors' vehicles. The terminals include a small screen, a full keyboard, and 10 megabytes of memory.

The system recommends up to eight mechanics who can be assigned to the order. The dispatcher chooses one of the recommended people and transmits the work order to that mechanic's truck. There, the screen displays a message stating an emergency has been assigned to that worker. The worker pushes a button on the terminal to transmit a signal back to the dispatching center to acknowledge receiving the emergency service request.

The system monitors the status of the order and continually updates, or maintains, the database. If the dispatcher does not assign the work order in a designated amount of time, a warning is displayed. If the mechanic assigned the order does not respond to the request, the dispatcher is notified and may reassign the job. The system records when the mechanic is en route to, working on, and finished with the job. Thus, the customer's record contains a complete picture of the job from start to finish.

Northern Illinois Gas's computer-aided dispatch system eliminates an estimated 700,000 pieces of paper per year, with each sheet representing one customer order. If it fails, however, the computer instantaneously switches to the former paper system, using 5-by-8-inch work order sheets and dispatchers giving orders using two-way radios.

When you smell gas at three o' clock in the morning, it is comforting to know that a utility company has developed a system to respond to your emergency in record time.

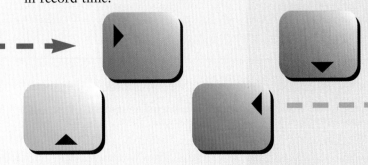

Microsoft
Access 7
Windows 95

Maintaining a Database Using the Design and Update Features of Access

Case Perspective

Mason Clinic has created a database and loaded it with patient and therapist data. The management and staff have received many benefits from the database, including the capability to ask a variety of questions concerning the data in the database. They now face the task of keeping the database up to date. They must add new records as they take on new patients and therapists. They must make changes to existing records to reflect additional charges, payments, change of addresses, and so on. Mason Clinic management also found that they needed to change the structure of the database in two specific ways. The clinic decided the database needed to include the type of insurance carrier that each patient has. They found the Last Name field was too short to contain the name of one of the patients. They also determined that they needed to improve the efficiency of certain types of database processing and found that to do so, they needed to create indexes, which are similar to indexes found in the back of books.

Introduction

Once a database has been created and loaded with data, it must be maintained. **Maintaining the database** means modifying the data to keep it up to date, such as adding new records, changing the data for existing records, and deleting records. **Updating** can include mass updates or deletions; that is, updates to, or deletions of, many records at the same time.

In addition to adding, changing, and deleting records, maintenance of a database can periodically involve the need to **restructure** the database; that is, to change the database structure. This can include adding new fields to a table, changing the characteristics of existing fields, and removing existing fields. It can also involve the creation of **indexes**, which are similar to indexes found in the back of books and which are used to improve the efficiency of certain operations.

Figure 3-1 summarizes some of the various types of activities involved in maintaining a database.

Project Three – Mason Clinic

You are to make the changes to the data in the Mason Clinic database as requested by the management of Mason Clinic. You must also restructure the database to meet the current needs of the clinic. This includes adding an additional field as well as increasing the width of one of the existing fields. You must also modify the structure of the database in a way that prevents users from entering invalid data. Finally, management is concerned that some operations, for example, those involving sorting the data, seem to be taking a little longer than they would like. You are to create indexes to attempt to address this problem.

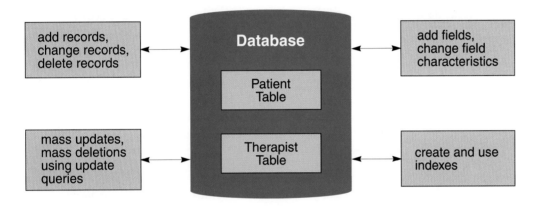

FIGURE 3-1

Overview of Project Steps

These steps give you an overview of how the Mason Clinic database will be maintained in this project. The following tasks will be completed in this project.

1. Start Access and open the Mason Clinic database.
2. Use a form to add a new record to the Patient table.
3. Locate the record for patient PE33 and then change the last name of the patient.
4. Delete the record for patient JG22.
5. Increase the width of the Last Name field to accommodate a patient name that will not fit in the current structure.
6. Add a field for insurance carrier (called Ins Carrier) to the Patient table.
7. Change the name of patient DI32 (the one that previously would not fit).
8. Resize the columns in Datasheet view.
9. Use an update query to initially set all the values in the Ins Carrier field to ORG, the most common carrier type.

10. Use a delete query to delete all patients in Zip Code 45621.
11. Create a validation rule to make the Last Name field a required field.
12. Create a validation rule to ensure that only values between $0.00 and $2,000.00 may be entered in the Balance field.
13. Specify that ORG is to be the default value for the Ins Carrier field.
14. Create a validation rule to ensure that only the values of ORG, GVT, or PRS may be entered in the Ins Carrier field.
15. Specify that any letters entered in the Patient Number field are to be converted automatically to uppercase.
16. Specify referential integrity between the Patient and Therapist tables.
17. Use the Sort buttons to sort records in the database.
18. Create and use indexes to improve performance.

Opening the Database

Before creating queries, first you must open the database. To do so, perform the following steps.

TO OPEN A DATABASE

Step 1: Click the Start button.
Step 2: Click Open Office Document, and then click 3½ Floppy [A:] in the Look in drop-down list box. If it is not already selected, click the Mason Clinic database name.
Step 3: Click the Open button.

The database is open and the Mason Clinic : Database window displays.

Adding, Changing, and Deleting

Keeping the data in a database up to date requires three tasks: adding new records, changing the data in existing records, and deleting existing records.

Adding Records

In Project 1, you added records to a database using Datasheet view; that is, as you were adding records, the records were displayed on the screen in the form of a datasheet, or table. When you need to add additional records, you can use the same techniques.

In Project 1, you used a form to view records. This is called **Form view**. You can also use Form view to update the data in a table. You can add new records, change existing records, or delete records. To do so, use the same techniques you used in Datasheet view. To add a record to the Patient table with a form, for example, use the following steps. These steps use the Patient form you created in Project 1.

Steps To Use a Form to Add Records

1 **With the Mason Clinic database open, point to the Forms tab (Figure 3-2).**

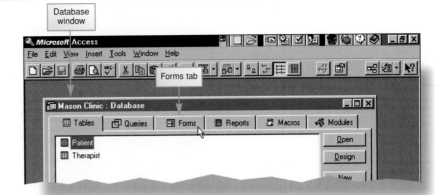

FIGURE 3-2

2 **Click the Forms tab. Right-click Patient.**

The shortcut menu displays (Figure 3-3).

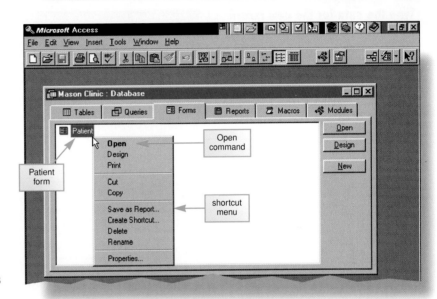

FIGURE 3-3

3 **Click Open.**

The form for the Patient table displays (Figure 3-4).

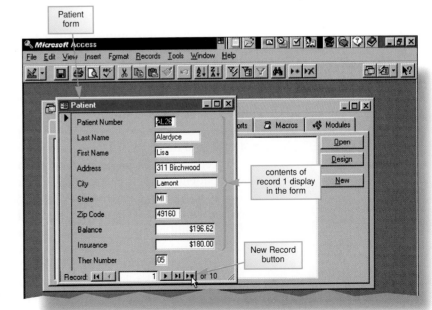

FIGURE 3-4

4 Click the New Record button.

The contents of the form are erased in preparation for a new record (Figure 3-5).

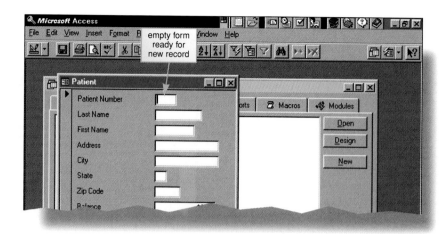

FIGURE 3-5

5 Type the data for the new record as shown in Figure 3-6. Press the TAB key after typing the data in each field. Once you press the TAB key after typing the final field (Ther Number), the record will be added and the contents of the form erased.

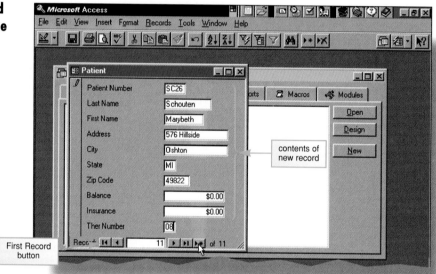

FIGURE 3-6

The record is now added to the Patient table.

Searching for a Record

In the database environment, **searching** means looking for records that satisfy some criteria. Looking for all the patients whose therapist number is 05 is an example of searching. The queries in Project 2 were examples of searching. Access had to locate those records that satisfied the criteria.

A need for searching also exists when using Form view or Datasheet view. To update patient PE33, for example, first you need to find the patient. In a small table, repeatedly pressing the Next Record button until patient PE33 is on the screen may not be particularly difficult. In a large table with many records, however, this would be extremely cumbersome. You need a way to be able to go directly to a record just by giving the value in some field. This is the function of the Find button. Prior to clicking the Find button, select the field for the search.

Perform the following steps to move to the first record in the file, select the Patient Number field, and then use the Find button to search for the patient whose number is PE33.

Steps To Search for a Record

1 **Make sure the Patient table is open and the form (Patient form) for the Patient table is on the screen. Click the First Record button (see Figure 3-6) to display the first record. If the Patient Number field is not currently selected (highlighted), select it by clicking the field name. Point to the Find button on the toolbar.**

The first record displays in the form (Figure 3-7).

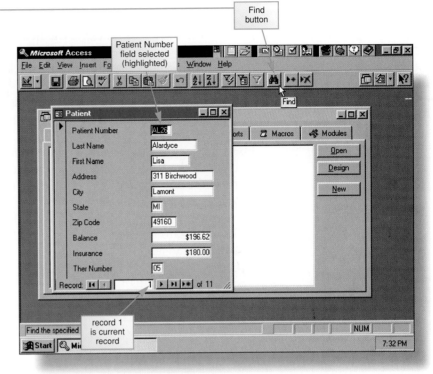

FIGURE 3-7

2 **Click the Find button. Type** PE33 **in the Find What text box.**

The Find in field: 'Patient Numbe' dialog box displays (Figure 3-8). The Find What text box contains the entry, PE33.

3 **Click the Find Next button and then click the Close button.**

Access locates the record for patient PE33.

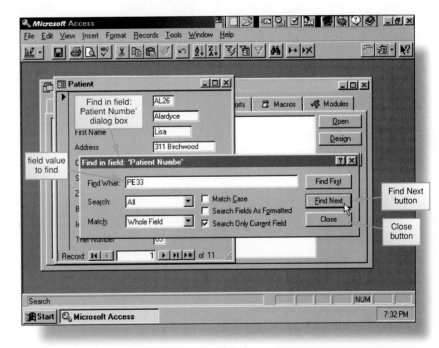

FIGURE 3-8

> **Other Ways**
> 1. On Edit menu click Find
> 2. Press CTRL+F

After locating a record that satisfies a criterion, to find the next record that satisfies the same criterion, repeat the same process. (You will not need to retype the value.)

More *About*
Changing the Contents of a Record

In changing a field, clicking within the field will produce an insertion point. Clicking the name of the field will select the entire field. The new entry typed then will completely replace the previous entry.

Changing the Contents of a Record

After locating the record to be changed, select the field to be changed by pressing the TAB key or clicking the field name. Then make the appropriate changes. Clicking the field name automatically produces an insertion point in the field name text box. If you press the TAB key, press F2 to produce an insertion point.

Normally, Access is in Insert mode, so the characters typed will be inserted at the appropriate position. To change to Overtype mode, press the INSERT key. The letters, OVR, will appear near the bottom right edge of the status bar. To return to Insert mode, press the INSERT key. In Insert mode, if the data in the field completely fills the field, no additional characters can be inserted. In this case, increase the size of the field before inserting the characters. You will see how to do this later in the project.

Complete the following steps to use Form view to change the name of patient PE33 to Pezzato by inserting an extra z. Sufficient room exists in the field to make this change.

Steps **To Update the Contents of a Field**

① **Position the mouse pointer in the First Name field text box for patient PE33 where the extra letter is to be inserted (that is, immediately after the z (Figure 3-9)).**

The mouse pointer appears as an I-beam.

② **Click to produce an insertion point, and then type z to insert the letter.**

The name is now Pezzato.

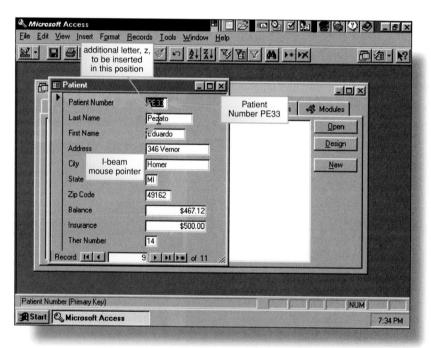

FIGURE 3-9

More *About*
Using the Form View Button

Repeatedly clicking the Form View button will transfer back and forth between Form view and the design of the form, called Design view. To move to Datasheet view, you *must* click the down arrow, and then click Datasheet View in the drop-down list that displays.

Switching Between Views

Sometimes, after working in Form view where you can see all fields, but only one record, it would be helpful to see several records at a time. To do so, switch to Datasheet view by clicking the Form View button down arrow and then clicking Datasheet View. Perform the following steps to switch from Form view to Datasheet view.

Steps To Switch from Form View to Datasheet View

① **Point to the Form View button down arrow on the toolbar (Figure 3-10).**

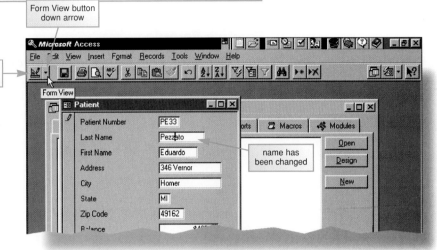

FIGURE 3-10

② **Click the Form View button down arrow. Point to Datasheet View.**

The Form View drop-down list displays (Figure 3-11).

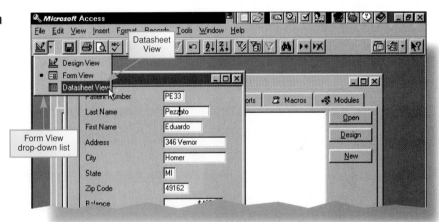

FIGURE 3-11

③ **Click Datasheet View, and then maximize the window containing the datasheet.**

The datasheet displays (Figure 3-12). The position in the table is maintained. The current record indicator points to patient PE33, the patient that displayed on the screen in Form view. The Last Name field, the field in which the insertion point displayed, is highlighted.

Patient Number	Last Name	First Name	Address	City	State	Zip
AL26	Alardyce	Lisa	311 Birchwood	Lamont	MI	49160
AT73	Acton	Thomas	312 Newcastle	Homer	MI	49162
BR31	Bryce	Roger	617 College	Lamont	MI	49160
DI32	Dalton	Irene	41 Lafayette	Madison	IN	42909
GC92	Gutierez	Carlos	476 Fulton	Jackson	OH	49401
GT43	Grant	Thomas	247 Fuller	Lamont	MI	49160
JG22	Jenkins	Glen	201 Plymouth	Madison	IN	42909
LI66	Lawrence	Irving	912 Devonshire	Beulah	MI	45621
PE33	Pezzato	Eduardo	346 Vernor	Homer	MI	49162
PE76	Perez	Enzo	216 Four Mile	Perry	MI	47211
SC26	Schouten	Marybeth	576 Hillside	Oshton	MI	49822

FIGURE 3-12

*Other***Ways**

1. On View menu click Datasheet

If you wanted to return to Form view, you would use the same process. The only difference is that you would click Form View rather than Datasheet View.

Deleting Records

When records are no longer needed, **delete the records** (remove them) from the table. If, for example, patient JG22 has moved and will no longer be coming in for therapy, that patient's record should be deleted. To delete a record, first locate it and then press the DELETE key. Complete the following steps to delete patient JG22.

Steps To Delete a Record

1 **With the datasheet for the Patient table on the screen, position the mouse pointer on the row selector of the record in which the patient number is JG22 (Figure 3-13).**

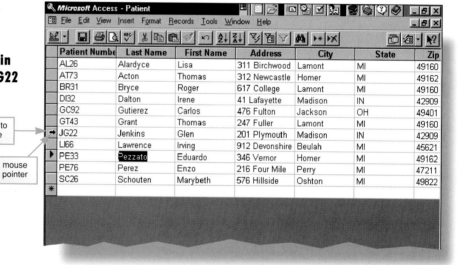

FIGURE 3-13

2 **Click the row selector to select the record, and then press the DELETE key to delete the record.**

The Microsoft Access dialog box displays (Figure 3-14). The message indicates that one record will be deleted.

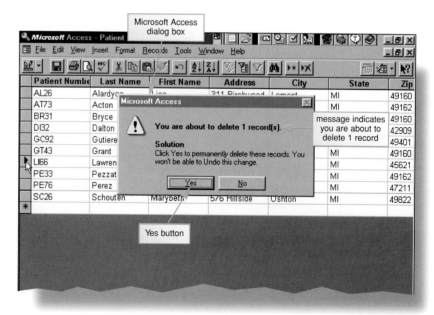

FIGURE 3-14

3 Click the Yes button to complete the deletion.

The record is deleted (Figure 3-15).

4 Close the window containing the table by clicking its Close button.

record has been deleted

Patient Numbe	Last Name	First Name	Address	City	State	Zip
AL26	Alardyce	Lisa	311 Birchwood	Lamont	MI	49160
AT73	Acton	Thomas	312 Newcastle	Homer	MI	49162
BR31	Bryce	Roger	617 College	Lamont	MI	49160
DI32	Dalton	Irene	41 Lafayette	Madison	IN	42909
GC92	Gutierez	Carlos	476 Fulton	Jackson	OH	49401
GT43	Grant	Thomas	247 Fuller	Lamont	MI	49160
LI66	Lawrence	Irving	912 Devonshire	Beulah	MI	45621
PE33	Pezzato	Eduardo	346 Vernor	Homer	MI	49162
PE76	Perez	Enzo	216 Four Mile	Perry	MI	47211
SC26	Schouten	Marybeth	576 Hillside	Oshton	MI	49822

FIGURE 3-15

Changing the Structure

When you initially create a database, you define its **structure**; that is, you indicate the names, types, and sizes of all the fields. In many cases, the structure you first defined will not continue to be appropriate as you use the database. A variety of reasons exist why the structure of a table might need to change. Changes in the needs of users of the database may require additional fields to be added. In the Patient table, for example, if it is important to store a code indicating the insurance carrier of a patient, you need to add such a field.

Characteristics of a given field might need to change. For example, the patient Irene Dalton's name is stored incorrectly in the database. It should be Irene Dalton-Manters. The Last Name field is not large enough, however, to hold the correct name. To accommodate this change, increase the width of the Last Name field.

It may be that a field currently in the table is no longer necessary. If no one ever uses a particular field, there is no point in having it in the table. Because it is occupying space and serving no useful purpose, it should be removed from the table. You would also need to delete the field from any forms, reports, or queries that include it.

To make any of these changes, click the Design button in the Database window.

Changing the Size of a Field

The steps on the next page change the size of the Last Name field from 10 to 14 to accommodate the change of name from Dalton to Dalton-Manters.

More *About*
Changing the Structure

The ease with which the structure of a table can be changed is a real advantage of using a database management system like Access. In a nondatabase environment, changes to the structure can be very cumbersome, requiring difficult and time-consuming changes to many programs.

Steps To Change the Size of a Field

1 **With the Database window on the screen, click the Tables tab, and then right-click Patient.**

The shortcut menu displays (Figure 3-16).

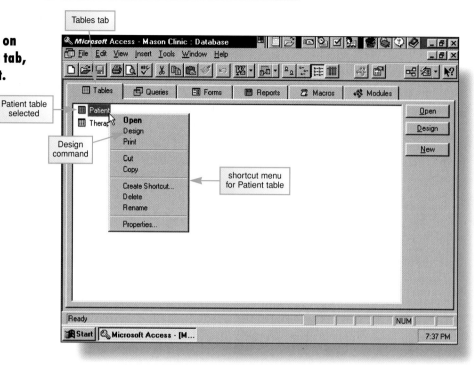

FIGURE 3-16

2 **Click Design, and then point to the row selector for the Last Name field.**

The Patient : Table window displays (Figure 3-17).

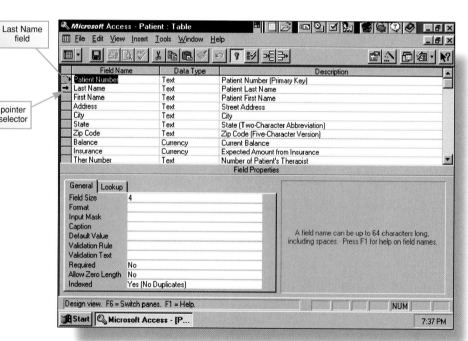

FIGURE 3-17

3 **Click the row selector for the Last Name field.**

The Last Name field is selected (Figure 3-18).

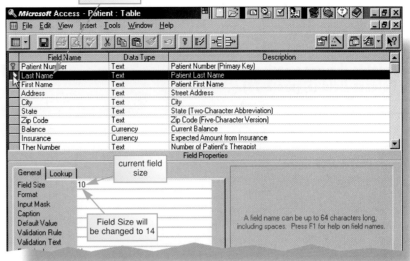

FIGURE 3-18

4 **Press F6 to highlight the field size, type 14 as the new size, and press F6 again.**

The size is changed (Figure 3-19).

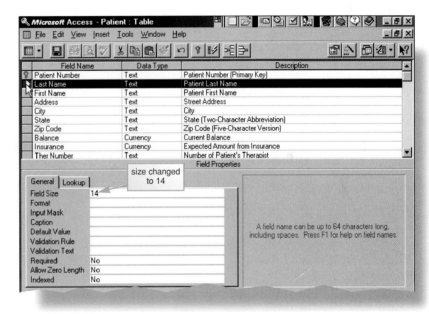

FIGURE 3-19

Adding a New Field

The following steps add a new field, called Ins Carrier, to the table. This field is used to indicate the type insurance coverage the patient has. The possible entries in this field are ORG (covered by insurance through an organization where the patient works), GVT (covered by government insurance), and PRS (covered by personal insurance). The new field will follow the Zip Code in the list of fields; that is, it will be the *seventh* field in the restructured table. The current seventh field (Balance) will become the eighth field, Insurance will become the ninth field, and so on. Complete the steps on the next page to add the field.

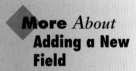

More *About*
Adding a New Field

A variety of reasons exists why new fields are added to tables. Users needs can change. The field may have been omitted by mistake when the table was first created. Government regulations may change in such a way that an organization needs to maintain additional information.

Steps To Add a Field to a Table

1 **Point to the row selector for the Balance field (Figure 3-20).**

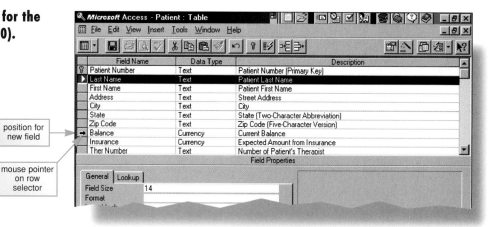

position for new field

mouse pointer on row selector

FIGURE 3-20

2 **Click the row selector for the Balance field and then press the INSERT key to insert a blank row.**

A blank row displays in the position for the new field (Figure 3-21).

space for new field

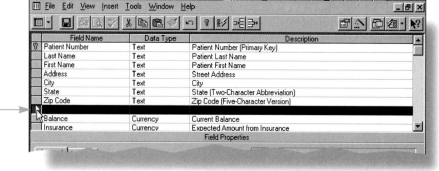

FIGURE 3-21

3 **Click the Field Name column for the new field. Type** Ins Carrier **(field name) and then press the TAB key. Select the Text data type by pressing the TAB key. Type** Insurance Carrier (ORG, GVT, or PRS) **as the description. Press F6 to move to the Field Size text box, type** 3 **(the size of the Ins Carrier field), and press F6 again.**

The entries for the new field are complete (Figure 3-22).

name of new field

data type for new field

description of new field

size of new field

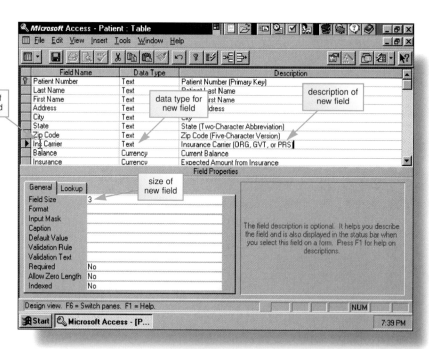

FIGURE 3-22

4 Close the Patient : Table window by clicking its Close button.

The Microsoft Access dialog box displays (Figure 3-23).

5 Click the Yes button to save the changes.

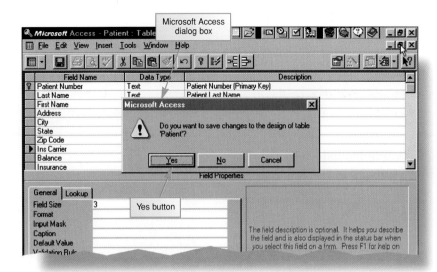

FIGURE 3-23

OtherWays

1. Click row selector below where new field is to be added, click Insert Row button on toolbar
2. Click row selector below where new field is to be added, on Insert menu click Field

Updating the Restructured Database

Changes to the structure are available immediately. The Last Name field is longer, although it does not appear that way on the screen, and the new Ins Carrier field is included.

To make a change to a single field, such as changing the name from Dalton to Dalton-Manters, click the field to be changed, and then type the new value. If the record to be changed is not on the screen, use the Navigation buttons (Next Record, Previous Record) to move to it. If the field to be corrected simply is not visible on the screen, use the horizontal scroll bar along the bottom of the screen to shift all the fields until the correct one displays. Then make the change.

Perform the following steps to change the name of Dalton to Dalton-Manters, and at the same time increase the column width so the entire name is visible.

 To Update the Contents of a Field

1 Right-click Patient.

The shortcut menu displays (Figure 3-24).

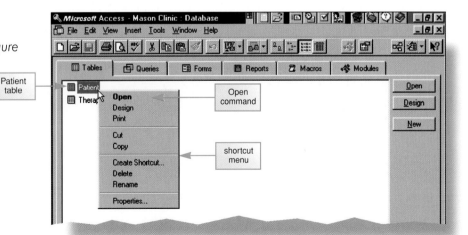

FIGURE 3-24

2 Click Open. Position the I-Beam mouse pointer to the right of the n of Dalton (customer DI32).

The datasheet displays (Figure 3-25).

3 Click in the field, and then type -Manters **as the addition to the name.**

The name is changed from Dalton to Dalton-Manters.

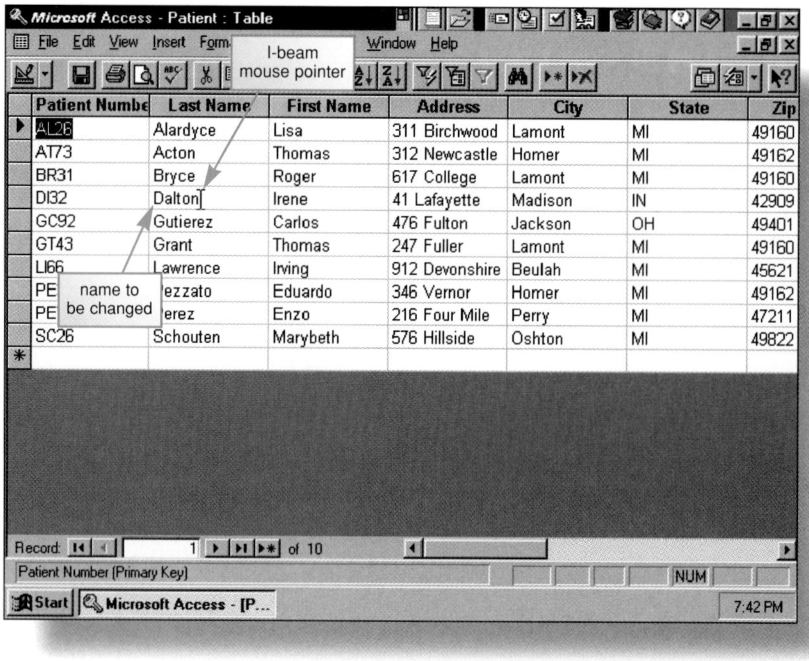

FIGURE 3-25

More *About*
Updating a Restructured Database

In a nondatabase environment, after changing a structure, it can take several hours before the new structure is available for use. Computer jobs to change the structure often would run overnight or even over a weekend. Having the changes available immediately is a major benefit to using a system like Access.

Resizing Columns

After changing the size of a field, you will often need to **resize the column** (change its size) for the field in the datasheet. In this case, because the larger name, Dalton-Manters, still displays, it is not necessary. In other cases, however, the expanded name might not completely display. To correct this problem, you would expand the size of the column.

In some instances, you may want to reduce the size of a column. The City field, for example, is short enough that it does not require all the space on the screen that is allotted to it.

Both types of changes are made the same way. Position the mouse pointer on the line in the column heading immediately to the right of the column to be resized. The mouse pointer will change to a double-headed arrow with a vertical bar. You then can drag the line to resize the column. Also, you can double-click in the column heading immediately to the right of the column to be resized. Access then determines the best size for the column.

The following steps illustrate the process for resizing the City column to the best size.

More *About*
Resizing Columns

Changes to the size of a field are not reflected automatically on the forms you have created. If you used the AutoForm command, you can change the field sizes by simply recreating the form. To do so, right-click the form, click Delete, and create the form as you did in Project 1.

Steps To Resize a Column

1 **Point to the line in the column heading immediately to the right of the column heading for the City field (Figure 3-26).**

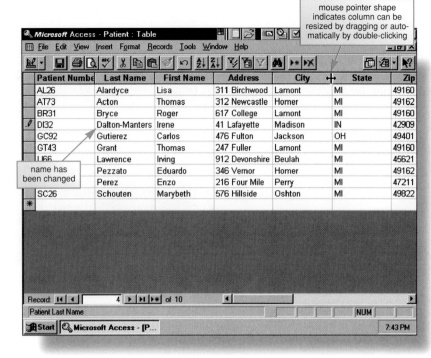

FIGURE 3-26

2 **Double-click the line in the column heading.**

The City column has been resized to the best size to fit the data (Figure 3-27).

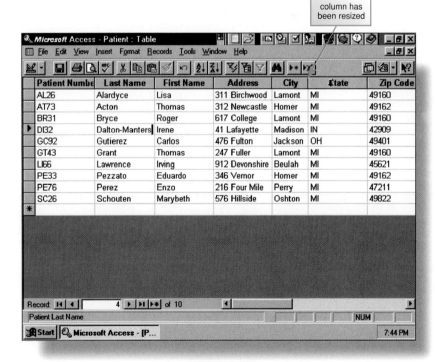

FIGURE 3-27

3 Close the Patient : Table window by clicking its Close button.

The Microsoft Access dialog box displays (Figure 3-28). If you wanted to save this change to the width of the City column, you would click the Yes button.

4 Click the No button.

The change is not saved. The next time the datasheet displays, the City column will have its original width.

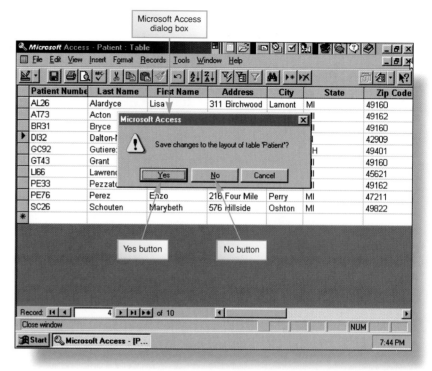

FIGURE 3-28

OtherWays

1. On Format menu click Column Width, click Best Fit

More About Update Queries

Each database management system offers some mechanism for updating multiple records at a time, that is, for making the same change to all the records that satisfy some criterion. Some systems, including Access, accomplish this through the query tool by providing a special type of query for this purpose.

Using an Update Query

The Ins Carrier field is blank on every record. One approach to entering the information for the field would be to step through the entire table, changing the value on each record to what it should be. If most of the patients have the same type, a simpler approach is available.

Suppose, for example, that more patients are type ORG (organization). Initially, you can set all the values to ORG. To quickly and easily accomplish this, you use a special type of query called an **update query**. Later, you can change the type for the patients covered by personal or by government insurance individually.

The process for creating an update query begins the same as the process for creating the queries in Project 2. After selecting the table for the query, click the Query Type button and then click Update on the menu that displays. An extra row, Update To:, displays in the design grid. Use this additional row to indicate the way the data will be updated. If a criterion is entered, then only those records that satisfy the criterion will be updated.

Perform the following steps to change the value in the Ins Carrier field to ORG for all the records. Because all records are to be updated, no criteria will be entered.

Steps   To Use an Update Query to Update All Records

1 With the Patient table selected click the New Object button down arrow on the toolbar.

The New Object drop-down list displays (Figure 3-29).

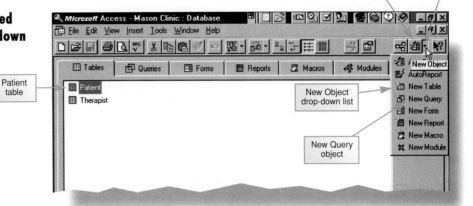

FIGURE 3-29

2 Click New Query.

The New Query dialog box displays (Figure 3-30). Design View is selected (highlighted).

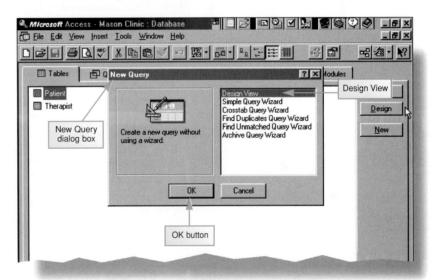

FIGURE 3-30

3 Click the OK button, and be sure the Query1 : Select Query window is maximized. Resize the upper and lower panes of the screen as well as the Patient field list so all fields in the Patient table display (see pages A 2.7 through A 2.10 in Project 2). Click the Query Type button down arrow on the toolbar.

The Query Type drop-down list displays (Figure 3-31).

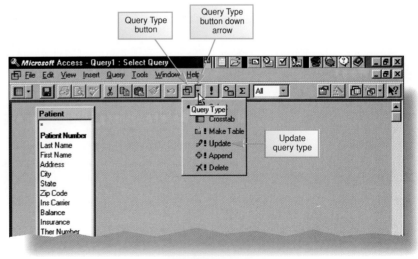

FIGURE 3-31

4 Click Update, double-click the Ins Carrier field to select the field, click the Update To text box in the first column of the design grid, and type ORG as the new value.

The Ins Carrier field is selected (Figure 3-32). The value to which the field is to be changed is entered as ORG. Because no criteria are entered, the Ins Carrier value on every row will be changed to ORG.

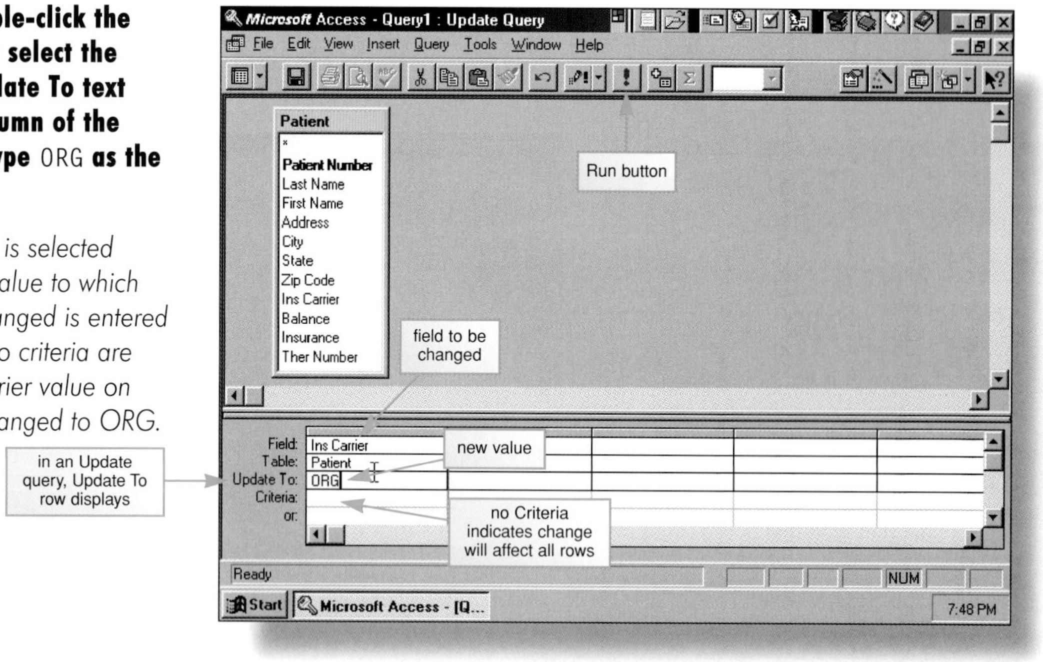

5 Click the Run button on the toolbar.

The Microsoft Access dialog box displays (Figure 3-33). The message indicates that 10 rows will be updated by the query.

6 Click the Yes button.

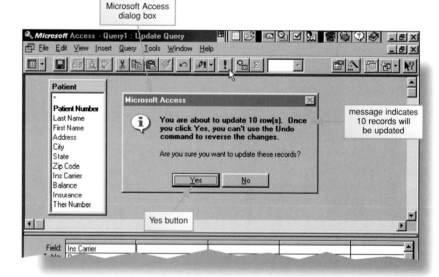

FIGURE 3-32

FIGURE 3-33

OtherWays

1. On Query menu click Update

Using a Delete Query to Delete a Group of Records

In some cases, several records are deleted at a time. If, for example, another neighboring clinic will be serving all patients in a particular Zip Code, all the patients who have this Zip Code can be deleted from the Mason Clinic database. Rather than deleting these patients individually, which would be very cumbersome, delete them in one operation by using a delete query.

Perform the following steps to use a delete query to delete all patients whose Zip Code is 45621.

Steps To Use a Delete Query to Delete a Group of Records

1 **Clear the grid by clicking Edit on the menu bar and then clicking Clear Grid. Click the Query Type button down arrow on the toolbar.**

The Query Type drop-down list displays (Figure 3-34).

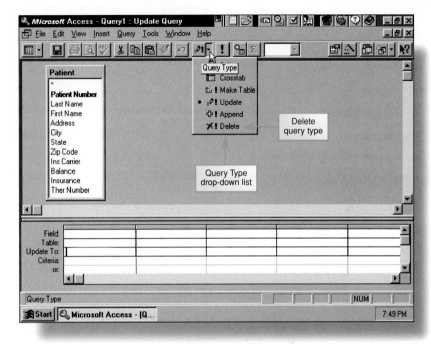

FIGURE 3-34

2 **Click Delete, double-click the Zip Code field to select the field, and click the Criteria box. Type** 45621 **as the criteria.**

The criteria is entered in the Zip Code column (Figure 3-35).

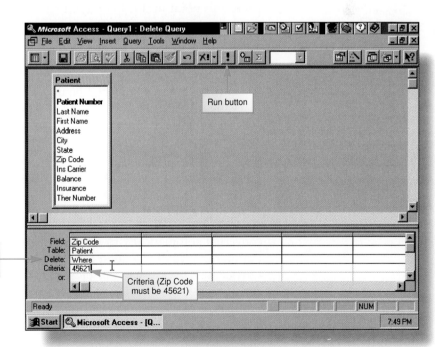

FIGURE 3-35

3 Run the query.

The Microsoft Access dialog box displays (Figure 3-36). The message indicates the query will delete 1 row (record).

4 Click the Yes button. Close the Query window. Do not save the query.

One patient (LI66) has been removed from the table.

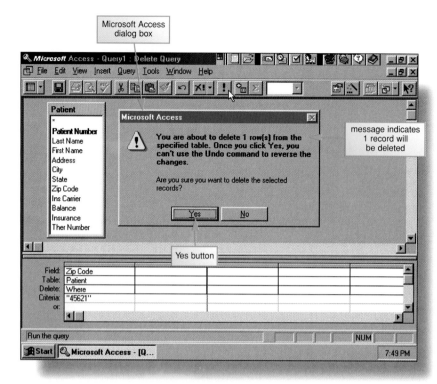

FIGURE 3-36

OtherWays
1. On Query menu click Delete

Creating Validation Rules

Up to this point in this book, you have created, loaded, queried, and updated a database. Nothing done so far, however, ensures that users enter only valid data. This section explains how to create **validation rules**; that is, rules that the data entered by a user must follow. As you will see, Access will prevent users from entering data that does not follow the rules. The steps also specify **validation text**, which is the message that will be displayed if a user violates the validation rule.

Validation rules can indicate a **required field**, a field in which the user must actually enter data. For example, by making the Last Name field a required field, a user must actually enter a name (that is, the user cannot leave it blank). Validation rules can make sure a user's entry lies within a certain **range of values**; for example, that the values in the Balance field are between $0.00 and $2,000.00. They can specify a **default value;** that is, a value that Access will display on the screen in a particular field before the user begins adding a record. To make data entry of patient numbers more convenient, you can also have lowercase letters converted automatically to uppercase. Finally, validation rules can specify a collection of acceptable values; for example, that the only legitimate entries for Ins Carrier are ORG, GVT, and PRS.

Specifying a Required Field

To specify that the Last Name field is to be a required field, perform the following steps.

 Steps To Specify a Required Field

---

1 **With the Database window on the screen and the Tables tab selected, right-click Patient.**

The shortcut menu displays (Figure 3-37).

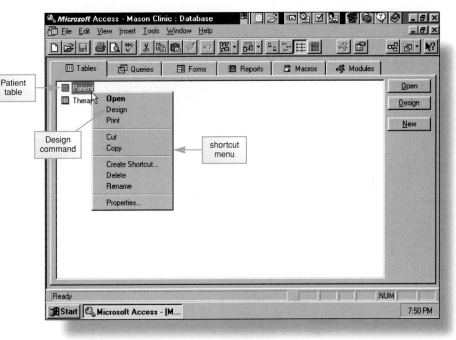

FIGURE 3-37

2 **Click Design, select the Last Name field by clicking its row selector. Point to the Required text box.**

The Patient : Table window displays (Figure 3-38). The Last Name field is selected.

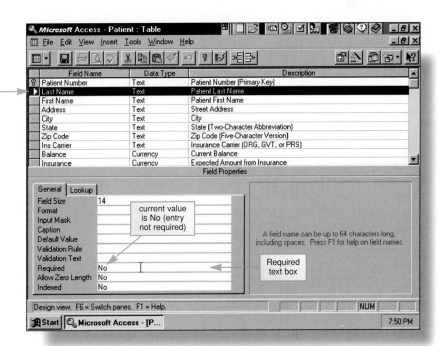

FIGURE 3-38

3 **Click the Required text box in the Field Properties area, and then click the down arrow that displays. Click Yes in the drop-down list.**

The value in the Required text box changes to Yes (Figure 3-39). It is now required that the user enter data into the Last Name field when adding a record.

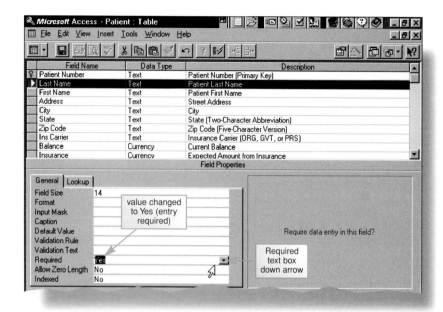

FIGURE 3-39

Specifying a Range

The following steps specify that entries in the Balance field must be between $0.00 and $2,000.00. To indicate this range, you will enter a condition that specifies that the balance must be both >= 0 (greater than or equal to zero) and <= 2000 (less than or equal to 2,000).

 Steps To Specify a Range

1 **Select the Balance field by clicking its row selector. Click the Validation Rule text box to produce an insertion point, and then type** >=0 and <=2000 **as the rule. Click the Validation Text text box to produce an insertion point, and then type** Must be between $0.00 and $2,000.00 **as the text. You must type all the text, including the dollar signs in this text box.**

The validation rule and text are entered (Figure 3-40).

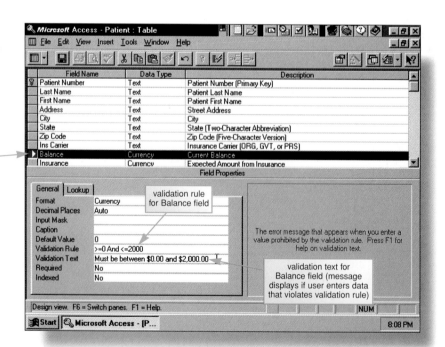

FIGURE 3-40

Users will now be prohibited from entering a balance that is either less than $0.00 or greater than $2,000.00 when they add records or change the value in the Balance field.

Specifying a Default Value

To specify a default value of ORG for the Ins Carrier field, complete the following step. By specifying this value, it simply means that if users do not enter an insurance carrier, the insurance carrier will be ORG.

 Steps To Specify a Default Value

1 **Select the Ins Carrier field. Click the Default Value text box and then type** =ORG **as the value.**

The Ins Carrier field is selected. The default value is entered in the Default Value text box (Figure 3-41).

Ins Carrier field selected

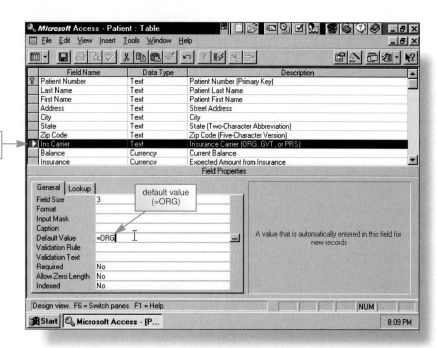

FIGURE 3-41

From this point on, if users do not make an entry in the Ins Carrier field when adding records, Access will set the value to ORG.

Specifying a Collection of Legal Values

The only legal values for the Ins Carrier field are ORG, GVT, and PRS. An appropriate validation rule for this field can direct Access to reject any entry other than these three possibilities. In other words, these three are the only **legal values**. Perform the step on the next page to specify the legal values for the Ins Carrier field.

Steps To Specify a Collection of Legal Values

1 **Make sure the Ins Carrier field is selected. Click the Validation Rule text box and then type** =ORG or =GVT or =PRS **as the collection of values. Click the Validation Text text box and then type** Must be ORG, GVT, or PRS **as the collection of values.**

The Ins Carrier field is selected. The validation rule and text have been entered (Figure 3-42). In the Validation Rule text box, Access automatically inserted quotation marks around the ORG, GVT, and PRS values and changed the lowercase letter, o, to uppercase in the word, or.

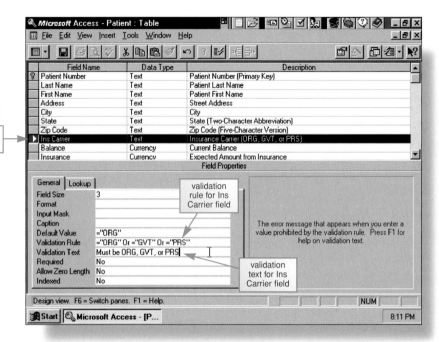

FIGURE 3-42

Users now will be allowed to enter only ORG, GVT, or PRS in the Ins Carrier field when they add records or make changes to this field.

Using a Format

To affect the way data is entered in a field, you can use a **format**. To do so, you enter a special symbol, called a **format symbol**, in the field's Format text box. The following step specifies a format for the Patient Number field in the Patient table. The format symbol used in the example is >, which causes Access to automatically convert lowercase letters to uppercase. The format symbol < causes Access to automatically convert uppercase letters to lowercase.

Steps: To Specify a Format

1 **Select the Patient Number field. Click the Format text box and then type > (Figure 3-43).**

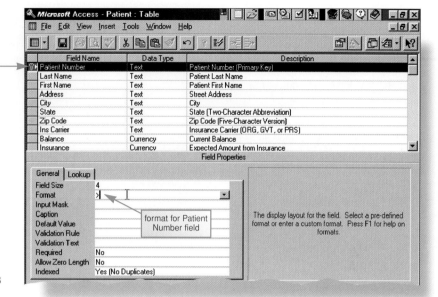

Patient Number field selected

format for Patient Number field

FIGURE 3-43

From this point on, any lowercase letters will be converted automatically to uppercase when users add records or change the value in the Patient Number field.

Saving Rules, Values, and Formats

To save the validation rules, default values, and formats, perform the following steps.

Steps: To Save the Validation Rules, Default Values, and Formats

1 **Click the Close button for the Patient : Table window to close the window.**
The Microsoft Access dialog box displays asking if you want to save your changes (Figure 3-44).

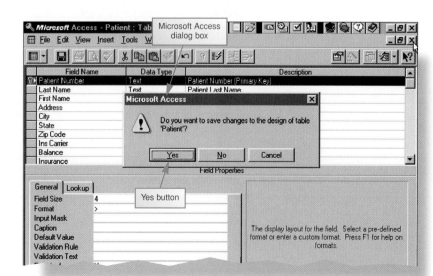

Microsoft Access dialog box

Do you want to save changes to the design of table 'Patient'?

Yes button

FIGURE 3-44

2 **Click the Yes button to save the changes.**

The Microsoft Access dialog box displays (Figure 3-45). This message asks if you want the new rules applied to current records. If this were a database used to run a business or to solve some other critical need, you would click Yes. You would not want to take the chance that some of the data already in the database violates the rules.

3 **Click the No button.**

The rules are not violated by the data in the Patient table. The changes are made.

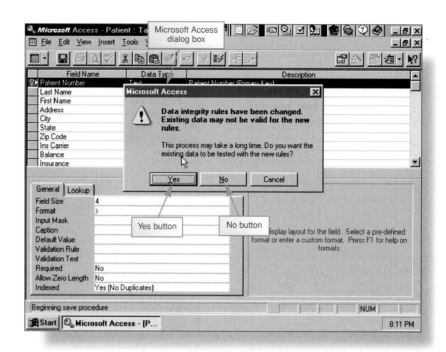

FIGURE 3-45

Updating a Table that Contains Validation Rules

When updating a table that contains validation rules, Access provides plenty of assistance in making sure the data entered is valid. It helps in making sure that data is formatted correctly. Access also will not accept invalid data. Entering a number that is out of the required range, for example, or entering a value that is not one of the possible choices, will produce an error message in the form of a dialog box. The database will not be updated until the error is corrected.

If the patient number entered contains lowercase letters, such as ab24 (Figure 3-46), Access will automatically convert the data to AB24 (Figure 3-47).

Patient Numbe	Last Name	First Name	Address	City	State	Zip
AL26	Alardyce	Lisa	311 Birchwood	Lamont	MI	49160
AT73	Acton	Thomas	312 Newcastle	Homer	MI	49162
BR31	Bryce	Roger	617 College	Lamont	MI	49160
DI32	Dalton-Manters	Irene	41 Lafayette	Madison	IN	42909
GC92	Gutierez	Carlos	476 Fulton	Jackson	OH	49401
GT43	Grant	Thomas	247 Fuller	Lamont	MI	49160
PE33	Pezzato	Eduardo	346 Vernor	Homer	MI	49162
PE76	Perez	Enzo	216 Four Mile	Perry	MI	47211
SC26	Schouten	Marybeth	576 Hillside	Oshton	MI	49822
ab24						

customer number contains lowercase letters

FIGURE 3-46

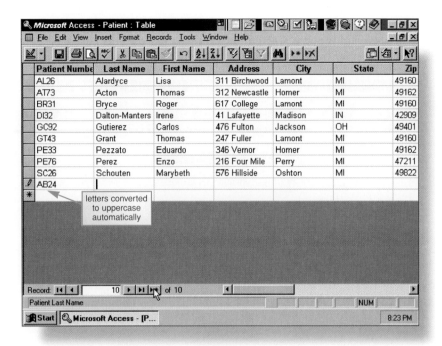

FIGURE 3-47

Instead of the Ins Carrier field initially being blank, it now contains the value ORG (Figure 3-48), because ORG is the default value. Thus, for any patient whose insurance carrier is ORG, it is not necessary to enter the value. By pressing the TAB key, the value ORG is accepted.

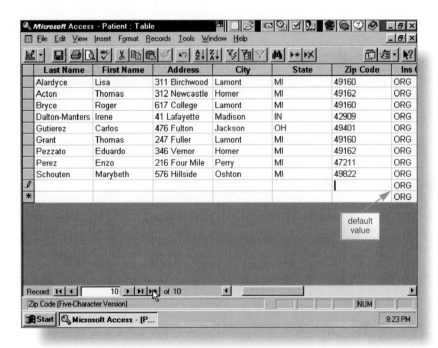

FIGURE 3-48

If the insurance carrier is not valid, such as xxx, Access will display the text message you specified (Figure 3-49) and not allow the data to enter the database.

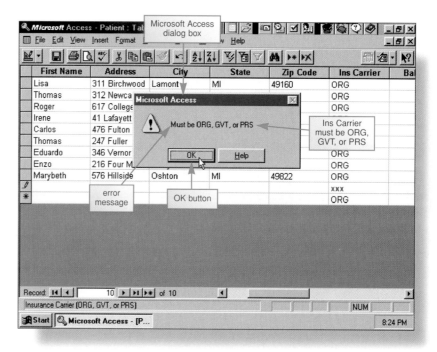

FIGURE 3-49

If the balance is not valid, such as 2200, Access also displays the appropriate message (Figure 3-50) and refuses to accept the data.

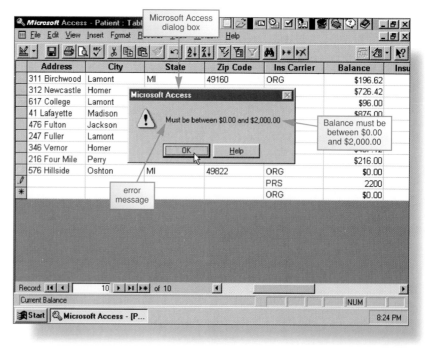

FIGURE 3-50

If a required field contains no data, Access indicates this by displaying an error message as soon as you attempt to leave the record (Figure 3-51). This field *must* be filled in before Access will move to a different record.

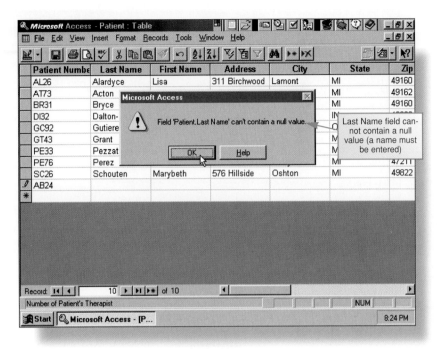

FIGURE 3-51

Take care when creating validation rules as you may come to an impasse where you can neither leave the field nor close the table because you have entered data into a field that violates the validation rule. It may be that you cannot remember the validation rule you created or it was created incorrectly.

First try to type an acceptable entry. If this does not work, repeatedly press the BACKSPACE key to erase the contents of the field and then try to leave the field. If, for some reason, this does not work, press the ESC key until the record is removed from the screen. The record will not be added to the database.

If you ever have to take such drastic action, you probably have a faulty validation rule. Use the techniques of the previous sections to correct the existing validation rules for the field.

Making Individual Changes to a Field

Earlier, you changed all the entries in the Ins Carrier field to ORG. You now have created a rule that will ensure that only legitimate values (ORG, GVT, or PRS) can be entered in the field. To make a change, click the field to be changed to produce an insertion point, use the BACKSPACE or DELETE key to delete the current entry, and then type the new entry.

Complete the steps on the next page to change the Ins Carrier value on the second and fourth records to PRS and on the fifth record to GVT.

Steps To Make Individual Changes

1 **Make sure the Patient table displays in Datasheet view. Click the right scroll arrow twice.**

The Patient table displays in Datasheet view (Figure 3-52).

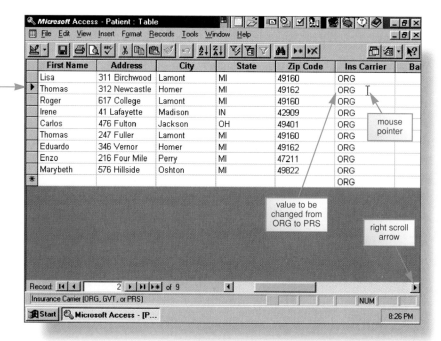

FIGURE 3-52

2 **Click to the right of the ORG entry in the Ins Carrier field on the second record to produce an insertion point. Press the BACKSPACE key three times to delete ORG and then type PRS as the new value. In a similar fashion, change the ORG on the fourth record by typing PRS and the fifth record by typing GVT (Figure 3-53).**

3 **Close the Patient : Table window by clicking its Close button.**

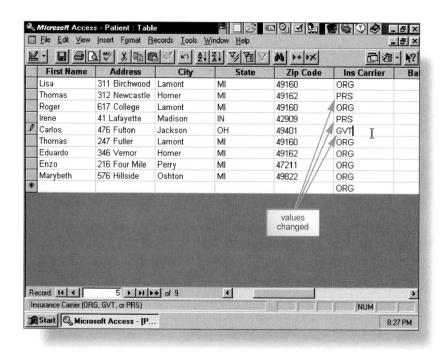

FIGURE 3-53

The Ins Carrier field changes are now complete.

Specifying Referential Integrity

A **foreign key** is a field in one table whose values are required to match the **primary key** of another table. For example, the therapist number in the Patient table must match the primary key of the Therapist table. In other words, the therapist number for any patient must be that of a *real* therapist; that is, a therapist currently in the Therapist table. A patient whose therapist number is 02, for example, should not be stored if therapist 02 does not exist. The property that affirms the value in a foreign key must match that of another table's primary key is called **referential integrity**.

In Access, to specify referential integrity, define a relationship between the tables by using the Relationships command. Access then prohibits any updates to the database that would violate the referential integrity. Access will not allow you to store a patient with a therapist number that does not match a therapist currently in the Therapist table. Access also will prevent you from deleting a therapist who currently has patients. Therapist 08, for example, currently has several patients in the Patient table. If you deleted therapist 08, these patients' therapist numbers would no longer match anyone in the Therapist table.

The type of relationship between two tables specified by the Relationships command is referred to as a **one-to-many relationship**. This means that one record in the first table is related to (matches) many records in the second table, but each record in the second table is related to only one record in the first. In the sample database, for example, a one-to-many relationship exists between the Therapist table and the Patient table. One therapist is associated with many patients but each patient is associated with a single therapist. In general, the table containing the foreign key will be the *many* part of the relationship.

The following steps use the Relationships command to specify referential integrity by specifying a relationship between the Therapist and Patient tables.

> **More** *About*
> **Referential Integrity**
>
> Enforcing referential integrity efficiently proved to be one of the most difficult tasks facing the developers of relational database management systems. Although the problem was worked on throughout the 1970s, it was not until the late 1980s that relational systems were able to satisfactorily enforce referential integrity.

Steps To Specify Referential Integrity

1 Close any open datasheet on the screen by clicking its Close button. Then, point to the Relationships button on the toolbar (Figure 3-54).

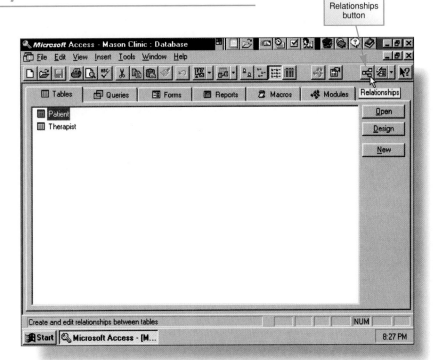

FIGURE 3-54

2 Click the Relationships button and then click the Therapist table. Point to the Add button.

The Show Table dialog box displays (Figure 3-55). The Therapist table is selected.

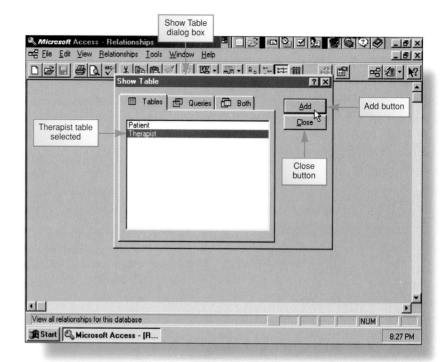

FIGURE 3-55

3 Click the Add button, click the Patient table, click the Add button again, and then click the Close button. Resize the field list boxes that display so all fields are visible. Point to the Ther Number field in the Therapist table.

Field list boxes for the Therapist and Patient tables display (Figure 3-56). The boxes have been resized so all fields are visible.

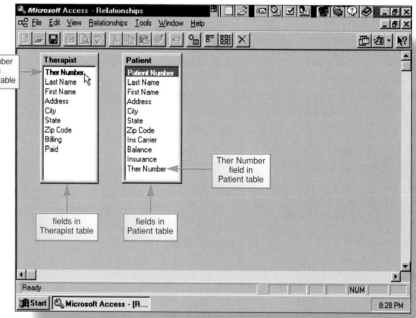

FIGURE 3-56

4 **Drag the Ther Number field in the Therapist table field list box to the Ther Number field in the Patient table field list box. Point to the Enforce Referential Integrity check box.**

The Relationships dialog box displays (Figure 3-57). The correct fields (the Ther Number fields) have been identified as the matching fields.

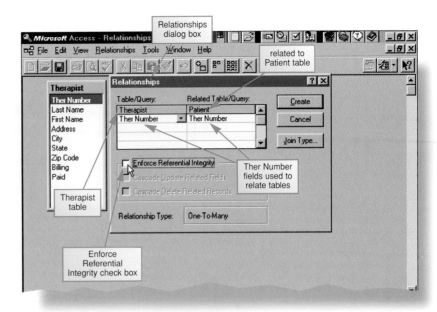

FIGURE 3-57

5 **Click Enforce Referential Integrity.**

Enforce Referential Integrity is selected (Figure 3-58). This will cause Access to reject any update that would violate referential integrity.

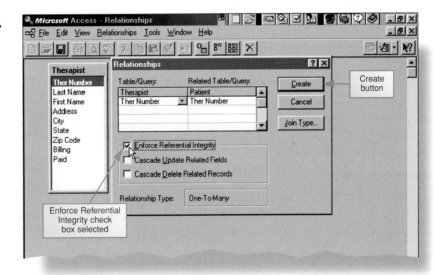

FIGURE 3-58

6 **Click the Create button.**

*Access creates the relationship and displays it visually with the **relationship line** joining the two Ther Number fields (Figure 3-59). The number 1 by the Ther Number field in the Therapist table indicates that the Therapist table is the one part of the relationship. The ∞ symbol at the other end of the line indicates that the Patient table is the many part of the relationship.*

FIGURE 3-59

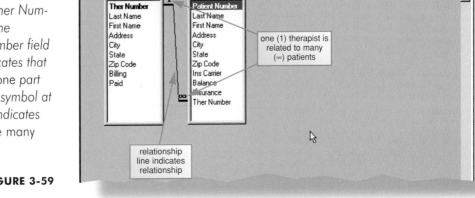

7 **Close the Relationships window by clicking its Close button.**

The Microsoft Access dialog box displays (Figure 3-60).

8 **Click the Yes button to save your work.**

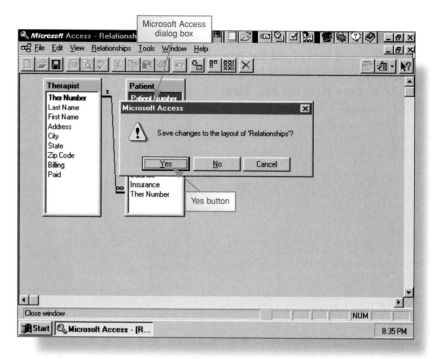

FIGURE 3-60

Access will now reject any number in the Ther Number field in the Patient table that does not match a therapist number in the Therapist table. Trying to add a patient whose Ther Number does not match would result in the error message shown in Figure 3-61.

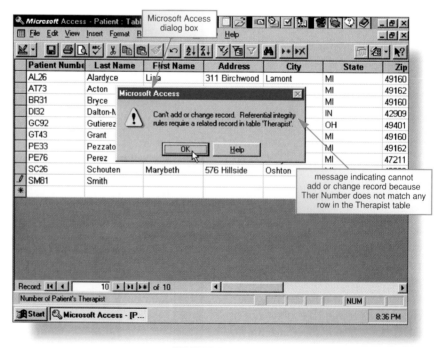

FIGURE 3-61

Deleting a therapist for whom there are related patients would also cause a problem. These patients would have a therapist number that does not match any therapist in the Therapist table. Deleting therapist 05 from the Therapist table, for example, would cause a problem for all records in the Patient table on which the therapist number is 05. To prevent this problem, Access will prohibit such a deletion. Instead of deleting the record, Access will display the message shown in Figure 3-62.

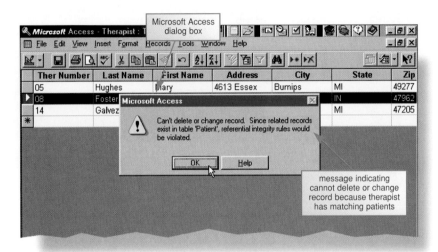

FIGURE 3-62

Ordering Records

Recall from previous discussions that Access sequences the records by patient number whenever listing them because patient number is the primary key. To change the order in which records appear, click the Sort Ascending or Sort Descending buttons on the toolbar. Either button reorders the records based on the field in which the cursor is located.

Perform the following steps to order the records by patient name using the Sort Ascending button.

Steps **To Use the Sort Ascending Button to Order Records**

1. **Open the Patient table in Datasheet view, and then click the Last Name field on the first record (any other record would do as well). Point to the Sort Ascending button on the toolbar (Figure 3-63).**

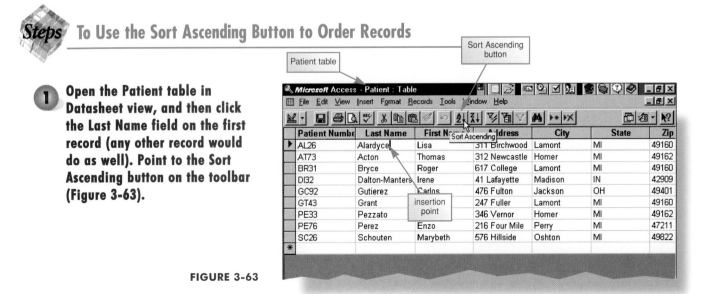

FIGURE 3-63

2 **Click the Sort Ascending button.**

The rows are now ordered by last name (Figure 3-64).

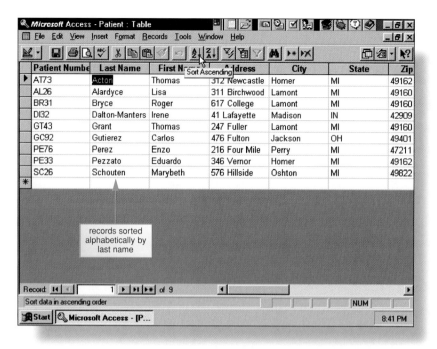

FIGURE 3-64

OtherWays

1. On Records menu click Sort, click Ascending or Descending

If you wanted to sort the data in reverse order, click the Sort Descending button instead of the Sort Ascending button.

Ordering Rows on Multiple Fields

Just as you can sort the answer to a query on multiple fields, you can also sort the data that displays in a datasheet on multiple fields. To do so, the major key and minor key must be next to each other in the datasheet with the major key on the left. (If this is not the case, you can drag the columns into the correct position. Instead of dragging, however, usually it will be easier to use a query that has the data sorted in the desired order.)

Provided the major and minor keys are in the correct position, select both fields and then click the Sort Ascending button on the toolbar. To select the fields, click the field selector for the first field (the major key). Next hold down the SHIFT key and then click the field selector for the second field (the minor key). A **field selector** is the small bar at the top of the column that you click to select an entire field in a datasheet.

Order records on the combination of insurance carrier and balance using the Sort Ascending button by completing the following steps.

Steps To Use the Sort Ascending Button to Order Records on Multiple Fields

1 Scroll the table to bring the rightmost fields into view. Click the field selector at the top of the Ins Carrier column to select the entire column. Hold down the SHIFT key and then click the field selector for the Balance column.

The Ins Carrier and Balance fields are selected (Figure 3-65).

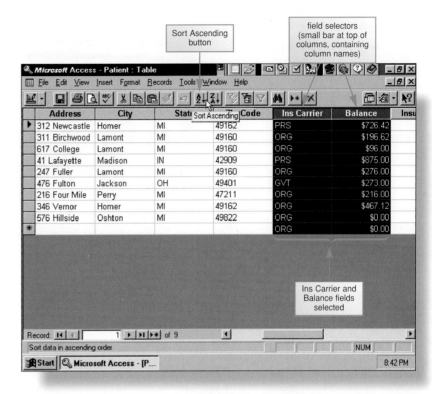

FIGURE 3-65

2 Click the Sort Ascending button on the toolbar.

The rows are ordered by insurance carrier (Figure 3-66). Within each group of Patients having the same carrier, the rows are ordered by balance.

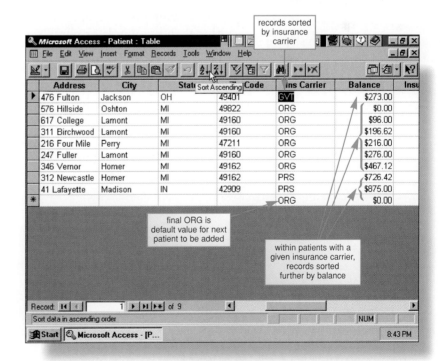

FIGURE 3-66

3 **Close the Patient : Table window by clicking its Close button.**

The Microsoft Access dialog box displays (Figure 3-67) asking if you want to save the changes to the design; that is, do you want to save the order in which the records currently display?

4 **Click the No button to abandon changes.**

The next time the table is open, the records will display in their original order.

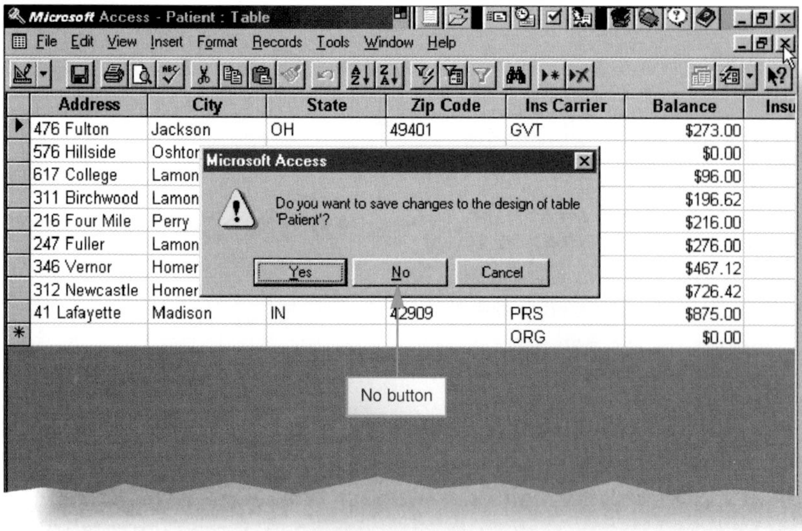

FIGURE 3-67

Creating and Using Indexes

What Is an Index?

You are already familiar with the concept of an index. The index in the back of a book contains important words or phrases together with a list of pages on which the given words or phrases can be found. An **index** for a table is similar. Figure 3-68, for example, shows the Patient table along with an index built on last names. In this case, the items of interest are last names rather than key words or phrases as is the case in the back of this book. The field or fields on which the index is built is called the **index key**. Thus, in Figure 3-68, the Last Name field is the index key.

Each last name occurs in the index along with the number of the record on which the corresponding patient is located. Further, the names appear in the index in alphabetical order. If Access were to use this index to find the record on which the last name is Grant, for example, it could rapidly scan

FIGURE 3-68

Index on Last Name Field

LAST NAME	RECORD NUMBER
Acton	2
Alardyce	1
Bryce	3
Dalton-Manters	4
Grant	6
Gutierez	5
Perez	8
Pezzato	7
Schouten	9

Patient Table

RECORD NUMBER	PATIENT NUMBER	LAST NAME	FIRST NAME	STREET	CITY	STATE	ZIP CODE	...
1	AL26	Alardyce	Lisa	311 Birchwood	Lamont	MI	49160	...
2	AT73	Acton	Thomas	312 Newcastle	Homer	MI	49162	...
3	BR31	Bryce	Roger	617 College	Lamont	MI	49160	...
4	DI32	Dalton-Manters	Irene	41 Lafayette	Madison	IN	42909	...
5	GC92	Gutierez	Carlos	476 Fulton	Jackson	OH	49401	...
6	GT43	Grant	Thomas	247 Fuller	Lamont	MI	49160	...
7	PE33	Pezzato	Eduardo	346 Vernor	Homer	MI	49162	...
8	PE76	Perez	Enzo	216 Four Mile	Perry	MI	47211	...
9	SC26	Schouten	Marybeth	576 Hillside	Oshton	MI	49822	...

Patient Table

RECORD NUMBER	PATIENT NUMBER	LAST NAME	FIRST NAME	STREET	CITY	STATE	ZIP CODE	...
1	AL26	Alardyce	Lisa	311 Birchwood	Lamont	MI	49160	...
2	AT73	Acton	Thomas	312 Newcastle	Homer	MI	49162	...
3	BR31	Bryce	Roger	617 College	Lamont	MI	49160	...
4	DI32	Dalton-Manters	Irene	41 Lafayette	Madison	IN	42909	...
5	GC92	Gutierez	Carlos	476 Fulton	Jackson	OH	49401	...
6	GT43	Grant	Thomas	247 Fuller	Lamont	MI	49160	...
7	PE33	Pezzato	Eduardo	346 Vernor	Homer	MI	49162	...
8	PE76	Perez	Enzo	216 Four Mile	Perry	MI	47211	...
9	SC26	Schouten	Marybeth	576 Hillside	Oshton	MI	49822	...

the names in the index to find Grant. Once it did, it would determine the corresponding record number (5) and then go immediately to record 5 in the Patient table, thus finding this Patient much more rapidly than if it had to look through the entire Patient table one record at a time. Indexes make the process of retrieving records very fast and efficient.

Because no two patients happen to have the same last name, the Record Number column contains only single values. This may not always be the case. Consider the index on the Zip Code field shown in Figure 3-69. In this index, the Record Number column contains several values, namely all the records on which the corresponding Zip Code appears. The first row, for example, indicates that Zip Code 42909 is found only on record 4; whereas, the third row indicates that Zip Code 49160 is found on records 1, 3, and 6. If Access were to use this index to find all patients in Zip Code 49160, it could rapidly scan the Zip Codes in the index to find 49160. Once it did, it would determine the corresponding record numbers (1, 3, and 6) and then go immediately to these records. It would not have to examine any other records in the Patient table.

Another benefit to indexes is that they provide an efficient alternative to sorting. That is, if the records are to appear in a certain order, Access can use an index rather than having to physically rearrange the records in the database file. Physically rearranging the records in a different order, which is called **sorting**, can be a very time-consuming process.

To see how indexes can be used for alphabetizing records, look at the record numbers in the index (Figure 3-68) and suppose you used these to list all patients. That is, simply follow down the Record Number column, listing the corresponding patients. In this example, first you would list the patient on record 2 (Acton), then the patient on record 1 (Alardyce), then the patient on record 3 (Bryce), and so on. The patients would be listed alphabetically by last name without actually sorting the table.

To gain the benefits from an index, you must first create one. Access automatically creates an index on the primary key as well as some other special fields. If, as is the case with both the Patient and Therapist tables, a table contains a field called Zip Code, for example, Access will create an index for it automatically. You must create any other indexes you feel you need, indicating the field or fields on which the index is to be built.

Index on Zip Code Field

ZIP CODE	RECORD NUMBER
42909	4
47211	8
49160	1, 3, 6
49162	2, 7
49401	5
49822	9

FIGURE 3-69

More *About*
Indexes

Indexes in Access, and in many other database management systems, are stored in a very special structure called a B-tree. This is a highly efficient structure that supports very rapid access to records in the database as well as a rapid alternative to sorting records.

Although the index key will usually be a single field, it can be a combination of fields. For example, you might want to sort records by balance within therapist number. In other words, the records are ordered by a combination of fields: Ther Number and Balance. An index can be used for this purpose by using a combination of fields for the index key. In this case, you must assign a name to the index. It is a good idea to assign a name that represents the combination of fields. For example, an index whose key is the combination of Ther Number and Balance, might be called Therbal.

How Does Access Use an Index?

Access creates an index whenever you request that it do so. It takes care of all the work in setting up and maintaining the index. In addition, it will use the index automatically.

If you request that data be sorted in a particular order and Access determines that an index is available it can use to make the process efficient, it will do so. If no index is available, it will still sort the data in the order you requested; it will just take longer.

Similarly, if you request that Access locate a particular record that has a certain value in a particular field, Access will use an index if an appropriate one exists. If not, it will have to examine each record until it finds the one you want.

In both cases, the added efficiency provided by an index will not be readily apparent in tables that have only a few records. Once your tables have more records in them, the difference can be dramatic. Even with only fifty to one hundred records, you will notice a difference. You can imagine how dramatic the difference would be in a table with fifty thousand records.

When Should You Create an Index?

An index improves efficiency for sorting and finding records. On the contrary, indexes occupy space on your disk. They also require Access to do extra work. Access must maintain all the indexes that have been created up to date. Thus, there are both advantages and disadvantages to indexes. Consequently, the decision as to which indexes to create is an important one. The following guidelines should help you in this process.

Create an index on a field (or combination of fields) if one or more of the following conditions are present:

1. The field is the primary key of the table (Access will create this index automatically)
2. The field is the foreign key in a relationship you have created (Access also will create this index automatically when you specify the relationship)
3. You will frequently need your data to be sorted on the field
4. You will frequently need to locate a record based on a value in this field

Because Access handles 1 and 2 automatically, you need only to concern yourself about 3 and 4. If you think you will need to see patient data arranged in order of patient balances, for example, you should create an index on the Balance field. If you think you will need to see the data arranged by balance within therapist number, you should create an index on the combination of the Ther Number field and the Balance field. Similarly, if you think you will need to find a patient given the patient's last name, you should create an index on the Last Name field.

Creating Single-Field Indexes

A **single-field index** is an index whose key is a single field. In this case, the index key is to be the Last Name field. In creating an index, you need to indicate whether to allow duplicates in the index key; that is, two records that have the same value. For example, in the index for the Last Name field, if duplicates are not allowed, Access would not allow the addition of a patient whose last name is the same as the last name of a patient already in the database. In the index for the Last Name field, duplicates will be allowed. Perform the following steps to create a single-field index.

 To Create a Single-Field Index

1 **Right-click Patient.**

The shortcut menu displays (Figure 3-70).

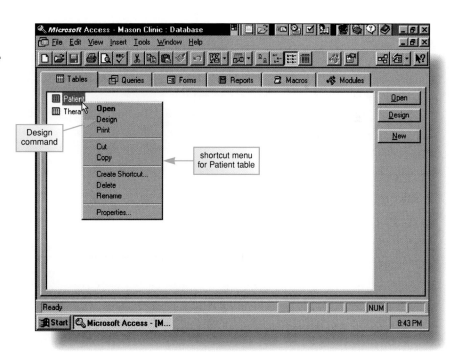

FIGURE 3-70

2 Click Design and then maximize the Patient : Table window if necessary. Click the row selector to select the Last Name field. Point to the Indexed text box.

A maximized Patient : Table window displays (Figure 3-71). The Last Name field is selected.

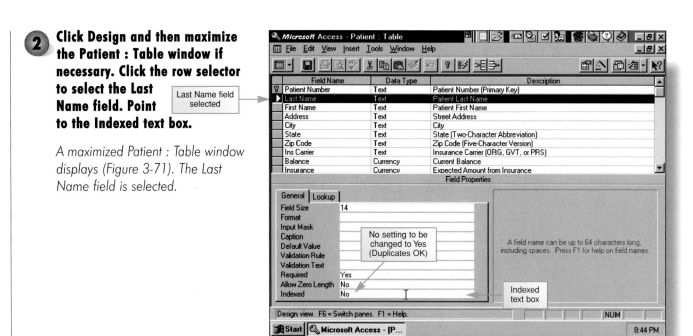

FIGURE 3-71

3 Click the Indexed text box in the Field Properties pane. Click the down arrow that displays.

The Indexed drop-down list displays (Figure 3-72). The settings are No (no index), Yes (Duplicates OK) (create an index and allow duplicates), and Yes (No Duplicates) (create an index but reject (do not allow) duplicates).

4 Click Yes (Duplicates OK).

The indexes on the Last Name field now will be created and are ready for use as soon as you save your work.

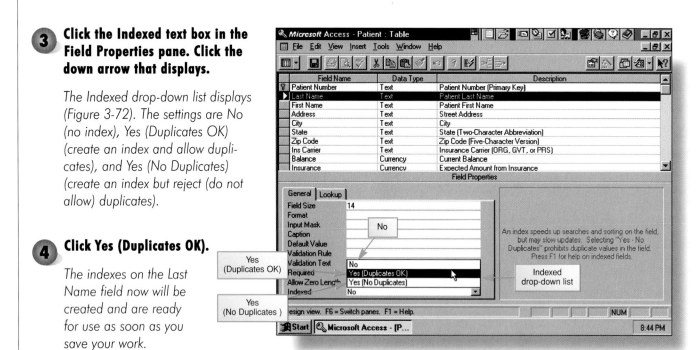

FIGURE 3-72

Creating Multiple-Field Indexes

Creating **multiple-field indexes**, that is indexes whose key is a combination of fields, involves a different process from creating single-field indexes. Click the Indexes button on the toolbar, enter a name for the index, and then enter the combination of fields that make up the index key. The following steps create a multiple-field index with the name Therbal. The key will be the combination of the Ther Number field and the Balance field.

Steps To Create a Multiple-Field Index

1 **Point to the Indexes button on the toolbar (Figure 3-73).**

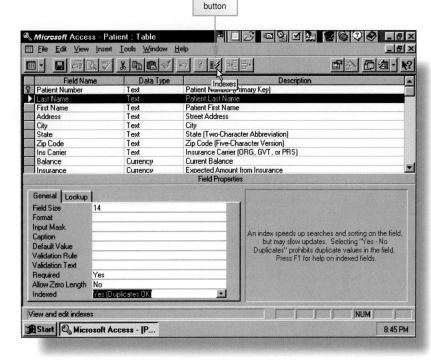

FIGURE 3-73

2 **Click the Indexes button.**

The Indexes: Patient dialog box displays (Figure 3-74). The index on Patient Number is the primary index and was created automatically by Access. The index on Last Name is the one just created. Access created an index automatically on the Zip Code field. Use this dialog box to create additional indexes.

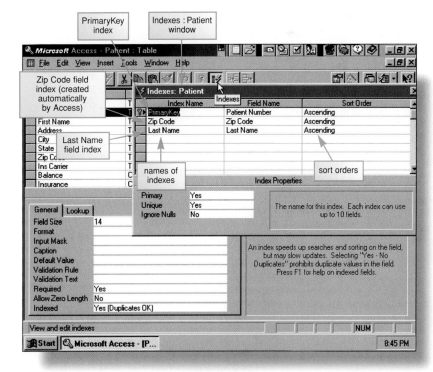

FIGURE 3-74

3 Click the Index Name entry on the row following Last Name. Type `Therbal` as the index name, and then press the TAB key. Point to the down arrow.

The index name has been entered as Therbal (Figure 3-75). An insertion point displays in the Field Name column.

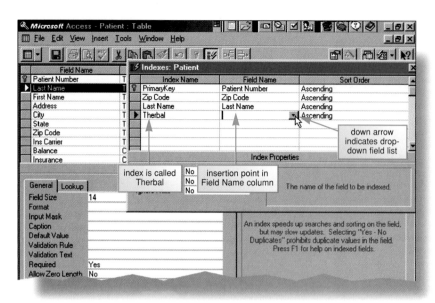

FIGURE 3-75

4 Click the down arrow in the Field Name column to produce a list of fields in the Patient table, scroll down the list, and select Ther Number. Press the TAB key three times to move to the Field Name entry on the following row. Select the Balance field in the same manner as the Ther Number field.

Ther Number and Balance are selected as the two fields for the Therbal index (Figure 3-76). The absence of an index name on the row containing the Balance field indicates that it is part of the previous index, Therbal.

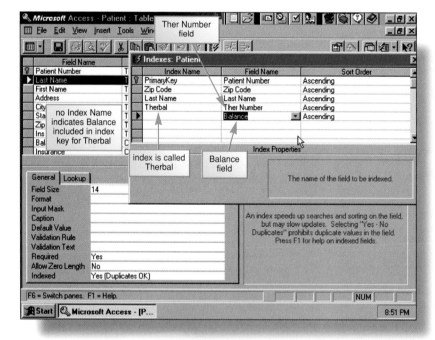

FIGURE 3-76

5 Close the Indexes: Patient dialog box by clicking its Close button.

6 Close the Patient : Table window by clicking its Close button. When asked if you want to save your changes, click the Yes button.

The indexes are created and the Database window displays.

1. On View menu click Indexes

Closing the Database

The following step closes the database by closing its Database window.

TO CLOSE A DATABASE

Step 1: Click the Close button for the Mason Clinic : Database window.

The indexes now have been created. Access will use them automatically whenever possible to improve efficiency of ordering or finding records. Access will also maintain them automatically. That is, whenever the data in the Patient table is changed, Access will automatically make appropriate changes in the indexes.

Project Summary

Project 3 covered the issues involved in maintaining a database. You used Form view to add a record to the Mason Clinic database and also searched for a record satisfying a criterion. You changed and deleted records. You changed the structure of the Patient table in the Mason Clinic database, created validation rules, and specified referential integrity between the Patient and the Therapist tables by creating relationships. You made mass changes to the Patient table. Finally, you created indexes to improve performance.

What You Should Know

Having completed this project, you should now be able to perform the following tasks:

- Add a Field to a Table *(A 3.16)*
- Change the Size of a Field *(A 3.14)*
- Close a Database *(A 3.49)*
- Create a Multiple-Field Index *(A 3.47)*
- Create a Single-Field Index *(A 3.45)*
- Delete a Record *(A 3.12)*
- Make Individual Changes *(A 3.34)*
- Open a Database *(A 3.6)*
- Resize a Column *(A 3.19)*
- Save the Validation Rules, Default Values, and Formats *(A 3.29)*
- Search for a Record *(A 3.9)*
- Specify a Collection of Legal Values *(A 3.28)*
- Specify a Default Value *(A 3.27)*
- Specify a Format *(A 3.29)*

- Specify a Range *(A 3.26)*
- Specify a Required Field *(A 3.25)*
- Specify Referential Integrity *(A 3.35)*
- Switch from Form View to Datasheet View *(A 3.11)*
- Update the Contents of a Field *(A 3.10, A 3.17)*
- Use a Delete Query to Delete a Group of Records *(A 3.23)*
- Use a Form to Add Records *(A 3.7)*
- Use an Update Query to Update All Records *(A 3.21)*
- Use the Sort Ascending Button to Order Records *(A 3.39)*
- Use the Sort Ascending Button to Order Records on Multiple Fields *(A 3.41)*

A+ Test Your Knowledge

1 True/False

Instructions: Circle T if the statement is true or F if the statement is false.

T F 1. Access sorts records automatically by the primary index.

T F 2. Indexes provide an efficient alternative to sorting.

T F 3. To force all letters in a field to display as uppercase, use the > symbol in the Format text box.

T F 4. You can add and change records using Form view, but you can only delete records using Datasheet view.

T F 5. To change the order in which records appear in a table, click the Sort Ascending or Sort Descending button on the toolbar.

T F 6. To delete a record from a table, click the row selector for the record, and then press CTRL+D.

T F 7. To delete a group of records that satisfy a criteria, use a query.

T F 8. A foreign key is a field in one table whose values are required to match a primary key of another table.

T F 9. The property that the value in a foreign key must match that of another table's primary key is called entity integrity.

T F 10. To specify referential integrity, click the Referential Integrity button on the toolbar.

2 Multiple Choice

Instructions: Circle the correct response.

1. Indexes _____.
   a. provide an efficient alternative to sorting
   b. allow rapid retrieval of records
   c. allow rapid retrieval of tables
   d. both a and b

2. To create a multiple-field index, click the _____ button in the Table Design window.
   a. Secondary Index
   b. Define Secondary Indexes
   c. Indexes
   d. Define Indexes

3. _____ are rules that the data entered by a user must follow.
   a. Data rules
   b. Edit rules
   c. Integrity rules
   d. Validation rules

 Test Your Knowledge

4. To search for a specific record in a table, select the field to search and click the _____ button.
   a. Search
   b. Locate
   c. Find
   d. Locator

5. To force all letters in a field to display as uppercase, use the _____ symbol in the Format text box.
   a. ?
   b. >
   c. @
   d. &

6. A(n) _____ is a field in one table whose values are required to match a primary key of another table.
   a. secondary key
   b. auxiliary key
   c. foreign key
   d. matching key

7. The property that the value in a foreign key must match that of another table's primary key is called _____ integrity.
   a. entity
   b. referential
   c. relationship
   d. inter-relation

8. To delete a record from a table, click the row selector for the record, and then press _____.
   a. CTRL+U
   b. CTRL+D
   c. DELETE
   d. CTRL+DELETE

9. To specify referential integrity, click the _____ button.
   a. Referential Integrity
   b. Integrity
   c. Relationships
   d. Primary Key

10. To add a field to a table structure, select the field below where you would like the new field inserted and then press _____.
    a. CTRL+N
    b. CTRL+INSERT
    c. INSERT
    d. ALT+INSERT

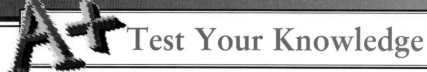

Test Your Knowledge

3 Adding, Changing, and Deleting Records

Instructions: Figure 3-77 shows the first record in the Client table in Form view. Use this figure to help explain how to perform the following tasks in Form view. Write your answers on your own paper.

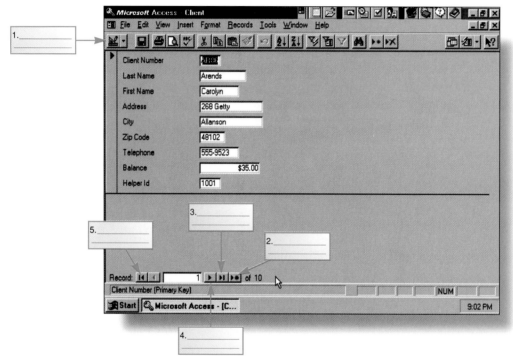

FIGURE 3-77

1. Change the Last Name from Arends to Arendsen.
2. Add a new record to the Client table.
3. Locate the record that contains the value MA21 in the Client Number field.
4. Switch to Datasheet view.
5. In Datasheet view, delete the record where the Client Number is MA21.

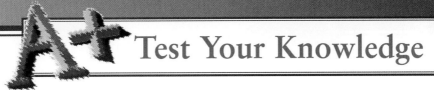

Test Your Knowledge

4 Understanding Validation Rules and Indexes

Instructions: Figure 3-78 shows the Helper table in Design view. Use this figure to help explain how to create the following validation rules and indexes. For each question, assume that the proper field already has been selected. Write your answers on your own paper.

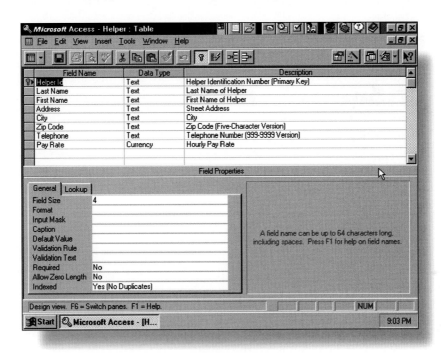

FIGURE 3-78

1. Make the Last Name field a required field.
2. Specify a default value of $5.00 for the Pay Rate field.
3. Specify that any value entered in the Pay Rate field must be greater than or equal to $5.00 and less than or equal to $10.00.
4. Create an index on the Last Name field that allows duplicates.

1 Reviewing Project Activities

Instructions: Perform the following tasks using a computer.

1. Start Access.
2. Double-click the Help button on the toolbar to display the Help Topics: Microsoft Access for Windows 95 dialog box.
3. Click the Contents tab. Double-click the Finding and Sorting Data book. Double-click the Finding Records or Data book. Double-click Find specific occurrences of a value in a field.
4. Read the Help information. Next, right-click within the box, and then click Print Topic. Hand in the printout to your instructor. Click the Help Topics button to return to the Help Topics: Microsoft Access for Windows 95 dialog box.
5. Click the Index tab. Type sort in box 1 and then double-click sorting records in tables in box 2. Double-click Working in table Datasheet view in the Topics Found dialog box. Click the Sort, filter, or find records link and then read the Help information. Click the remaining four links and read their Help information. Click the Close button.
6. Double-click the Help button on the toolbar. Click the Find tab. Type validation in box 1. Click Validation in box 2. Double-click Define validation rules to control what values can be entered into a field in box 3. When the Help information displays, read it, ready the printer, right-click, and click Print Topic. Hand in the printout to your instructor. Click the Help Topics button to return to the Help Topics: Microsoft Access for Windows 95 dialog box.
7. Click the Answer Wizard tab. Type how do i create indexes in box 1. Click the Search button. Double-click Decide if and when to use an index in box 2 under How Do I. Read and print the Help information. Hand in the printout to your instructor.

? Use Help

2 Expanding the Basics

Instructions: Use Access online Help to better understand the topics listed below. Begin each of the following by double-clicking the Help button on the toolbar. If you are unable to print the Help information, then answer the question on your own paper.

1. Using the Creating, Importing, and Linking Tables book on the Contents sheet on the Help Topics: Microsoft Access for Windows 95 dialog box, answer the following questions:
   a. How do you delete an index?
   b. You cannot create indexes on fields of certain data types. What are these data types?
   c. What is the maximum number of fields in a multiple-field index?
   d. How can you create a primary key that includes more than one field?
2. Using the key term *update* and the Index tab in the Help Topics: Microsoft Access for Windows 95 dialog box, display and print information on update queries. Then, answer the following questions:
   a. How can you see a list of records that will be updated?
   b. How can you stop a query after you start it?
3. Use the Find tab in the Help Topics: Microsoft Access for Windows 95 dialog box to display and then print information about replacing specific occurrences of a value in a field. Then answer the following questions:
   a. What are the advantages of using the Replace command instead of an update query?
   b. What is a null value?
4. Use the Answer Wizard in the Help Topics: Microsoft Access for Windows 95 dialog box to display and print information on defining a custom data display format for a field.

Apply Your Knowledge

1 Maintaining the Extra Hands Database

Instructions: Start Access. Open the Extra Hands database from the Access folder on the Student Floppy Disk that accompanies this book. Perform the following tasks:

1. Open the Client table in Design view as shown in Figure 3-79.
2. Increase the size of the Last Name field to 15.
3. Format the Client Number field so any lowercase letters display in uppercase.
4. Make the Last Name field a required field.
5. Specify that balance amounts must be greater than or equal to $0.00 and less than or equal to $150.00. Include validation text.
6. Create an index that allows duplicates for the Last Name field.
7. Save the changes to the structure.
8. Open the Client table in Datasheet view.
9. Change the last name of Client Number JO12 to *Johns-Rivers*.
10. Print the table.
11. Delete the record of Client Number MA21.
12. Print the table.
13. Sort the data in ascending order by Zip Code within City.
14. Print the table. Close the table. If you are asked to save changes to the design of the table, click the No button.
15. Establish referential integrity between the Helper table (the *one* table) and the Client table (the *many* table).

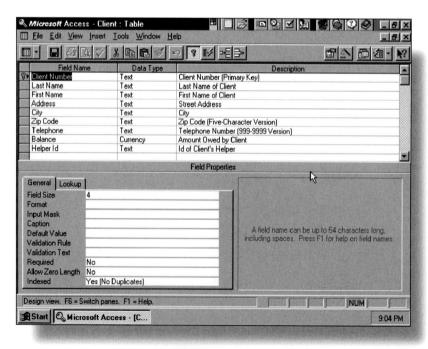

FIGURE 3-79

1 Maintaining the Symphony Shop Database

Problem: The Symphony Shop volunteers have determined that they would like to make some changes to the database structure. They need to increase the size of the Description field and add an additional index. Because several different individuals update the data, the volunteers also would like to add some validation rules to the database. Finally, there are some novelty items that must be added to the database.

Instructions: Use the database created in the In the Lab 1 of Project 1 for this assignment. Perform the following tasks:

1. Open the Symphony Shop database and open the Novelty table in Design view as shown in Figure 3-80 on the next page.
2. Create an index for the Description field. Be sure to allow duplicates.
3. Create and save the following validation rules for the Novelty table. List the steps involved on your own paper.
   a. Make the Description field a required field.
   b. Ensure that any lowercase letters entered in the Novelty Id field are converted to uppercase.
   c. Ensure that any lowercase letters entered in the Dist Code field are converted to uppercase.
   d. Specify that Units On Hand must be between 0 and 100. Include validation text.
4. Save the changes.
5. Open the Novelty form you created in Project 1, and then add the following record to the Novelty table:

P04	Pencil Cases	20	$.95	$1.50	MM

6. Switch to Datasheet view and sort the records in ascending order by Description.
7. Print the table. Close the table. If you are asked to save changes to the design of the table, click the No button.
8. Create a new query for the Novelty table.
9. Using a query, delete all records in the Novelty table where the Description starts with the letter K. (Hint: Use information from Use Help Exercise 2 to solve this problem.) Close the query without saving it.
10. Print the Novelty table.
11. Open the Distributor table in Design view, change the field width of the Name field to 22, and save the change.
12. Open the Distributor table in Datasheet view, and then change the name on the first record to *AAA Arts Distributor*. Resize the column so the complete name displays.
13. Print the table. Save the change to the layout of the table.
14. Specify referential integrity between the Distributor table (the *one* table) and the Novelty table (the *many* table). List the steps involved on your own paper.

(continued)

Maintaining the Symphony Shop Database *(continued)*

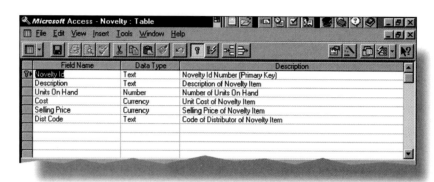

FIGURE 3-80

2 Maintaining the College Telephone System Database

Problem: The manager of the College Telephone System has determined that she would like to make some changes to the database structure. Another field must be added to the database, and the size of the Last Name field must be increased. Because several different individuals update the data, the manager also would like to add some validation rules to the database. Finally, there are some additions and deletions to the database.

Instructions: Use the database created in the In the Lab 2 of Project 1 for this assignment. Perform the following tasks:

1. Open the College Telephone System database and open the User table in Design view as shown in Figure 3-81.
2. Create an index for the Last Name field. Be sure to allow duplicates.
3. Create an index on the combination of the Dept Code and Last Name fields. Name the index Deptname.
4. Change the field width of the First Name field to 14.
5. Save these changes and display the User table in Datasheet view.
6. Change the first name for User Id T4521 to *Catherine Anne*.
7. Print the table.
8. Sort the records in ascending order by Dept Code.
9. Print the table. Close the table. If you are asked to save changes to the design of the table, click the No button.
10. Open the User table in Design view, and then add the Staff Code field to the User table. Define the field as Text with a width of 3. Insert the Staff Code field after the Extra Charges field. This field will contain data on whether the user is faculty (FAC), professional (PRO), or Administrative (ADM). Save the changes to the User table.
11. Create a new query for the User table.

In the Lab

12. Using this query, change all the entries in the Staff Code column to FAC. This will be the status of most users. Do not save the query.

13. Print the table.

14. Open the User table in Design view and create the following validation rules for the User table. List the steps involved on your own paper.

    a. Make First Name and Last Name required fields.

    b. Specify the legal values, FAC, PRO, and ADM for the Staff Code field. Include validation text.

    c. Ensure that any letters entered in the User Id, Office, and Dept Code fields are converted to uppercase.

    d. Specify a default value of $15.00 for the Basic Charge field.

15. Save the changes.

16. You can use either Form view or Datasheet view to add records to a table. To use Form view, you must replace the form you created in Project 1 with a form that includes the new field, Staff Code. With the User table selected, click the New Object button down arrow on the toolbar. Click AutoForm. Use this form that contains staff code to add the following record:

T8967	Schleer	Lois	3578	225SSH	$15.00	$0.00	ADM	ENG

17. Close the form. Click the Yes button when asked if you want to save the form. Save the form as *User*. Click the Yes button when asked if you want to replace the User form you created in Project 1.

18. Open the User form and then locate the users with User Ids T2389 and T8521. Change the Staff Code for each record to PRO.

19. Change to Datasheet view and print the table in order by last name. Close the table. If you are asked to save changes to the design of the table, click the No button.

20. Create a new query for the User table.

21. Using a query, delete all records in the User table where the Dept Code is HIS.

22. Close the query without saving it.

23. Print the User table.

24. Specify referential integrity between the Department table (the *one* table) and the User table (the *many* table). List the steps involved on your own paper.

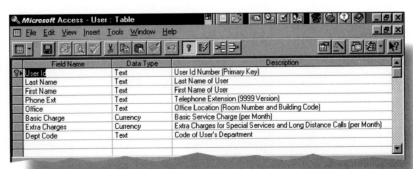

FIGURE 3-81

In the Lab

3 Maintaining the WWWW Radio Station Database

Problem: The radio station manager has determined that some changes must be made to the database structure. Another field must be added and the size of the Name field must be increased. Because several different individuals update the data, the manager also would like to add some validation rules to the database. Finally, there are some additions and deletions to the database.

Instructions: Use the database created in the In the Lab 3 of Project 1 for this assignment. Perform the following tasks:

1. Open the WWWW Radio Station database and open the Accounts table in Design view as shown in Figure 3-82.
2. Create an index for the Name field. Be sure to allow duplicates.
3. Create an index on the combination of the State and Zip Code fields. Name the index Statezip.
4. Save these changes and display the Accounts table in Datasheet view.
5. Order the records in the Accounts table by Zip Code within State.
6. Print the table. Close the table. If you are asked to save changes to the design of the table, click the No button.
7. Open the Accounts table in Design view, and then change the field width of the Name field to 25.
8. Add the field Acc Type to the Accounts table. Define the field as Text with a width of 3. Insert the Acc Type field after the Zip Code field. This field will contain data on the type of account. Accounts are classified as retail (RET), service (SRV), and industry (IND).
9. Save these changes and display the Accounts table in Datasheet view.
10. Change the name of account G075 to *Geo's Tires & Balancing*. Change the name of account C046 to *Boan-Carter Shoes*.
11. Resize the Name column to fit the changed entries. Decrease the width of the State, Zip Code, and Acc Type columns.
12. Print the table. If necessary, change the margins so the table prints on one page in landscape orientation. Close the table. Save the layout changes to the table.
13. Create a new query for the Accounts table.
14. Using this query, change all the entries in the Acc Type column to RET. This will be the type of most accounts. Do not save the query.
15. Open the Accounts table and order the records by name. Print the table. Close the table. If you are asked to save changes to the design of the table, click the No button.
16. Open the Accounts table in Design view, and then create the following validation rules. List the steps involved on your own paper.
    a. Make Name a required field.
    b. Specify the legal values RET, SRV, and IND for the Acc Type field. Include validation text.
    c. Ensure that any letters entered in the Account Number and State fields are converted to uppercase.
    d. Specify that balance must be between $0.00 and $500.00. Include validation text.

In the Lab

17. Save the changes to the Accounts table.

18. You can use either Form view or Datasheet view to add records to a table. To use Form view, you must replace the form you created in Project 1 with a form that includes the new field, Acc Type. With the Accounts table selected, click the New Object button down arrow on the toolbar. Click AutoForm. Use this form that contains Acc Type to add the following record:

S001	Stand Electric	12 Benson	Germantown	PA	19113	IND	$0.00	$0.00	21

19. Close the form. Click the Yes button when asked if you want to save the form. Save the form as *Accounts*. Click the Yes button when asked if you want to replace the Accounts form you created in Project 1.

20. Open the Accounts form and locate the accounts with Account Numbers B133, M012, and R111 and then change the Acc Type for each record to SRV.

21. Change to Datasheet view and print the table.

22. Create a new query for the Accounts table.

23. Using the query screen, delete all records in the table where the account has the Acc Type of IND.

24. Close the query without saving it.

25. Print the Accounts table.

26. Specify referential integrity between the Account Reps table (the *one* table) and the Accounts table (the *many* table). List the steps involved on your own paper.

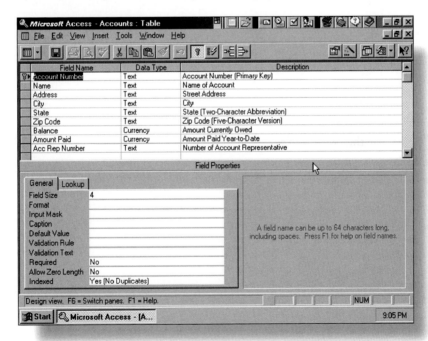

FIGURE 3-82

Cases and Places

The difficulty of these case studies varies:

▶ Case studies preceded by a single half moon are the least difficult. You are asked to create the required database based on information that has already been placed in an organized form.

▶▶ Case studies preceded by two half moons are more difficult. You must organize the information presented before using it to create the desired database.

▶▶▶ Case studies preceded by three half moons are the most difficult. You must choose a specific topic, and then obtain and organize the necessary information before using it to create the required database.

1 ▶ Use the restaurant database created in Case Study 1 of Project 1 for this assignment. Execute each of these tasks and then print the results: (a) Del Licious now occupies the storefront formerly occupied by Hat Dancers, which has gone out of business. Del Licious serves American cuisine, is open from 6:00 a.m. to 11:00 p.m., and has carryout but no delivery service. Its phone number is (714) 555-3628. You are fond of the all-you-can-eat special on Tuesdays. (b) Pablo's Tacos and Mr. Ming's now offer delivery service. (c) New Orient now opens at 11:00 a.m. and closes at 11:00 p.m. (d) Taranio's has moved to 532 S. Madison. (e) Parthenon and Taranio's have changed their specials from Tuesday to Monday. (f) Madras Ovens now offers carryout service.

2 ▶ Use the textbook database created in Case Study 2 of Project 1 for this assignment. Execute each of these tasks and then print the results: (a) Margaret Healy has dropped the price of her textbook from $36 to $30. (b) Mary Nord has sold her book, so you can delete her record from your database. (c) John Mote informs you he gave you the wrong course number for his textbook. It is used in Ast 120 instead of Ast 210. (d) You decide to sell your computer book you are using in this class for $35. It is in good condition. (e) The Psychology department has changed textbooks in the introductory course for the upcoming semester. Delete the books listed for Psy 101. (f) Dave Corsi's book is in poor condition. (g) Sandi Radleman has changed her phone number to 555-1782.

Cases and Places

3 ▶▶ Use the nutritional content database created in Case Study 3 of Project 1 for this assignment. Execute each of these tasks and then print the results: (a) Other meat also can be considered lean. For example, pork tenderloin has the same calories and fat as eye of round and has 65 mg of cholesterol. Top pork loin chop and center chop both have 170 calories, 7 grams of fat, and 70 mg of cholesterol. Boneless ham is one of the most nutritional meats, with 125 calories, 4 grams of fat, and 45 mg of cholesterol. Lamb loin chop has 180 calories, 8 grams of fat, and 80 mg of cholesterol, and whole leg of lamb has 160 calories, 7 grams of fat, and 75 mg of cholesterol. Add these cuts of meat to the database. (b) Display and print the cuts of meat with less than 70 milligrams of cholesterol in a three-ounce serving. (c) Display and print the cuts of meat with more than 160 calories in a three-ounce serving. (d) Your nutritionist has told you to consume less than 20 grams of fat daily. During the day, you have eaten food with a total fat gram content of 15. Display and print the cuts of meat that would be within the nutritionist's advice.

4 ▶▶ Use the movie collection database created in Case Study 4 of Project 1 for this assignment. Add five of your favorite movie titles to the table. Print the entire table sorted by movie title in ascending order.

5 ▶▶▶ Many national brokers offer IRAs. Call three of these brokerage companies and obtain the same information for investing $1,000 that you needed to complete Case Study 5 of Project 1 in the financial institutions database. Add these records to the table. Then display and print the following: (a) The names of all the financial institutions in the table and total values of the IRAs at age 65 in descending order. (b) The names and phone numbers of the financial institutions and total amounts of interest earned at age 65 in descending order. (c) The average value of the IRAs at age 65. (d) The average interest rates for the banks, savings and loans, credit unions, and brokerage companies. (e) The name, address, and interest rate of the financial institution with the highest interest rate. (f) The name, phone number, and interest rate of the financial institution with the lowest interest rate. (g) The names of the financial institutions and penalties for early withdrawal in two years in ascending order. (h) The names of the financial institutions and annual fees in ascending order. (i) A bar graph indicating the amount of interest you would earn and the total value of your IRA at age 65 for each financial institution.

Cases and Places

6 ▶▶▶ You have found the campus directory database you created in Case Study 6 of Project 1 to be invaluable. You have been handwriting additional names and numbers and making changes to the printout, and now you want to update the table. Add a new category called secretaries, and add the names, phone numbers, and room numbers of secretaries you call. In the faculty category, list your favorite instructors from previous semesters. Add your current instructors' office hours to the table. In the administration category, add data for the president and vice president of the school. In the services category, add the library circulation desk, athletic office, and theatre box office data. Print the entire table. Then print the instructors' names in ascending order, along with their phone numbers, office hours, and office room numbers. Create a similar printout for the administrators and for the secretaries. Finally, print the services in ascending order, including phone numbers and room numbers.

7 ▶▶▶ Use the product comparison database you created in Case Study 7 of Project 1 for this assignment. Often generic items are available for products on your shopping list. During your next shopping trip, locate any generic items that you could substitute for the 20 items in the table. Create a new field in the table and add the generic prices. Then, print the five items in each of the four categories in ascending order, along with the sizes and prices.

Integrating Excel Worksheet Data into an Access Database

Case Perspective

Eastern Office Supply has been using Excel to automate a variety of tasks for several years. Employees at Eastern have created several useful worksheets that have simplified their work tremendously. Along with the worksheets, they have created attractive charts for visual representation of the data.

When Eastern decided it needed to maintain customer data, the familiarity with Excel led to the decision to maintain the data as an Excel worksheet. For a while, this seemed to work fine. As time passed, however, they began to question whether Excel was the best choice. Their counterparts at other companies indicated that they were using Access to maintain customer data. Access had worked well for them. As the structure of their data became more complex, Access adapted easily to the increased complexity. They appreciated the power of the query and reporting features in Access. Finally, officials at Eastern decided that they should follow the lead of the other companies. They decided to convert their data from Excel to Access.

Introduction

It is not uncommon for people to use an application for some specific purpose, only to find later that another application may be better suited. For example, a company such as Eastern Office Supply might initially keep data in an Excel worksheet, only to discover later that the data would be better maintained in an Access database. Some common reasons for using a database instead of a worksheet are:

1. The worksheet contains a great deal of redundant data. As discussed in Project 1 on pages A 1.54 through A 1.56, databases can be designed to eliminate redundant data.
2. The worksheet would need to be larger than Excel can handle. Excel has a limit of 16,384 rows; whereas in Access, no such limit exists.
3. The data to be maintained consists of multiple interrelated items. For example, at Mason Clinic, they need to maintain data on two items, Patients and Therapists, and these items are interrelated. A patient has a single therapist and each therapist treats several patients. The Mason Clinic database is a very simple one. Databases can easily contain thirty or more interrelated items.
4. You want to use the extremely powerful query and report capabilities of Microsoft Access.

More *About* **Converting Data: Worksheets**

In Microsoft Excel, you can convert a single worksheet within a multiple-worksheet workbook to an Access table. This is not true with other spreadsheet packages, in which you must first save the worksheet as an individual file and then convert the individual file.

Regardless of the reasons for making the change from a worksheet to a database, it is important to be able to make the change easily. In the not-too-distant past, converting data from one tool to another often could be a very difficult, time-consuming task. Fortunately, an easy way of converting data from Excel to Access is available.

Figure 1 illustrates the conversion process. The type of worksheet that can be converted is one in which the data is stored as a **list**, that is, a labeled series of rows in which each row contains the same type of data. For example, in the worksheet at the top of Figure 1, the first row contains the labels, which are entries indicating the type of data found in the column. The entry in the first column, for example, is Customer Number, indicating that all the other values in the column are customer numbers. The entry in the second column is Name, indicating that all the other values in the column are names. Other than the first row, which contains the labels, all the rows contain precisely the same type of data: a customer number in the first column, a name in the second column, an address in the third column, and so on.

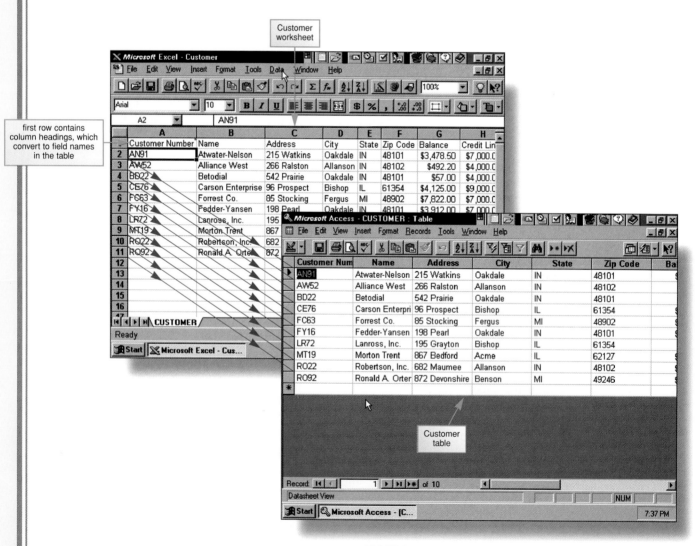

FIGURE 1

As Figure 1 illustrates, the worksheet, shown at the upper left of the figure, is converted to a database table, shown at the lower right. The columns in the worksheet become the fields. The column headings in the first row of the worksheet become the field names. The rows of the worksheet, other than the first row, which contains the labels, become the records in the table. In the process, each field will be assigned the data type that seems the most reasonable, given the data currently in the worksheet.

The conversion process, which uses the Import Spreadsheet Wizard, can begin from either Excel or Access. The steps are very similar in both cases. The wizard takes you through some basic steps, asking a few simple questions. Once you have answered the questions, the wizard will perform the conversion.

Once the data has been converted, you can use a wizard to analyze the table data in case you are not sure your design is appropriate. The wizard then will attempt to find redundancy; that is, duplication, in the data (see Project 1, pages A 1.54 through A 1.56 for a discussion of redundancy in a database). If the wizard finds redundancy, it will suggest a way of splitting your table to remove the redundancy. If, for example, you were to create a worksheet containing the data as shown in Figure 1-86 on page A 1.54, the resulting table would contain all the problems with redundancy that were discussed in that section. To correct these problems, the wizard will recommend the splitting shown in Figure 1-87 on page A 1.55. If you accept the wizard's recommendation, it will split the tables for you automatically.

Opening an Excel Workbook

Before converting the data, open the workbook in Excel by performing the following steps.

TO OPEN AN EXCEL WORKBOOK

Step 1: Click the Start button.

Step 2: Click Open Office Document, select 3½ Floppy [A:] in the Look in drop-down list box, and select the Access folder. Make sure the Customer workbook is selected.

Step 3: Click the Open button.

The Excel worksheet displays (Figure 2).

More *About*
Converting Data:
Databases

In addition to converting data from a worksheet to a database, you can also convert data from one database management system to another. Access, for example, provides tools for easily converting data from such database systems as dBASE III, dBASE IV, and Paradox.

More *About*
Converting Data:
Other Formats

Data can be converted to a database from a variety of formats, such as delimited and fixed-width text files. If you cannot convert directly from another worksheet or database to Access, often you can convert to one of these special formats and then convert the resulting file to Access.

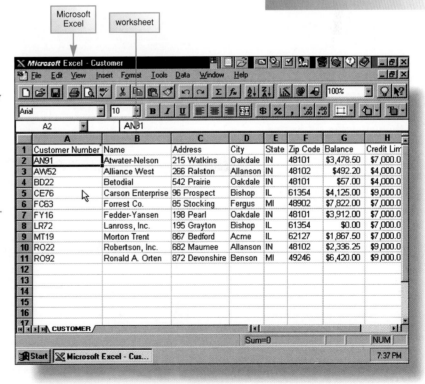

FIGURE 2

Converting an Excel Worksheet to an Access Database

To convert the data, you will use the Import Spreadsheet Wizard. In the process, you will indicate that the first row contains the column headings. These column headings will then become the field names in the Access table. In addition, you will indicate the primary key for the table. As part of the process, you can, if you desire, choose not to include all the fields from the worksheet in the resulting table. Some of the steps may take a significant amount of time for Access to execute.

Steps **To Convert an Excel Worksheet to an Access Database**

1 **Click any cell in the worksheet, click Data on the menu bar, and then click Convert to Access.**

The Convert to Microsoft Access dialog box displays (Figure 3). Use this dialog box to indicate whether the table that is created is to be placed in a new database or an existing database.

FIGURE 3

2 **Make sure the New database option button is selected and then click the OK button.**

The Import Spreadsheet Wizard dialog box displays (Figure 4). It displays a portion of the worksheet that is being converted. In this dialog box you indicate that the first row of the worksheet contains the column headings. The wizard uses these values as the field names in the Access table.

FIGURE 4

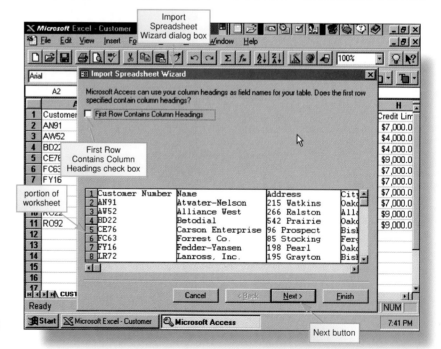

3 **Click First Row Contains Column Headings and then click the Next button.**

The Import Spreadsheet Wizard dialog box displays giving you the opportunity to specify field options (Figure 5). You can specify that indexes are to be created for certain fields. You also can specify that certain fields should not be included in the Access table.

FIGURE 5

4 **Click the Next button.**

The Import Spreadsheet Wizard dialog box displays (Figure 6). Use this dialog box to indicate the primary key of the Access table. You can allow Access to add a special field to serve as the primary key as illustrated in the figure. You can choose an existing field to serve as the primary key. You also can indicate no primary key. Most of the time, one of the existing fields will serve as the primary key. In this worksheet, for example, the Customer Number serves as the primary key.

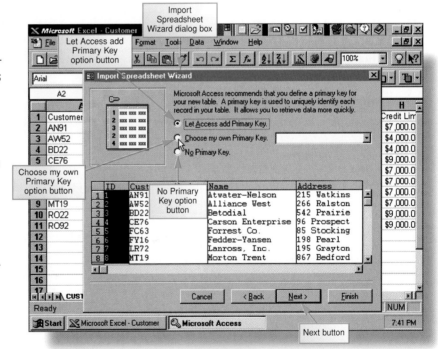

FIGURE 6

⑤ Click Choose my own Primary Key.

The Customer Number field will be the primary key (Figure 7).

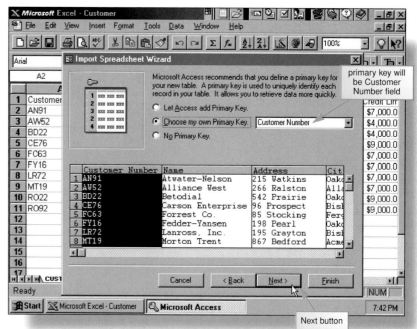

FIGURE 7

⑥ Click the Next button. Be sure CUSTOMER displays in the Import to Table text box and the button requesting a wizard to analyze the table is not checked.

The Import Spreadsheet Wizard dialog box displays (Figure 8). The name of the table will be CUSTOMER.

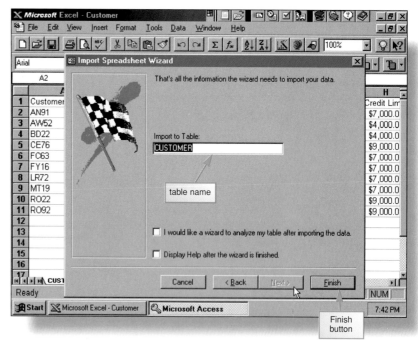

FIGURE 8

7 Click the Finish button.

The worksheet will be converted into an Access table. When the process is completed the Import Spreadsheet Wizard dialog box will display (Figure 9).

8 Click the OK button.

The table has now been created (see Figure 1 on page AI 1.2).

9 Close Access, and then close Excel. Do not save the worksheet.

The customer table has been created in a database also called Customer.

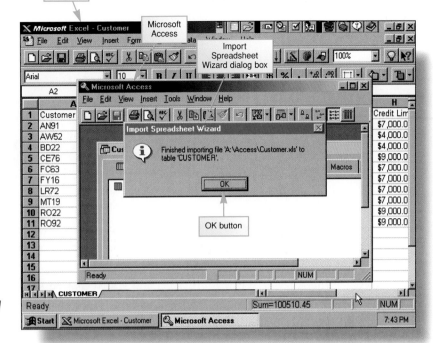

FIGURE 9

Using the Access Table

Once the Access version of the table has been created, you can treat it as you would any other table. After first opening the database containing the table, you can open the table in Datasheet view (Figure 1 on page AI 1.2). You can make changes to the data. You can create queries that use the data in the table.

By clicking Design on the table's shortcut menu, you can view the table's structure and make any necessary changes to the structure. The changes may include changing field sizes and types, creating indexes, or adding additional fields. To accomplish any of these tasks, use the same steps you used in Project 3.

Summary

The Integration Feature covered the process of integrating an Excel worksheet into an Access database. To convert a worksheet to an Access table, you learned to use the Import Spreadsheet Wizard. Working with the wizard, you identified the first row of the worksheet as the row containing the column headings and you indicated the primary key. The wizard then created the table for you and placed it in a new database.

What You Should Know

Having completed this Integration Feature, you should be able to perform the following tasks:

▶ Convert an Excel Worksheet to an Access Database *(AI 1.4)*

▶ Open an Excel Workbook *(AI 1.3)*

In the Lab

1 Using Help

Instructions: Perform the following tasks using a computer.

1. Start Access.
2. Double-click the Help button on the toolbar to display the Help Topics: Microsoft Access for Windows 95 dialog box. Click the Index tab. Type import in box 1 and then double-click spreadsheets under importing data in box 2. Double-click Import or link a spreadsheet in the Topics Found dialog box. When the Help information displays, read it. Next, right-click within the box, and then click Print Topic. Hand in the printout to your instructor. Click the Help Topics button to return to the Help Topics: Microsoft Access for Windows 95 dialog box.
3. Click the Answer Wizard tab. Type how do i use the table analyzer wizard in box 1. Click the Search button. Double-click Normalize a table using the Table Analyzer Wizard in box 2 under How Do I. Read and print the Help information. Hand in the printout to your instructor.

2 Converting the Software Worksheet

Problem: Great Lakes Educational Software has been using Excel to keep track of its inventory. Employees at Great Lakes use several worksheets to re-order software, keep track of carrying costs, and graph trends in software buying. The company is expanding rapidly and branching out into other educational products. They now need to maintain additional data and would like to produce more sophisticated reports and queries. The company management has asked you to convert its inventory data to an Access database.

Instructions: Perform the following tasks.

1. Open the Software worksheet (Figure 10) in the Access folder on the Student Floppy Disk that accompanies this book.
2. Convert the Software worksheet to an Access table. Use Software as the name of the Access table and Software Number as the primary key.
3. Open and print the table in Access.

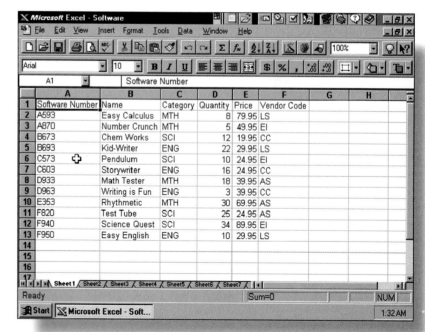

FIGURE 10

3 Converting the Employee Worksheet

Problem: The Great Outdoors Catalog Company has been using Excel to keep track of its inventory and do limited tracking of its employees. Employees at Great Outdoors Catalog Company use several worksheets to re-order products, keep track of carrying costs, and maintain employee records. The company realizes that employee data would be better handled in Access. The company management has asked you to convert its employee data to an Access database.

Instructions: Perform the following tasks.

1. Create a new database in which to store all the objects related to the employee data. Call the database Great Outdoors.
2. Import the Employee worksheet shown in Figure 11 into Access. Open the Employee worksheet in the Access folder on the Student Floppy Disk that accompanies this book. (Hint: Using Help on the previous page can help you solve this problem.)
3. Use Employee as the name of the Access table and SS Number as the primary key.
4. Open and print the Employee table.

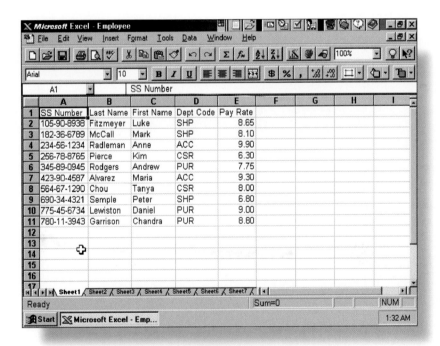

FIGURE 11